"*Why We Argue, Second Edition* is a timely and important book. The inability to have productive discussions on matters on which we deeply disagree poses a threat to our democracy, and it can affect our mental health as citizens as well. In their wide-ranging discussion, Aikin and Talisse characterize the nature of the challenges involved, and they make useful suggests as to how we might go about addressing them. I highly recommend their book."

Sanford Goldberg, *Northwestern University, USA*

Why We Argue (And How We Should)

Why We Argue (And How We Should): A Guide to Political Disagreement in an Age of Unreason presents an accessible and engaging introduction to the theory of argument, with special emphasis on the way argument works in public political debate. The authors develop a view according to which proper argument is necessary for one's individual cognitive health; this insight is then expanded to the collective health of one's society. Proper argumentation, then, is seen to play a central role in a well-functioning democracy.

Written in a lively style and filled with examples drawn from the real world of contemporary politics, and questions following each chapter to encourage discussion, *Why We Argue (And How We Should)* reads like a guide for the participation in, and maintenance of, modern democracy. An excellent student resource for courses in critical thinking, political philosophy, and related fields, *Why We Argue (And How We Should)* is an important contribution to reasoned debate.

What's New in the Second Edition:

- Updated examples throughout the book, including examples from the 2016 U.S. election and first years of the Trump presidency;
- Expanded coverage of dialectical fallacies, including coverage of new types of fallacies and of sites where such fallacies thrive (e.g., cable news, social media);
- Revised **For Further Thought** questions and definitions of **Key Terms**, included at the end of each chapter;
- The addition of five new chapters:
  - o Deep Disagreements
  - o Arguments by Analogy
  - o Argumentation Between the Ads
  - o The Owl of Minerva Problem
  - o Argumentative Responsibility and Argument Repair.

Scott F. Aikin is Assistant Professor of Philosophy at Vanderbilt University. His previous books include *Evidentialism and the Will to Believe* (2014) and *Epistemology and the Regress Problem* (Routledge 2011).

Robert B. Talisse is W. Alton Jones Professor of Philosophy and Professor of Political Science at Vanderbilt University. He is the author of five books, including *Engaging Political Philosophy* (Routledge 2016), *Pluralism and Liberal Politics* (Routledge 2011), and *Democracy and Moral Conflict* (2009).

For Professor Talisse and Aikin's frequently-updated observations of contemporary arguments and other matters related to
Why We Argue (And How We Should),

follow them on Twitter at:

@WhyWeArgue

Why We Argue (And How We Should)

A Guide to Political Disagreement in an Age of Unreason

Second Edition

Scott F. Aikin and Robert B. Talisse

Routledge
Taylor & Francis Group

NEW YORK AND LONDON

Second edition published 2019
by Routledge
711 Third Avenue, New York, NY 10017

and by Routledge
2 Park Square, Milton Park, Abingdon, Oxon OX14 4RN

Routledge is an imprint of the Taylor & Francis Group, an informa business

First edition published 2014 by Routledge

Library of Congress Cataloging-in-Publication Data
A catalog record for this title has been requested

ISBN: 978-1-138-08741-5 (hbk)
ISBN: 978-1-138-08742-2 (pbk)
ISBN: 978-1-315-11049-3 (ebk)

Typeset in Times New Roman
by Taylor & Francis Books

For our friends, colleagues, and students at Vanderbilt University

Contents

PART III
Repairing Public Argument   175

Praise for the First Edition

"*Why We Argue* is a superb book for students of philosophy, politics, and argumentation. Moreover it is a necessary read for anyone seeking a clear introduction to the ethical importance of well-reasoned public argument. In my ideal world, this text would be required reading for college students and politicians alike."

Lawrence Torcello, *Rochester Institute of Technology, USA*

"Aikin and Talisse offer a guide to political disagreement and argument that takes seriously both the cognitive health of the individual arguer and the collective health of democratic society. Their clear prose and theoretically engaged analyses of current case studies effectively skewer the argumentative foibles of both the political left and the political right. This lively and engaging book effectively connects the epistemology of argument quality with the political demands of decent democratic life."

Harvey Siegel, *University of Miami, USA*

"*Why We Argue* makes a compelling case for the significance of argument in our everyday lives, but what sets this book apart is the insistence on the importance of what we owe to others when we are arguing. This emphasis on the social aspects is an important contribution to the literature on teaching the nature and purpose of argument."

Emily Esch, *College of Saint Benedict/Saint John's University, USA*

Preface to the Second Edition

Times change. The first edition of *Why We Argue (And How We Should)* was published in 2014; we wrote the book in the midst of the 2012 U.S. presidential election. Now we are writing this Preface in the wake not only of the 2016 presidential election in the U.S., but also of the Brexit Referendum in the UK and several European elections where populist and nationalist candidates who did not win office nonetheless enjoyed disconcertingly high levels of support. What's more, the communicative landscape of democracy seems to have changed dramatically in only a few years. The current U.S. president communicates to the world primarily by way of Twitter, and we are only now coming to realize the full impact on the U.S. election of foreign agents acting strategically on social media. Further, the vernacular of democratic politics now features terms like "fake news," "alternative facts," and "post-truth." Naturally, all signs point to amplified levels of distrust among democratic citizens.

In light of these developments, the vision of democratic citizenship driving this book is likely to seem quaint, a relic of a freshly bygone age. We defend the idea that democracy is centrally, though certainly not exclusively, the epistemological proposal that intelligent and responsible persons who sincerely disagree about fundamental moral, social, and political questions can nonetheless regard each other as fellow citizens who, despite the depth and severity of their disagreements, have something to contribute to the collective cognitive well-being of society. The recurring metaphor is that of cognitive health, and the core argument of the book is that if we wish to maintain our own cognitive health, we need to interact with others who are also cognitively healthy; in order to maintain our collective cognitive health, we need a suitably functioning cognitive environment. Maintaining a proper cognitive environment is a collective project, and we all must pitch-in. Doing our part in this endeavor requires us to try to argue well, and this in turn calls us to develop the skills and virtues of argumentation. *Why We Argue (And How We Should)* diagnoses some of the ways in which we can fall short and offers some guidance on how we can improve.

Central to our account is the idea that argumentation fails when interlocutors are insufficiently *dialectical*. Dialecticality is a complex collection of norms, and is discussed at length in Chapter 14. In this preliminary context, however, dialecticality has two main components. First, it has to do with an arguer's ability to connect their reasons with their opponent, rather than with, for example, a caricature thereof. Second, it has to do with an arguer's rational engagement with their opposition rather than with an onlooking audience. This latter feature of dialecticality forms the crucial interface between proper argumentation and proper democracy. In a democracy, a good deal of argumentation is engaged in the presence of an audience. What's more, these argumentative exchanges frequently are engaged for the sake of the onlookers. Political candidates debate each other on stage so that an audience can evaluate their command of the issues; television news centrally features segments where political commentators discuss the latest stories so that the viewing audience can witness the clash of opinion and thereby become informed.

Publicly visible debate is an important part of democratic politics. However, when debate is conducted before (and for the sake of) an audience, there emerge distinctive ways in which it can fail. To take an obvious kind of failure, the public forum can encourage arguers to play to the audience, striving to look good to a particular public rather than perform rationally in the exchange. Winning smiles and snappy sloganeering are how mass audiences are moved, after all. Thus there is a long tradition in philosophy, beginning with Plato, which denounces the practice of trying to reason in large groups. The claim is that when we try to reason together in large forums, the sweet-talkers and confident liars win.

According to a common response to this criticism, the public forum in which debate is enacted must be designed so that interlocutors are compelled to address each other. Hence public debates are often moderated by a neutral third party who is charged with ensuring that the interlocutors avoid rhetorical excesses and stay engaged with each other. However, as we stress in this book, there are ways for public argument to fail dialectically even when interlocutors are precluded from overtly mugging to the crowd and are forced to speak only to each other. We call these kinds of failures *dialectical fallacies*, and although they vary in significant ways, they share a core structure. Dialectical fallacies are modes of argumentative exchange that are designed to mislead an onlooking audience about the state of play between the disputants in a public debate. They are ways of implicitly communicating to an audience that one's interlocutor, and the position he or she espouses, is cognitively disordered, inept, or incompetent. Importantly, dialectical fallacies often involve no overt mistreatment of one's interlocutor; they work simply to promote among the onlookers the impression that the dialectical situation that obtains between the interlocutors is not one of equality. Accordingly, when they are successful, dialectical fallacies both sway the audience to one's own viewpoint and leave them with the impression that the opposition is incompetent, deluded, and ignorant. One not only wins the audience over to one's position, but also convinces them that no further discussion with the opposing side could be fruitful.

Part Two of this book catalogues and examines several kinds of dialectical fallacy, and we have identified several new types in the Second Edition. We need not rehearse these forms here. However, it is worth emphasizing that dialectically fallacious modes of public argument pose a special threat to democracy. A democracy is a community of political equals that governs itself; democracy is centrally the proposition that the governed must share equal power in setting the direction of their government. The direction of democratic government is set by means of majoritarian elections where each citizen is granted exactly one vote. The reason that majoritarian elections are used is that, in a democracy, it is expected that citizens will not only have different opinions about what direction government should take, but they will reasonably disagree about such matters. We might say, then, that democracy is committed to the idea that sincere, well-intentioned, competent, informed, and rational citizens might nevertheless disagree severely about moral and political questions. Democracy is partly the project of creating a stable social and political order in which disagreement of that kind could be fruitfully engaged; it is therefore also the project of collective self-government among equal citizens despite ongoing disagreement about fundamental matters. Given this, we might say that the key to democracy is the view that respectful disagreement is possible among proper citizens. Hence our ongoing disagreements need not undermine the bases for a stable and decent political order.

The dialectical fallacies undermine this fundamental democratic commitment. Again, they are modes of argumentative exchange that foster among audiences the idea that, with respect to certain fundamental questions, no reasoned disagreement is possible. This idea strikes at the heart of democracy, even as it poses as a bulwark against democracy's opponents. Our aim in *Why We Argue (And How We Should)* remains that of helping students and citizens to guard themselves from this fundamental yet understandably seductive cognitive error. To this end, the Second Edition expands our account of the dialectical fallacies. That is, we have not only updated our examples. We have introduced new kinds of dialectical fallacy, and identified new sites where they thrive. In particular, we have added new chapters that deal with the kind of political debate that is commonly engaged on cable news, and on online forums. We have also included a chapter on how arguments by analogy can be dialectically fallacious.

Alongside the updated and new material, the Second Edition also introduces a new theme that now runs throughout our account of public argument, and which is discussed explicitly in Part Three. The mechanisms and venues of public argument are so fluid and fast-paced that our efforts to argue well now confront a distinctive obstacle: the diagnostic vocabulary that must be developed in order to diagnose lapses of good argument is itself subject to a kind of opportunistic and distorting cooptation. To be more specific, in order to do their evaluative work, the concepts by which we assess the character of one another's argumentative performances must be second-order. That is, the vocabulary of fallacies is a metalanguage in that it assesses argumentative performance in a content neutral way. Consequently, charging an arguer with, say, begging the question or deploying a straw man does not entail that one rejects her conclusion. Fallacies are errors in making a case, they are not defects of the content of one's premises or conclusion. However, our contemporary cognitive environment allows for the concepts in our metalanguage of argumentation to be captured and deployed as first order assessments of the conclusions one opposes.

To see how this works, consider the fate of the *ad hominem* fallacy in our popular political vernacular. It is now common for political arguers to charge their interlocutors with deploying the *ad hominem* as a way of rebuffing their opponent's views. But the resulting argument ("My opponent has employed an *ad hominem*, therefore his conclusion is false") is *itself* fallacious. What's more, it is common for those who charge their opponents with the *ad hominem* to use that very charge as a kind of personal insult to their interlocutor. In other words, the charge of *ad hominem* has itself become a form of *ad hominem* attack! It's almost comical. Nonetheless, the philosophical point is serious: our second-order vocabulary for assessing one another's argumentative performances has been deployed for first-order engagement. In Chapter 14, we call this cooptation *weaponizing* the metalanguage, and we call the general problem that second-order concepts can be easily weaponized the *Owl of Minerva Problem*.

We now think that the Owl of Minerva Problem captures a fundamental challenge to contemporary democracy. We see it at work in all of our newly and recently minted political concepts, including "fake news." Note that the term *fake news* was introduced to signify that some websites present themselves as engaged in journalism while in fact being devoted to some other objective (rumor mongering, propagandizing, misinformation campaigns, and so on). Very quickly, though, the term mutated, and it is now used as a way of deriding journalists and news outlets who report stories with which one disagrees. The troubling lesson, of course, is that any concept that might be developed to help identify and diagnose instances in which second-order concepts have been weaponized will itself be liable to weaponization. It seems, then, that our argumentative metalanguage is destined to lag behind the argumentative practices, and so our attempts to theorize the breakdowns in public argument are, in a way, doomed. By the time newly crafted theoretical tools get the degree of uptake that is necessary in order for them to do reparative work, they will have been weaponized, transmogrified into new ways to merely mimic proper argument.

As our new subtitle suggests, this Second Edition takes a more cautious and foreboding view of the prospects for healthy democracy. And yet we remain relatively optimistic. After all, the Owl of Minerva Problem can emerge only when people are deeply invested in arguing well. And so we have tried, specifically in Chapter 14, to present an account of how we might repair our argumentative culture so that it more closely realizes the cognitive norms we share. The task of democracy, like the task of rationality, is fraught with hazards. Our attempts to manage the hazards by means of sustained reflection on our aims and practices might, in the end, fall short. But at the very least these attempts help to keep before our minds the fact that such hazards exist. And to lose sight of the very existence of the hazards we inevitably confront is simply to augment the threat they pose.

We have incurred many debts in writing this book and in the many years we have spent talking, thinking, writing, and arguing about argument. We would like to thank the following people, all of whom have contributed considerably to this book: Jason Aleksander, Colin Anderson, Theano Apostolou, Jody Azzouni, James Bednar, Ophelia Benson, Joanne Billett, Thom Brooks, Steven Cahn, Michael Calamari, John Casey, Meng-Ju Chuang, Caleb Clanton, Allen Coates, Elizabeth Edenberg, Andrew Forcehimes, Susan Foxman, Marilyn Friedman, Steve Gimbel, Sandy Goldberg, Lenn Goodman, David Miguel Gray, Michael Harbour, Nicole Heller, D. Micah Hester, Michael Hodges, Angelo Juffras, David Kaspar, Chris King, Michael Lynch, Mason Marshall, Grace Matelich, Larry May, David McCullough, Emily McGill, Jose Medina, C. D. Myers, John O'Connor, John Peterman, Yvonne Raley, Brian Ribeiro, Mike Santasiero, Luke Semrau, Sandra Skene, Rob Tempio, Lawrence Torcello, Jeffrey Tlumak, Eric Webber, and Julian Wuerth. Portions of some chapters are revised versions of our previously published essays in the journal *Think*, and we thank our editor, Stephen Law, for permission to draw from those materials. A special note of gratitude is also due to S. Abbas Raza. Many of the chapters in this book derive from ideas that were initially presented in our monthly column on Abbas's blog, *3 Quarks Daily* (3quarksdaily.com). Additionally, we received special help in working out the details of the second edition of the book from Mary Butterfield, Thomas Dabay, Ian Dove, David Godden, Hans Hansen, Andrew Howat, Michael Hoppmann, Catherine Hudleby, Lisa Madura, Amy McKiernan, Joshua Miller, Lyn Radke, Andrew Riggs, Eric Ritter, and Boomer Trujillo. And we received extensive feedback and useful suggestions all along the way from John Patrick Casey. Finally, we thank Andy Beck, our editor at Routledge, and the Routledge editorial team for their support.

Preface to the First Edition

This book aspires to be an accessible and engaging introduction to the theory of argumentation. Topically, then, the book resides at the intersection of several areas of philosophy that are most often treated as more or less distinct, including logic, epistemology, philosophy of language, social philosophy, and political philosophy. Although we will be addressing topics that are native to these distinct areas of inquiry, we have tried to avoid presupposing any prior knowledge of philosophy. Our hope is that argument—as an activity and a subject of concern in these various domains—is familiar enough to our readers to allow us to simply dive into the issues. However, the subject-matter is nonetheless complex. Hence at certain junctures, our discussion employs some of the technical apparatus of professional philosophy. At those moments, we have supplied the necessary background. So whereas we have aspired to write a book about a cluster of philosophical topics that is accessible to non-philosophers, we do not suppose that we have written a book that is *easy* to read. We think that a book about argument that is also an easy read would necessarily be a book that presents a simplistic and ultimately inadequate view of its subject.

Although we have tried to write for a general readership, we understand that this book will be read mostly by students enrolled in Informal Logic, Critical Thinking, or Introduction to Philosophy courses. Consequently, in addition to trying to write accessibly, we have also tried to make the book maximally versatile, that is, useable in a broad range of pedagogical contexts. Thus this is a short book. It can be used alongside material of other kinds. It is also a self-contained book. It can be read as a stand-alone treatment of some fundamental issues about argument and its connection to politics. In order to facilitate readability and accessibility, we have abandoned many of the usual conventions of academic writing. For one thing, we have resisted the habit of introducing long footnotes containing references to the vast academic literature on the topics we discuss. In addition, apart from the Introduction and the Conclusion, each chapter concludes with a list of Key Terms and a short series of questions "For Further Thought." The questions do not attempt to point readers in the direction of the main contentions of the foregoing chapter, they should not be taken to be "study questions" in the standard sense. Rather, they are intended to stimulate additional thoughts, many of which we hope will provide grounds for criticism of the views we have presented. We hope that in wrestling with some of our more controversial claims, our readers will sharpen the dialectical virtues we hold are so valuable.

Introduction

This book is about argument. As the "we" in its title may suggest, it places special emphasis on the social nature and political significance of argument. Accordingly, this book is a contribution to the area of logic known as *critical thinking*. However, this book differs in several respects from what is typical of works in that genre. For one thing, we employ an expansive conception of what argument is. Throughout the following chapters, we take argument to be any attempt to discover, discern, and evaluate reasons for belief or action. Argument also includes our responses to others' attempts to examine reasons. Argument in the sense to be employed here refers to any attempt to think things through, talk things over, or figure things out, by means of processes aimed at sharing and evaluating reasons.

Books about critical thinking tend to employ a more restrictive view of what arguments are. Often they adopt the view that an argument is a set of statements, where a subset of statements (the premises) is proposed to provide support for another statement (the conclusion). From this starting point, they present the needed distinctions between formal and informal reasoning, deduction and induction, validity and soundness, and cogency and non-cogency. Then they develop strategies for evaluating arguments of various kinds. In the case of deductive arguments, the focus is on formal rules of inference and methods for detecting formal fallacies. In the case of inductive and informal arguments, things tend quickly to get rather messy; various informal fallacies are catalogued, methods for extracting the argumentative content from ordinary uses of language are presented, and processes for estimating the strength supplied by the premises for the conclusion are suggested. Interestingly, but perhaps not surprisingly, the work on formal reasoning and deductive arguments tends to be uniform across the literature, while the work on informal and inductive logic admits staggering variety.

This book does not fit this mold. Although we will have a lot to say about cogent reasoning and responsible argument, our focus is not on standard methods of evaluating inferences and detecting fallacies. Those who seek work of this more typical kind should look elsewhere. Our emphasis is fixed instead on the ways in which people argue (again, in our expanded sense of the term) together. Insofar as we are interested here in fallacy detection, we are concerned to identify a range of argumentative failures that are perhaps best described as *dialectical fallacies.*

Although the whole of this book is aimed at developing the idea of a dialectical fallacy, the very idea calls for some initial elaboration. To do this, we must contrast dialectical fallacies with other kinds of fallacies—to see what's unique about them, we must see them in contrast. And this requires us to address some of the topics we just claimed would not be central to the book. Life is brimming with such ironies.

Let us begin with the regular observation that arguments are sets of claims with two subsets: premises and conclusions. The premises are supposed to be reasons given for accepting the conclusion. Now, given this setup, there are three core questions to ask about arguments.

Question 1: Is the argument successful in convincing its audience of the conclusion? Call this the question of *Rhetorical Success.*

Question 2: Are the premises of the argument true or acceptable? Call this the question of *Material Success.*

Question 3: Assuming the premises true, do they provide support for the argument's conclusion? Call this the question of *Logical Success.*

With these three questions in hand, we have a useful set of categories for reflection on argument.

Think for a moment about an argument someone gave you that you didn't find convincing at all but others around you found quite compelling. Perhaps an uncle had a particularly wild conspiracy theory or a roommate had a line of thought on taxation that you thought implausible. And despite the fact that these arguments didn't seem very good to you, others thought them quite good. What initially distinguishes you from all those other folks is that for you, the argument is not *rhetorically* successful, but for them it is. But note that this result isn't the end of the story, since there's a reason why you don't and they do find those conclusions acceptable. The big difference is that they think the argument was both logically and materially successful, but you think those arguments fail at least one of those criteria.

Consider, perhaps, your roommate's proposal about taxation. Let's imagine that she holds that by raising taxes on the poor, that policy will motivate many not to be poor any more. And so, since we provide motive not to be poor, we can expect people to work harder to not be poor. And if they work harder, they will make more money. And if they make more money, they won't be poor anymore. So, if we raise taxes on the poor, your roommate concludes, we reduce poverty. Now, that's quite an argument, but we take it that you're probably not moved by it. And it's likely for the reason that it seems highly unlikely that taking more money from the poor will have any other result than making them more poor. Very few of the economically challenged are in that position only because they don't have enough of a motivation to be more economically well-off. It's often because there just aren't opportunities to acquire more diverse skills, develop a network, or get experience that one needs to make more money. Now, notice that in this case, the reason why you don't accept this argument is because you did not accept one of the argument's premises. Premises can show the conclusion acceptable only if they themselves are acceptable. False or simply unacceptable premises, then, are a *material failure* of an argument. So your reason for not being moved by your roommate's taxation argument was that it had a false premise. And now we can explain why those others were moved by the argument – they found that premise acceptable. Material success of an argument for an audience is a precondition for its rhetorical success.

Now, let's turn to your uncle's conspiracy theory. Imagine it runs like this: we are not allowed to know all the things the military does, so they must be hiding aliens and their technology. Perhaps the reason why you don't accept your uncle's conspiracy theory argument is that, despite the fact that you agree that the government has many secret programs and bases we are not allowed to inspect, that doesn't mean they are hiding aliens and their technology from us. There's no clear connection between those facts. In that case, the problem with your uncle's argument is that even though the premises are acceptable, they aren't relevant to the conclusion. And so you can agree with the premises of an argument but still hold it not to be any good, because arguments must also be *logically* successful, too. The premises not only need to be true, but you have to see them supporting the conclusion, showing why the conclusion is true. In cases where there is a failure of logical support, we often call these *fallacies*. In the case of your uncle, the fallacy is what's often called *the fallacy of ignorance* – just because you don't have evidence that aliens *aren't* on those bases, it doesn't mean that they *are*. The challenge is to articulate what exactly it is for an argument to be fallacious, and what it takes for them to be fallacious in the manner we take to be of particular interest. We need an account of what a *dialectical fallacy* is.

We must start with an examination of what makes dialectical fallacies different from the more familiar kind of fallacy, what is known as a *formal fallacy*. Here is a common formal fallacy. It is called *affirming the consequent*:

If Bill's a bachelor, Bill is male.
Bill is male.
Therefore Bill is a bachelor.

The trouble with this argument is that it presents an *invalid inference*. This is a fancy way of saying that the truth of the premises does not guarantee the truth of the conclusion. In the above argument, it is possible for the premises to be true, but the conclusion false. (Bill may be a married man.)

So even were the premises true and the conclusion true, this is still a sloppy piece of reasoning.

The objective of formal fallacy detection is to show when the truth of the premises does not yield the proper degree of support for the conclusion. The highest degree of support premises can provide for a conclusion is the *guarantee* of its truth, given their truth. Arguments that have that feature are called deductively *valid*. Some, but not all, valid arguments have premises that are in fact true. But the truth of the premises is not necessary for formal validity. Consequently, the following argument is formally valid:

> All logicians are robots.
> Willard is a logician.
> Therefore, Willard is a robot.

What makes this inference formally valid is that the premises and conclusion take a determinate and recognizably valid form. The forms that these valid arguments take and the ways in which they can be made systematic are the objects of study comprising *formal logic*. Now, in calling the above argument formally valid, one simply calls attention to the fact that the truth of the premises guarantees the truth of the conclusion. *Whether* the premises are in fact true is not a question that matters for validity. Consequently, one can acknowledge the *formal logical success* of this argument—that the truth of its premises does indeed guarantee the truth of its conclusion—while still resisting its conclusion. The argument fails because its premises are in fact not true. This is, again, a good reason to keep the *material* and *logical* evaluations as separate matters. In order to evaluate whether an argument is *logically* acceptable, we have to grant the premises and see if, given their truth, they make the conclusion true. That's a different kind of enterprise from asking whether those premises are true, as we do with *material* evaluation. And again, this point should be clear: it is possible for an argument to be materially acceptable but not logically successful (as we saw with the bachelors argument above), and there can be logically acceptable but materially unsuccessful arguments (as we saw with the logicians argument above).

This set of evaluative criteria points us to a second metric of argument evaluation. As we have said, an argument is formally valid when the truth of its premises guarantees the truth of its conclusion. It seems, then, that a valid argument with premises that are *in fact* true would be an unmitigated success.

Arguments that are valid and have true premises are called *deductively sound*. Notice that all deductively sound arguments are deductively valid. But, as we have already seen, not all deductively valid arguments are deductively sound. It is obvious why deductive soundness is often considered to be the gold standard for argumentative success. Deductively sound arguments are *demonstrations* of the truth of their conclusions. It seems natural to think that one can't get better than that. Who could ask for anything more?

As it turns out, there are problems with taking deductive soundness to be the criterion of argumentative success. For one thing, deductive soundness sets a highly demanding standard for success. As we know all too well, the world is messy and complicated. We very rarely find ourselves in situations where matters are so clear-cut as to be resolved by a formal argument. Guarantees are definitely splendid things, but life offers very few of them. In the rough-and-tumble world of actual reasoning, we require arguments that are *good enough* for our given purposes. We don't want to make the perfect the enemy of the good in logic, so we must look for a more forgiving standard than deductive soundness.

But there is another reason to be concerned about the criterion of deductive soundness as benchmark for success in argument. Imagine a dispute over the identity of the only president of the United States who served two non-consecutive terms. One disputant claims it is Chester A. Arthur. Another contends that it is Grover Cleveland. An argument is needed to resolve the dispute. Imagine our second disputant proposing the following argument:

> Grover Cleveland was the only president of the United States to serve non-consecutive terms.
> *Therefore*, Grover Cleveland was the only president of the United States to serve non-consecutive terms.

This argument is obviously impotent. But notice, first, that *it is deductively valid*. The truth of its premise indeed guarantees the truth of its conclusion. Now notice that its premise is in fact true. Consequently, *the argument is deductively sound*! Yet something is obviously amiss. The supposed gold standard for argument success just failed.

It seems, then, that deductive soundness is not all it is cracked up to be. When we engage in argument, we are not looking only for a formal demonstration of the truth of our conclusion; we are also looking to address questions, resolve disagreements, move inquiry along, and find out new things. More importantly, we are often attempting to *address* others, to *engage* with those with whom we disagree, and to *settle* disputes with them. To be sure, the formal criteria help, but they are not all there is to success in argument. We need a conception of argumentative success that goes beyond the formal properties.

Let us return briefly to our three questions of *rhetorical, logical,* and *material* success. One of the things that we'd done with the question of *rhetorical* success is that we indexed an audience with it. So an argument can move some people, but not others. And this, again, is explained by whether or not they judge the argument materially and logically successful. If arguments aren't just formal arrangements of sentences, but are communicative actions we take on to resolve disagreements with particular people, we have got to have as a requirement that their material and logical success be accessible to their audiences. If an audience can't see the premises as acceptable or as supporting the conclusion, then how is the argument supposed to give them a reason to accept the conclusion? What arises is what we've been calling a *dialecticality requirement* for arguments – they must have premises and logical support that are acceptable to their audiences, and they must address the objections and concerns the audience may have on the issue. Not only must an argument live up to the formal requirements for good reasoning, but it must live up to the dialectical requirements of addressing disagreement.

Now we have the grounds to say that the trouble with the Grover Cleveland argument is that it *begs the question*. The conclusion is identical to the premise, so the argument attempts to settle a disputed question by merely asserting one disputant's answer. But, again, disputes arise between people who disagree, and arguments among disputants must be designed to address disputes in ways that could provide a *resolution* to disagreements. In order to resolve a disagreement, the arguments provided must actually address the disputants and attempt to provide them with reasons to come to agree. Accordingly, even a formally unimpeachable argument can fail if it is unable to fulfill the social role of argumentation. To put the matter in a nutshell: in order to be successful, arguments must be sufficiently *dialectical*.

Consider another disagreement. Imagine that it's Saturday and Kelly is at work. Her friends, Simone and Carl, are trying to figure out where she is. Simone thinks Kelly is at home. Carl thinks that Kelly is either at school or at work. Carl reasons as follows:

It's Saturday, so Kelly can't be at school. So she must be at work.

That's a valid piece of reasoning, given that he's only deliberating between school and work. And it's sound, too, since Kelly is at work, and it is Saturday. So another piece of sound formally valid reasoning, that from an exclusively formal perspective would be unimpeachable. The problem is that Carl's reasoning, though sound, does not address Simone's thought – that Kelly is at home. We have the term *false dilemma* for reasoning along these lines – where one has unjustifiably restricted the range of possibilities to consider and eliminate, leaving plausible (even if ultimately false) alternatives unaddressed. Carl's reasoning, even though it gets the truth, doesn't sync up with those around him, and so is rendered socially inert.

These considerations provide a rough sense of what a *dialectical fallacy* is. An argument presents a dialectical fallacy when it fails to play its proper *social role*, most typically by failing to actually *address* those to whom the argument is purported to be offered. Arguments are not merely collections of propositions that must be composed of proper formal relations, but they are exchanges between people aiming to resolve a disagreement or answer a question. Consequently, such fallacies are unique in that they propose to establish their conclusions on the basis of insufficient support by way of a distortion of the *dialectical situation* among the disputants. This, again, returns us to the *dialecticality requirement* for arguments – they must have premises and logical support that are acceptable to their audiences, and they must address the objections and concerns the audience may have on the issue.

Fallacies of begging the question and false dilemma are most often aimed not simply at convincing one's interlocutor of the truth of some conclusion, but rather (and more importantly) at convincing an *onlooking audience* that one's interlocutor is inept, vicious, ignorant, benighted, untrustworthy, malicious, or worse. Of course, these fallacies can also be employed first-personally, as attempts to convince ourselves that those who oppose our views are not worth engaging with. In a democratic society, adopting the view that those who disagree with you are for that reason intellectually deficient is potentially dangerous. We hold that proper practices of argument are crucial for the health of a democratic society. Consequently, democratic citizens should be very careful when dismissing disagreement as merely a symptom of the stupidity or wickedness of one's opponents. We also hold that the most pervasive argumentative failures in contemporary public political discourse are of this dialectical kind.

We proceed in three steps, which are reflected in the three parts of our book. Our first task is to lay out in very general terms our conception of the nature, purpose, and significance of argument. We first make a case for thinking that argument is continuous with and required by the more general aims of our cognitive lives. Engaging in argument is necessary if we are responsibly to attempt to believe the true, and reasonably avoid believing the false. On this view, argument is a process of cognitive hygiene, and a requirement for intellectual health. Consequently, it matters not only that we engage in argument, but also that we argue well, or at least competently. By the close of our third chapter, we will have laid out a conception of the social and political role of argument, and the norms for responsible argument. Importantly, one of our objectives is to show that well-run argument is part of a well-run democracy.

With this groundwork in place, we turn in Part II to a series of case studies in argumentative failure. Again, the emphasis of these chapters is placed upon the ways in which some people fail at proper argument, not only by drawing an incorrect inference or improperly assessing the degree to which a piece of evidence supports some conclusion, but also by distorting or misrepresenting (again, to themselves or to others) the dialectical situation that obtains between their views and those of their opponents. In discussing these matters, we make considerable use of examples drawn from contemporary political discourse. Importantly, however, we resolutely decline to pronounce our own views concerning the issues under discussion. Our task is not that of political advocacy. We instead want to present a view of proper political argument that will look correct to anyone, regardless of where his or her political commitments lie.

With Part III, we lay out some problems that our program of argumentative improvement faces. In particular, we think we must wrestle with the simple fact that training in logic and critical thinking doesn't guarantee any improvement in our performances in argument. In fact, as we will show, it actually makes new and unique forms of errors of reasoning possible. That is, logic, critical thinking, and fallacy theory makes new fallacies and abuses of reason possible. So there's a sense that theories of good reasoning and vocabularies pointing out how we fail at it can contribute to failures. We call this the *Owl of Minerva Problem*, and we try to outline a few ways to mitigate its effects. One of the main contributing factors, we think, to bad argument is that argument is a practice that is under-valued in our broader culture. That is, practices can be rich and worthwhile only if they are valued and given space to be taken on in our cultures, and our observation is that a good deal of what's needed to repair argumentative practice is some cultural repair. One thought we've had is that arguing well can contribute to that repair, but that plan can only go so far. If argument's not valued, then it can't do the repair work needed. We outline some other strategies for repairing our civic culture so that argument can work. Our final chapter attempts to distill everything into a three-part requirement for civility in argument.

Key terms

Rhetorical Success	The argument convinces its audience of the conclusion.
Material Success	The argument's premises are true or acceptable.
Logical Success	The argument's premises, assuming they are true, support the conclusion.
Formal Validity	The argument's premises, if true, guarantee the truth of the argument's conclusion.
Formal Soundness	The argument is valid and its premises are true.
Formal Fallacy	An argument that purports to have formally valid support, but does not.
Dialectical Failure	An argument that fails to properly take up with the commitments of its audience.

Part I

A Conception of Argument

1   Why Do We Argue?

The ancient Greek philosopher Aristotle was an especially astute observer of human nature. Among his many famous pronouncements and ideas, the following two claims may already be familiar to you:

1   Humans by nature are political creatures.
2   Humans by nature desire to know.

The first of these quotations comes from Aristotle's book titled *Politics* (1253a2), and it is often interpreted as saying that humans are naturally "political" in our current colloquial sense of that term. To say that we are political in this sense is to say that we are competitive, ambitious, cunning, shrewd, manipulative, and perhaps ruthless. But this is not the sense of "political" that Aristotle intends. In claiming that we are by nature political, Aristotle means to say that we are by nature social and sociable beings. That is, Aristotle saw that it is no accident that human beings live together in families, neighborhoods, communities, and other social forms of association, including political associations.

Not only are we social in the sense that we enjoy the company of others, we also *depend* on each other in various ways. We need others if we are going to live lives that exhibit the familiar characteristics of a *human* life. From the time we are very young, we need others to nurture and care for us; we need others to teach us how to get along in the physical and social world. Moreover, there are certain distinctively human capacities—capacities for friendship, loyalty, love, gratitude, sincerity, generosity, kindness, and much else—that can exist only given the presence of others. For example, one cannot be a friend all by oneself, and generosity can be exercised only toward needy others. Finally, it seems that the ability to use language—to communicate, to express ourselves—is one of the most central features of human life, and communication presupposes a social life. In order to be fully human, we need others.

As Aristotle also observed, our dependence on others is not a one-way street. Others need us, too. Our dependence is mutual. This is most obvious in the case of friendship. Our friends need us, and, though it may sound odd to say so, we not only need them, but *we also need to be needed by them*. That's just what friendship is. Even infants, arguably the most helpless among us, provide for adults occasions for the development and exercise of the distinctive dispositions and attitudes appropriate to care-givers, nurturers, and guardians. We depend on others even when they depend on us. Dependence is not necessarily a one-way street. As human beings, we are interdependent. We need each other, and we need to be needed by each other.

Importantly, this inevitable and pervasive mutual dependence is not a sign of weakness or deficiency in human beings. As Aristotle also claimed, interdependence is *proper* to human beings. That's simply who we are. We are the kind of creature that needs others of its kind. Our relationships with others are what *make us properly human*. In fact, Aristotle went so far as to say that any creature that is not dependent on others in these distinctively human ways is thereby not a human being at all, but rather something either greater than or less than human—a god or a beast, he said.

Although our dependence on each other is not a defect, our mutual dependency does make our social relations complex and sometimes even problematic. It's obvious that our interdependence means that we must *rely* on others. We *count* on others to be sincere, to think and behave rationally, to follow the agreed-upon rules, to play fair, and so on. Conse-quently, in order to have the humanizing effect we all need, our relations of mutual interdependence must be in some sense *reciprocal*. They must have as their aim some *mutual* benefit. Or, to put the matter in a different way, we are not made more human when our relations with others are one-sided and inequitable, aimed at dispensing benefits only to one party to the relationship at the expense of the other party. Takers need Givers and perhaps Givers need Takers, too; but unless the taking and giving are aimed at some kind of mutual benefit for *both* parties in the long run, their relationship becomes merely a case of someone taking advantage of another. We sometimes speak of one person *using* another. The term *using* captures the one-sidedness of the relationship's benefit.

Perhaps more importantly, if our relationships are to have a humanizing effect, they must involve more than a simple *quid pro quo* or exchange of benefits, as when you scratch your neighbor's back so that he will in turn scratch yours when the time comes. Living socially involves relying on others, and in relying on others we seek not only a *mutual* benefit, but a *common* benefit, a benefit that accrues to *us*. In other words, properly ordered social relations aim at a common good among those who participate in the relation.

Consider, for example, the norms for standing in line. When someone cuts the line, the people behind that person in line have been wronged to some degree, at least by the fact that they must now wait a little longer, or they may miss out on the finite resource being doled out. It is certainly right for those folks to object to this instance of line-cutting. But it does not seem out of place for someone *in front* of the person cutting the line to object, too. This is because cutting in line is not simply a case of one person inconveniencing others; it also involves the breaking of a social rule, and following the rule in question provides for everyone a more peaceful and cooperative social environment than the one that would result from a mad scrum for counter service. A mark of civic-mindedness is that even those not wronged by an infraction can and will object to it.

The humanizing element of our social relations makes possible civic-mindedness, the disposition to think not merely of one's individual good (good for me), but to consider also the shared good of the group (good for us). Families are the first places where these group-minded goods begin to motivate humans, but that civic-mindedness grows to larger associations, and ultimately to the state.

As mentioned above, these features of our mutual interdependence make our social relations complex, and this complexity gives rise to complications. Our mutual dependence creates opportunities for some to take advantage of others. Sometimes people enter into relations with others that are in fact not nurturing and mutually beneficial, but instead are lopsided, manipulative, stifling, or even abusive. What is philosophically interesting (and personally vexing) about relations of this kind is that those who are on the losing end of them often do not realize that they are being harmed; they do not see that they are being manipulated and used by the other. Frequently these are cases of misplaced trust and outright manipulation. These cases are possible because of our mutual dependence, and it is often because of the dependencies that people who are exploited in these relationships cannot recognize their exploitation.

Consequently, our natural dependence gives rise to a kind of vulnerability. In relying on others, we place a degree of trust in them; we interact "in good faith," and we count on others to reciprocate. In some sense this initial expression of trust and good faith is made blindly. We trust others so that they may prove worthy of trust; we rely on others, at least initially, in the hope that they will prove to be reliable. As we know all too well, sometimes we trust the wrong people to the wrong extent. Hence we not only depend upon others, we depend on others to be worthy of our dependence; we trust them to be responsible, reciprocating, and cooperative. And sometimes we learn a difficult lesson, and we consequently know that some others, under certain circumstances, are not to be trusted. And there are certain people who not only should not be trusted, but rather should be positively distrusted. It's an unpleasant fact. But that's life.

We are inherently social creatures, we depend on each other. This, in turn, means that it often matters to us how others live their lives. Since the question of whether those upon whom we depend are in fact trustworthy is a recurring issue for us, we must make the lives of others our business. We must sometimes make it our business to discover and evaluate what others do, even in private, as it were. That your neighbor stores dangerous chemicals under unsafe conditions in her garage is your business. That the store-owner downtown engages in unfair hiring practices is also your business. Perhaps it is also your business how the couple across the street raises their children. Of course, it has been a main occupation of political philosophers to discern the limits to the concern we should have with the lives of others. We depend and rely on each other, and so the lives of others are our business, at least to some extent; nonetheless, we must not become busybodies. The philosophical project of drawing a proper line between having a healthy regard for others and being a nuisance or busy-body is notoriously difficult. The history of philosophy is replete with varied attempts to do just this. Luckily, we need not undertake this task at present, because our concern is with an area of our shared social lives where we tend to think that the line is easier to discern.

To be more specific, one of the most obvious features of our social lives is that we depend on each other *epistemically*. *Epistemology* is the area of philosophy that examines the nature of knowledge, evidence, belief, and the like. Epistemologists are also concerned with the ways in which knowledge is transferred and accumulated, how new knowledge is achieved, and how knowledge differs from other phenomena, such as wishful thinking, blind faith, and lucky guessing. We need not delve deeply into the field of epistemology to make our central point, which is this: Much of what we believe and take ourselves to know derives in large measure from others.

Think about it. Apart from what you believe based on your own memories ("I had Cheerios for breakfast this morning"; "Tomorrow is my mother's birthday") and current bodily sensations ("I have a mild headache"; "I see an apple"), most of what you believe involves reliance on reports, information, findings, testimony, and data that are provided by others. You depend on these others to be reliable, accurate, sincere, and honest. Accordingly, we often regard what others think, and especially what others claim to know, as our business.

And this brings us to the second of Aristotle's claims from the beginning of this chapter. In his book titled *Metaphysics* (980a22), Aristotle observes that we each desire to know. Aristotle is often taken to be saying that humans are naturally or insatiably curious and eager to learn. This is a claim that is obviously disputable. Some of our fellow professors would go so far as to say that, in light of their many years teaching college students, it is obviously false. According to a more plausible interpretation of the quotation, Aristotle is asserting that we take ourselves to know quite a lot, and we are disturbed when we discover that we are wrong about some thing or another. We do not like being mistaken. We hate being wrong. We all desire to know insofar as we desire to avoid being duped, confused, incorrect, or deluded. If this is what Aristotle meant, then it looks as if he may be correct. Again, we try to avoid error, and we do not like having to change our minds about things, especially when it comes to the things we think are important.

The interest we have in knowing, the importance we place on getting things right, and the corresponding discomfort and frustration we feel when we discover that we have erred are all easy to understand. Our actions, plans, and projections are to a large extent based upon the things we believe to be the case. Consider even the mundane example of planning to meet a friend for lunch at a local restaurant. In setting your plans, you take yourself to know the location of the restaurant at which you are to meet your friend. You also take yourself to know that the restaurant in question is open for lunch. And in setting your plan, you take your friend to also know the location of the restaurant, and to understand that you are to meet at the determined time of day. And so on. To be mistaken in any of these beliefs will likely result in a failure to meet your friend for lunch. So, if it is important to you that you succeed in meeting your friend for lunch, it is important that you actually know the things you take yourself to know. The same is true in examples involving more important matters. Suppose you think that your health is very important, and accordingly try to keep to a healthy diet. Now imagine that you (mistakenly) believe that banana-splits are extremely healthy, and so you eat one or more banana-splits every day. Your false belief about what foods are healthy undermines your attempt to preserve your health.

More generally, your behavior is based on what you believe to be the case. If your beliefs are false, you are more likely to act in ways that contravene your intentions and undermine your aims. In a very literal sense, when your actions are based on false beliefs, you don't know what you're doing. Hence we tend to think that knowledge is highly valuable, and, correspondingly, we think it is important to avoid error. Consequently, it makes sense that we attempt to *manage* our cognitive lives, to exercise some kind of control over the processes by which we form, evaluate, sustain, and revise our beliefs.

The main way in which we try to manage our cognitive lives is by trying to attend to our reasons. When we hold beliefs, we typically take ourselves to have good reasons for them, reasons that provide sufficient support for the beliefs we hold, while also suggesting that we should reject competing beliefs. Consider an example. You look out the window and see that it is sunny. You consequently form the belief that it is not raining outside. Your observation of the clear sky and the bright sun provides you with reasons for your belief that it is not raining, while also giving reason to reject the belief that it is raining. Moreover, your belief that it is not raining outside provides you with reasons to act in various ways. If you were planning to go outside, you would probably not wear your raincoat nor carry an umbrella, and so on. Additionally, you think that your reasons for thinking that it is not raining outside can readily be made available to others. Were someone to doubt that it is sunny, you could show her the clear sky and bright sun or you could tell her that you just saw it was a nice day, and then she, too, would have good reason to believe that it is not raining outside.

It all seems rather easy, right? We believe for reasons. Or, to put the point more precisely, when we believe, we typically take our belief to be the product of what our reasons say we should believe. And this is exactly as it should be. There seems to be something odd, perhaps irrational or even idiotic, about believing *against* the reasons we have. Someone who insists that it is raining while gazing out the window onto a sunny day is not only making the error of believing what is false; she is also failing at rationally managing her beliefs. She not only fails to believe what her best reasons say she should believe; she also believes against them. That is, she not only denies what is obviously true, she denies something whose truth should be obvious *to her*. In such cases, we may say to her, "Look out the window! Can't you see that it is sunny?" And if our interlocutor persists in asserting that it is raining outside, we are likely to conclude that she's playing some kind of joke or just being stubborn. In either case, we take it that she doesn't *really* believe that it is raining, but only *says* that she does. We may scratch our heads, and then move on.

The sunny day case involves a *low-cost error*. Our friend may be wrong about the rain, and so she may take her umbrella with her when she goes outside. No biggie—she carries an umbrella with her on a sunny day. However, change the case a bit. Imagine that it's raining, it's clear from the available visual evidence that it's raining (that is, if she looked out the window she'd see a rainy day), and yet she believes it's not raining but sunny. So she's wrong, again. But now add one more thing to the case: she's planned a large picnic. She's taking the kids, some grandparents, the neighbors out to the park for a day in the grass and sun. Imagine she reasons as follows: *it can't be raining, because rain would ruin the picnic*. Not only does our friend reason badly (this is a case of simple wishful thinking), this is a *high-cost error*, and the cost in this case isn't paid only by her, but by the kids, the grandparents, and the neighbors. There they are in the rain with their cute little picnic baskets, which now are full of soggy sandwiches. That's a biggie, and one that our friend should want to avoid not just for the sake of having true beliefs about the weather, but to avoid ruining a Saturday for her friends and family. Her beliefs and how she forms them, then, matter not just to her, but to all those folks involved.

Recall from earlier our point about civic-mindedness. Even those who aren't directly impacted by those breaking the rules nonetheless have grounds for objecting to the violation. Originally our point was about the norms of standing in line, that even those *in front* of the person cutting the line are right to criticize the person who cuts the line behind them. Well, the same thing goes for cognitive norms, too. With the rainy picnic case, not only do the neighbors, kids, and grandparents who got wet have reason to criticize the reasoning, but even those who'd never go on the picnic are right to criticize it, too. And it's not just because the picnic got ruined, but also because it was bad reasoning.

Again, consider the line-cutting case. Imagine that the inconvenience to those back in line was negligible, and the line moved quickly, and nobody missed out on anything. It still is reasonable to criticize the line-cutter for the simple reason that they broke the rule of lines—*no cuts, wait your turn.* That's because it was just a lucky accident that nobody was inconvenienced. The rule exists in order to make the inconvenience of line-standing equitable and so that we can reasonably manage our time. Well, the same goes for the picnic. Even if the picnic came out fine, the reasoning behind it was still worthy of criticism. This is because it put the picnic and others' Saturdays in jeopardy of ruin, and that ruin was avoided merely by a stroke of good luck. The reasoning was, in a word, careless. We depend on each other to make plans responsibly, follow the rules, and reason well. Those who don't do those things deserve criticism, even if things turn out just fine in the end. Why? Because in being careless, they break the trust we place in them as social creatures.

We are now in a position to pull Aristotle's two insights together. That we are social creatures means that we are interdependent; we rely on each other in various ways in order to develop the attitudes, dispositions, and capabilities most characteristic of human life. Our interdependence involves relations that are mutual and reciprocal. Hence our lives are, at least to some extent, properly the business of others. This is most obviously the case when it comes to the ways in which our beliefs are dependent on information provided by others. We depend upon others to be honest, precise, careful, and accurate. When we rely on others who turn out to be deceitful, malicious, careless, or sloppy, our lives can be damaged. The health of our cognitive lives depends in large part on the health of the cognitive lives of others.

Now, one of the persistent, and perhaps permanent, facts of social life is that people disagree with each other about many of the most important matters. To live socially is to encounter others who believe things that differ from what you believe. What's more, to live socially is to encounter others who believe things that you believe to be patently false. And on top of that, living socially involves encountering others who believe that the things you believe are patently false. In short, social life is rife with disputes and disagreements. This is evident to anyone who reads the newspaper or watches the news on television or has ever read a political blog. It is also evident that not all disputes can be solved by a casual glance out the window, as with the cases we discussed a moment ago. That is, not all disputes are cases in which one party has grasped the relevant facts and the other has simply failed to do so. When people disagree, often they also disagree about what their reasons say they should believe. And sometimes they disagree about what reasons there are.

Perhaps it is unsurprising to find that disagreements over the things we tend to think most important are often of this latter kind. When it comes to Big Questions—matters of how to live, the meaning of life and death, the natures of justice, liberty, dignity, and equality, and the like—we often not only disagree about what to believe, we also disagree about what should count as a good reason to believe one thing rather than another. For sure, these are cases in which errors can be high-cost. If you're wrong about the nature of justice or the meaning of life, you're likely to do many unjust things and do things with your life that don't actually contribute to its meaning. It's important to figure such things out. The trouble is that disputes over Big Questions are often messy, and, consequently, seemingly interminable. Moreover, they are also *persistent*: that is, despite their messiness and seeming interminability, we nonetheless *continue* to debate these matters. Debate concerning these matters continues precisely because we want to get them right. In fact, even the view that Big Questions are nonsensical and that hence the debates over them are pointless is *itself* a view about which there is great and ongoing debate. Whether we should spend our time debating Big Questions is itself a Big Question! (And whether it's a very costly error to continue to discuss Big Questions is one too!) The point is that we can't stop caring about these matters, and so debate over them persists, despite the fact that it seems likely that no one will ever have the last word.

Imagine a trolley which just keeps going along its track, never reaching a destination. Would it be wise to board such a trolley? More importantly, once on the trolley, would it be wise to not get off if given the chance? Students in our courses sometimes contend that philosophy is like a trolley that just keeps going around in circles. They say that this means that philosophy is a pointless voyage that goes nowhere. Maybe they are correct in the simile. Philosophical debates do seem to go endlessly around and around. But we think our students are wrong to draw the conclusion that philosophy is for that reason *pointless*. Again, to claim that ongoing, perhaps never-ending, debate about things that matter is pointless is to take oneself to know something about what really matters. It is to take oneself to know something about what is a waste of time and what is worthwhile. The claim that philosophy is pointless is itself a philosophical position about a Big Question, one about which there is, as usual, lots of room for prolonged debate. Once again, we confront our puzzling, perhaps even mysterious, condition. We are creatures for whom argument over Big Questions is inescapable—some would say that it is irresistible—yet it is, it seems, without termination. To put the matter succinctly, we are incurable arguers. The question is why we bother.

So why do we bother? Why do we engage in argument? It might help to begin by asking what argument is. As it turns out, it is not easy to say what argument is. In fact, there are long-standing debates among philosophers about the matter. Yet we have to start somewhere. So we begin with the following. In the most general sense, argument is the attempt to make clear the reasons why we believe something that we believe. That's not bad for a start, but it is insufficient. Argument has an additional dimension that must be introduced. Argument is the attempt not only to make clear what our reasons are, but also to *vindicate* or *defend* what we believe by showing that our belief is well-supported by compelling reasons. We may say, then, that argument has an *inward-looking* and an *outward-looking* aspect. On the one hand, argument is the attempt to articulate the basis for the beliefs we hold; it is an attempt to explain why we believe what we believe. On the other hand, argument is the attempt to *display to others* that they have reason to believe as we do.

Given this latter formulation, we see that argument is one kind of response to disagreement. Since it involves an attempt to respond to disagreement by stating and examining the weight of our reasons, we may say that argument is the *rational* response to disagreement. Argument addresses disagreement by trying to resolve it by means of reasons. To put the point in a different way, an argument is an attempt to put a disagreement to rest by showing those with whom you disagree that they should be compelled by reasons to adopt your belief.

Assuming that this is at least minimally acceptable as a starting-point, it is important to notice that an argument is not simply a verbal fight or a contest of words. To repeat, it is an attempt to *rationally respond to a disagreement*. But notice also that, when we argue, our aim is not simply to resolve a disagreement by winning agreement. Rather, the aim of argument is to win agreement *in the right way*, namely, by presenting reasons and compelling those who disagree with us to recognize their quality. Consequently, when you and your neighbor argue about, say, the death penalty, you do not aim for your neighbor to simply *say* that she believes what you believe; rather, you want her to come to actually believe what you believe. Moreover, you want her to come to believe what you believe *for the good reasons you (take yourself to) have to believe it*. You don't seek merely to persuade your neighbor, you want her to *rationally adopt* your belief. And so you must attempt to show her that the most compelling reasons support your belief (and not hers). To seek simply to persuade her to *say* that she believes what you believe is not to attempt to resolve the disagreement so much as to merely cover it up. But covered-up disagreement is disagreement nevertheless.

To return now to our main query, why should you care about whether your neighbor agrees with you about the best answer to some Big Question, such as, for example, the justice of the death penalty? Why should you care about what your neighbor thinks about anything, for that matter?

The insights from Aristotle that we discussed earlier can help us. We are by nature social creatures for whom believing the truth and avoiding error is of high importance. Consequently, disagreement is troubling to us. This is not only to say that we typically find disagreement uncomfortable, especially in face-to-face contexts. It is also to say that we often find the *fact* that others disagree with us to be troubling. The simple reason is that the fact that others believe things that you reject can sometimes be evidence that you are wrong. To be sure, this is not to say that widespread agreement about some belief is evidence that it is correct (though it can be, especially when there is widespread agreement among those who have thoroughly investigated the belief in question); nor is it to say that when others disagree with you there is sufficient reason to take yourself to be wrong. The point rather is that when others who seem relatively intelligent, informed, sincere, and rational reject a belief that you accept, you have good reason to worry that you have made a mistake. Perhaps you have misjudged the force of your evidence? Maybe you have overlooked some important consideration or misunderstood the significance of some piece of data? Could there be some new reason or argument that you have not considered? Or perhaps you have been misinformed, mislead, or deceived? In other words, disagreement is often an appropriate cause for concern about our beliefs.

But it is important to note that to be concerned about your beliefs is not to stop believing. That others deny what you accept is not in itself cause for skepticism, or the suspension of belief. Believing that Madrid is the capital of Spain is consistent with feeling the need to double-check or reassess the evidence you have for that belief. When one feels concern about a belief, and consequently reviews one's reasons and evidence, one engages in an act of *cognitive hygiene*, not self-doubt. In fact, in our next chapter, we will present reasons for thinking that cognitive health requires us to *maintain* our beliefs, rather than simply holding them steady. That is, we will argue that cognitive health is much like health of other kinds. For example, dental health requires us to make regular trips to the dentist, even when we have no special reason for thinking that our teeth are unhealthy. Other forms of physical health require us to exercise our muscles and consume healthy foods. We do these things even when we have no special reason to believe ourselves unwell. In fact, in the cases of dental and bodily health, if one does not engage in routine check-ups, one incurs certain risks; health problems that would otherwise be minor and easily treated can become serious if they are not diagnosed in their early stages. Moreover, we have regimens of maintaining the health of our teeth and our bodies—we brush regularly and have exercise regimens. Similarly, our cognitive health requires us to occasionally *check* and *maintain* our beliefs and the reasons we have for holding them.

And here's the rub. Cognitive health requires us to maintain a regimen of cognitive hygiene. In order to be healthy believers, we must on occasion reexamine, reassess, and reevaluate the reasons we have for holding our beliefs. Now, these processes are inevitably social in that our reasons, evidence, and data in large measure derive from the experiences, testimony, and expertise of others. We must rely on others in order to remain cognitively healthy. We need others in order to manage our cognitive lives.

People tend to see disagreements and the arguments they occasion to be signals of disharmony and unhealthy conflict. To be sure, face-to-face disagreements sometimes are hostile and unfriendly affairs. But recall that in the sense we are employing here, argument is not necessarily aggressive or unsociable. Our claim is that properly conducted argument and reasoned disagreement is a normal and necessary feature of social life. In fact, we have suggested further that disagreement is a kind of cognitive resource, and thus a good. Those who disagree with the things you believe provide an occasion for you to check your beliefs and your reasons.

And this gives rise to two results that may seem surprising: There is a sense in which argument is an expression of our *respect* and *care* for each other. That is, when you argue with your neighbor, you exhibit concern not only for your own beliefs, but for hers. Again, in arguing, you not only try to win agreement from your neighbor, but you also address her as a fellow rational agent, a person both capable of following and being moved by reasons, and one who can be a source of reasons that can move you. In this sense, engaging in argument with others is a way of showing *respect* for them. But we also see that arguing is also a way of *caring* for others. In arguing, we help others to check their own beliefs and reasons; we provide the resources by means of which they can maintain their cognitive health. It does seem strange, we admit, to say that arguing with others is a way of showing that you care, but everything hangs on what argument is and how it is conducted. If you conduct yourself properly in argument, arguing with others indeed shows that you care for them. If you behave badly in argument, it most certainly alienates others and gets in the way of our cognitive health. And as a consequence, we'd say it's a failure of care. Consequently, arguing well is very important, and what we call the *dialectical* notion of argument captures this social element of arguing well.

So let us ask once more: Why do we bother with argument? We bother with argument because it matters to us that we believe responsibly, and it bothers us when we find that we have made a mistake or have been duped. The fact that others disagree with the things we believe occasions in us the concern that, in forming our beliefs, we have overlooked or misjudged some important piece of evidence or some compelling kind of reason. In cases where the beliefs in question are important, we often call upon those who reject what we believe to provide their own reasons, and we subsequently attempt to weigh their reasons against our own. Even though some arguments over Big Questions seem to go on and on, we engage in the activity of arguing for the sake of caring for our beliefs. You see, it is not so puzzling or mysterious after all.

Not all communication is argumentative. Sometimes people speak in order to haggle, bargain, jockey, compete, flatter, insult, amuse, inform, threaten, and charm. As was said earlier, argument is the attempt to resolve disagreement rationally. The discussion so far has emphasized the positive aspects of argumentation. However, as everyone knows, in the real world, things are not nearly as rosy. People often evoke the apparatus of argument in order to accomplish aims other than rational persuasion.

Under the guise of earnest reason-giving, they seek to embarrass, discredit, ridicule, humiliate, stigmatize, and silence those with whom they disagree. Further, there are those who are simple rationalizers; they have preferred beliefs and pretend to argue for them, but they do not put forth the reasons on the basis of which they truly hold their beliefs. They'll just say anything that they think will place their beliefs in a favorable light. Such is what might be called *pseudo-argument*. It is often difficult to tell the difference between proper argumentation and its counterfeits. In other words, there is a dark side to argumentation. The rest of this book consists of an attempt to provide guidance on how to argue properly, and how to distinguish proper argument from its imposters.

For Further Thought

1   According to the view developed in this chapter, we argue primarily because we encounter disagreement, and we need to find a way to respond rationally to it. But maybe a better response to disagreement is simply to avoid it altogether. Is there any reason why one should not attempt simply to interact only with those with whom one agrees about the things that matter most?

2   Might the answers to certain Big Questions be a matter not of evidence but of faith? Does the answer to this question affect the overall view presented in this chapter?

3   Many philosophers think that almost no one forms beliefs on the basis of reasons, arguments, and evidence. They say that our beliefs are most frequently the products of non-rational phenomena, such as habituation and acculturation. Suppose they are correct. Does this render argument pointless? Might there be a difference between *how we come to believe* what we believe and *how we maintain* our beliefs?

4   Is it really other people's business what you believe? Is it your business how your neighbor forms her beliefs, even if they have nothing to do with you?

5   In this chapter we argue that if people think it's pointless to argue over Big Questions, they must take themselves to have answered a Big Question. Is that right? If we are right, does it mean that the view that it's pointless to argue about Big Questions is self-refuting? Or is there another option?

Key Terms

Epistemology	The philosophical analysis of knowledge. The key questions are: What is Knowledge? What do we know? How do we show that we know?
Big Questions	Roughly, questions about central values and truths at the foundation of a meaningful human life. There is

wide and persistent disagreement about these questions and their answers.

Dialectical View of Argument	The take on argument that it is an attempt to rationally resolve a disagreement and answer critical questions. Argument is best seen as an instance of dialogue in search of truth.
Pseudoargument	The argumentative product of rationalization, where one finds a preferred conclusion and goes looking for premises to support it.

2   Why Argument Matters

Here's where things stand. We know why we argue. Argument is a natural activity for social beings that desire to know. Insofar as humans are by nature political beings who value knowledge, we might say that arguing is an essential part of what it is to be human. Now a new consideration emerges. That argument is a natural activity for humans does not mean that humans are naturally *adept* at argument. It only means that we are *prone* to argue. That we tend to engage in argument does not mean that we tend to argue properly, or even adequately. Some claim that it is obvious that most people argue poorly. In fact, after you take a logic class and learn the fallacy lists, you will likely come to believe that people reason more poorly than you had thought. It's a regular occurrence among students in our logic classes to bemoan the fact that once they've gotten good at detecting fallacies, they can't look anywhere without seeing them. Bad arguments are pretty much the only arguments around.

But before things get too cynical, let's be clear about what arguing well is all about. The topic of the present chapter is the importance of arguing well. After examining this issue, we will be prepared to examine *how* to argue well, which is the subject of the remainder of this book. Only once we've gotten clear about what comprises a good argument can we really see what's going wrong with bad ones.

When you think about it, arguments—or at least what are *presented* as arguments—are everywhere. In our everyday lives we are constantly subjected to purportedly rational appeals that attempt to alter our beliefs or create wholly new ones. These come from our friends and associates, teachers, authors of books, news media, celebrities, talk-show hosts, advertisers, leaders, and governments. It is easy to see why this is so. As was already noted, our beliefs frequently guide or determine our behavior, and others care about how we behave. Thus they have reason to care about what we believe.

That we care about how others behave and thus what others believe is, as we emphasized in the previous chapter, a consequence of the fact that our social interdependence requires us to rely on each other in various ways. And, once again, this mutual reliance can give rise to troubling complications. To put the matter bluntly, not everyone who cares about what we believe cares about our believing what the best reasons say we should believe. Not everyone who cares about what we believe cares about our cognitive health. Not all of those who care about *what* we believe care about *how* or *why* we believe. They just want us to believe the things that will make it most likely that we will act as they wish. They care about what we believe because they want to control us.

Thus we see one very important reason why studying argument matters. We want to avoid being duped or deceived. Wanting to avoid being duped is part of wanting to believe what is true and avoid believing what is false. Wanting to avoid being deceived is part of wanting to believe for your own reasons, to be in charge of your own life, to exhibit self-control. We might say then that skills at argument are like skills of self-defense—they protect against being duped.

This thought requires further elaboration. Again, some people care about what we believe because they wish to *manipulate* us in various ways. For example, advertisements often aim to generate buying behavior on the basis of reasons that are stunningly absurd. Crucially, the function of many advertisements is to cause us to lose sight of the quality of the reasons being offered. For example, we are encouraged by advertisements to believe that buying expensive sports cars will make us more successful, that drinking alcohol will make us more attractive and popular, or that smoking cigarettes will make us healthier. When baldly stated like this, we know better than to believe such things. However, when presented alongside polished and titillating imagery of successful and attractive people, we can be moved to adopt such beliefs, or at least act in accordance with them. Advertisements, that is, often attempt to get us to believe (and so to behave) on the basis of bad reasons by diverting our attention away from the quality of the reasons that are being offered. When ads of this kind are successful, we come to believe things on the basis of reasons that we have not taken care to evaluate. To use a phrase whose familiarity should strike you as revealing and even a little disconcerting, we are told to "just do it." Our rational faculties are more or less circumvented.

Here is an experiment to try next time you are watching television. Take out a notebook and write down what is said in the commercials—just copy their linguistic content. Do this for several commercials. Wait a few days, or maybe a week, and return to the notebook. You will find that, once divorced in your mind from the accompanying imagery, often the linguistic content of television commercials does not even make sense, much less present cogent reasons for buying the product being advertised. This is hard to notice when watching television because the words are accompanied by highly stimulating images. The images are there for the purpose of diverting attention away from what is being said.

Now try another experiment. Try watching commercials with the sound off on your television. Pay close attention to the images. Again, we think you are likely to find that the images and the way in which they are presented are attention-grabbing, but nonetheless they tend to be strange, erratic, and disjointed. Indeed, when it comes to the more stylized commercials, often it is impossible to discern what is being advertised on the basis of the images alone.

This is because the images and the words in commercials often serve different purposes. The images are intended to capture the attention of the eye, and the words are meant to give *the appearance of* reasons. Skilled advertisers know that when the images are especially captivating, good reasons are not really necessary. What matters is presenting you with what *sound like* reasons, but in fact are merely dressed-up versions of the command to "just do it."

Diverting attention away from the quality of our reasons is not the only way in which people try to manipulate us. There is one particular kind of manipulation in which we are overtly encouraged to focus our attention on reasons, and, moreover, strongly urged to evaluate them. How could such a direction of our attention to reasons be a strategy of obscuring reasons? Here's how. In these cases we are presented with a deliberately distorted or deprived image of what reasons there are. For example, let's say that Jack wants Jill to believe that she should vote for Sally for president. One strategy he might employ is to present Jill with his reasons for favoring Sally over the other candidates. A different tactic would be to convince Jill that those who oppose Sally are stupid and uninformed. Employing this second strategy, Jack's message to Jill is that there is no reasonable opposition to the view that Sally is the best candidate. So reasons are given, but those reasons, if considered seriously, block out all the others we should survey when making a decision.

One way to get someone to believe what you want them to believe is to convince them that all opponents of the belief are silly, stupid, ignorant, unreliable, or evil. The aim of this kind of manipulation, then, is not to circumvent our rational faculties, but rather to *channel* them in a specific, predetermined direction. This mode of belief manipulation is perhaps most popular in the realm of contemporary popular political commentary, where pundits often present their opponents as not merely mistaken, but irrational, ignorant, depraved, or demented. Hence they write books with titles like *Liberalism is a Mental Disorder* and *The Republican Noise Machine*. Authors of books like these try to convince you to adopt their favored beliefs by trying to convince you that there is no intelligent alternative to their own point of view.

The aim of this kind of manipulation is to encourage those who are like-minded to insulate themselves from discussion or even interaction with those with whom they might disagree. But there is a problem with this kind of insulation. When groups of like-minded individuals insulate themselves in this way, they not only deny themselves the cognitive benefits of hearing the considerations that favor opposing beliefs; they also deprive themselves of the relevant information that those outside of their group might have. And, as we will see later in this chapter, there are other risks as well.

Thus far, we have claimed that one crucial reason why we should care about proper argument is that arguing properly helps us to avoid getting duped. We have called special attention to a particular way in which one can be duped, namely, *manipulation*. And we have identified two distinct forms of manipulation, which we can characterize as *diverting* manipulation and *distorting* manipulation. These two ways of getting others to believe what one wants are cases of manipulation because they both involve processes of belief production that are insufficiently attentive to reasons. To repeat, when we believe, we aim to believe what is true; and we aim to believe what is true by striving to believe what the best reasons endorse. This is why, for example, falsity is a *fatal objection* to a belief. To come to see one of your beliefs as false is to come to see the belief as defective.

Yet our ambition to believe only what our best reasons suggest is not explained solely by the importance of believing the truth and rejecting what is false. Truth is, to be sure, a principal goal of cognitive life. But it is not the only goal. We strive to believe in accordance with our best reasons because, in addition to the goal of believing what is true, we also aim to be *in possession of* the truth. We aim to believe in such a way that enables us to *see* the truth of our beliefs, to grasp *why* what we believe is true and *understand it*. And this is so because we desire not only truth, but also to *be in control* of our cognitive lives.

To get a feel for the distinction between aiming to believe what is true and aiming to be *in possession of* the truth, imagine the following scenario. Dr. Know has developed a truth serum. But let's say that Know's serum is different from the truth serum commonly encountered in spy novels and science fiction. Let us say that whereas the more familiar kind of truth serum compels those who take it to say only what they *believe* to be true, Dr. Know's serum compels anyone who takes it to say only what *is true*. That is, one who takes the serum will report that the capital of Spain is Madrid only if Madrid is the capital of Spain; one will report that there are exactly twenty people in Central Park right now only if there are exactly twenty people there now; one will report that the death penalty is unjust only if it is; and so on. Importantly, Dr. Know's serum does not enable those who take it to see *how* they're able to report the truth. When you ask one of Know's patients how she came to believe, say, that the death penalty is unjust, she can give no response. She believes sincerely that the death penalty is unjust, and can report confidently that it is true that the death penalty is unjust, but nonetheless she cannot see what reasons there are for her belief. The best she could do, perhaps, is to explain that she came to believe it by drinking the truth serum.

In one way, those who take Dr. Know's serum are in an enviable cognitive position. They believe only what is true, and do not believe anything that is false. But it is hard to see the development of the serum as an unqualified success. Those who take it have only true beliefs, but they have no access to the reasons which show why their beliefs are true. They unerringly believe what is true, but nonetheless they do not *possess* the truth. Their cognitive lives are in this regard less than successful.

Return now to our two kinds of manipulation. To believe without an adequate evaluation of our reasons is a kind of cognitive shortfall. Even if we wind up believing what is true, we reach our goal by luck, and luck is notoriously fickle. Maybe next time we won't be so lucky. Similarly, to believe on the basis of a trumped-up or distorted presentation of the available reasons is, again, to fail cognitively, even if we wind up believing the truth. In both cases, we satisfy the goal of believing what is true and rejecting what is false, but both cases nevertheless involve a kind of mismanagement of our cognitive faculties. In both cases, when we reach the truth, we do so by a kind of fluke. We get the truth, but, alas, we have not earned it.

Luck is what is problematic in these cases. When we say that someone has achieved a goal by way of good luck, we both praise the goal as worthy and take a critical stance toward that person's performance in reaching it. Consider a few cases. When someone hits an incredible shot on the golf course, that person may say, "I was just lucky." In so doing, he is not saying the shot was not successful; rather, he is saying that the success was not entirely his own doing. It was not the result of his skill and effort. It was luck. Alternately, when your neighbor wins the lottery, you might say she was lucky. You, yourself, may have bought a ticket and put the same thought into selecting the numbers as she did. Yet she won and you did not. When we call her a "lucky winner" we are on the one hand saying she certainly is a winner, but also that it was simply luck that made it so, not effort or skill.

When it comes to our lives, we do not want to be merely lucky winners. We want our successes to be the products of our efforts; we want to *deserve* the goods when they come. Those who diligently practice their golf swings are not simply lucky when they hit those fabulous shots. They are skillful and in control of their swing. And those shots are the result of the exercise of those skills. Similarly, those who carefully manage their finances, save their nickels, and make good investments are not mere lucky winners when they discover their bank accounts burgeoning. They are thrifty. And their financial success is theirs in a way that is very different from those we call "clearing house lucky," even if they end up in the same place.

The point is that we want success at reaching our cognitive goals of believing the truth and rejecting falsehood, but it is important to note that success consists in achieving those goals in a particular way. We want not only to achieve our aims, but to succeed in a sense that the success is *ours*. Only success that results from our effort, skill, and vigilance is success that is truly our own. To put the point in a different way, we want truth, but we want to attain it not just in any old way. We want it in a way that enables us to possess the truth, to have command of what we believe. This is what those who take Dr. Know's serum lack.

These considerations put us in a position to make a distinction between the values of *cognitive success* and *cognitive command*. One can have a cognitive success by way of good luck—a lucky guess can still be true. But cognitive command is an understanding of an issue, a set of explanations for how and why things are one way and not another, and even an account of how others might have objections and what the replies to them are. Those who only have a correct belief have nothing to say back to someone who has doubts or needs an explanation, except to just say what they believe again. Having cognitive command, however, makes it so that success isn't just a matter of luck—it's the result of having done one's homework, understanding the situation, and having a story to tell. And so those with cognitive command have something to say when others have doubts or request more information.

Note, however, that cognitive command does not guarantee truth. That is, it is possible for those with cognitive command to be wrong. Experts, for example, have cognitive command of the subject of their expertise. That's what makes them experts. But experts sometimes disagree, and when they do, at least one expert is wrong. That doesn't mean that at least one purported expert isn't really an expert. It just means that at least one expert is wrong. So a pro golfer can hit the ball into the water hazard or into the thicket and still be an excellent golfer, and someone who has command of an issue can still get things wrong. Having cognitive command doesn't make us infallible, and this isn't too much of a surprise. We know already that with many issues, we can acknowledge that there are well-researched and impressively thought-out ideas that are nevertheless wrong.

That cognitive command does not guarantee truth or infallibility in no way undercuts its value. The reason why is that achieving cognitive command enables one to *rationally correct* oneself in light of countervailing evidence and counter-considerations. One who has achieved cognitive command of an issue understands how best to revise their belief should it be shown to be incorrect. Additionally, cognitive command enables us to *assess* new evidence, to *address* critics, and to *answer* objections. Cognitive command may not necessarily get us truth, but it does put us in contact with the relevant reasons and evidence. In this way, we come to understand an issue, and thus we are able to manage disagreement.

This point directs us back to the importance of argument. Achieving command of ourselves in forming and holding our beliefs is necessary if we are going to be able to defend our beliefs in the face of challenges to them. It is also necessary if we are going to be able to assess new evidence and unfamiliar considerations that bear on the truth of our beliefs.

Furthermore, having a firm grasp of the reasons why we hold our beliefs is crucial when we are faced with the need to change, revise, or amend them.

Argumentation—again, the processes of giving reasons in support of one's beliefs, proposing considerations that tell against opposing beliefs, and assessing the reasons offered by those who disagree with us—is the activity by which we come into possession of our beliefs. If we argue poorly or carelessly, we may yet believe what is true, but we lose control of our cognitive lives. Often when we lose control of ourselves, there are others who are eager to take control for us, and, when they do so, they gain control *of* us. As we have said above, proper argumentation, or at least competent argumentation, is important as a matter of cognitive hygiene. But now we are able to see that proper argumentation is also a form of cognitive self-protection, a way of avoiding getting duped.

Much of what we have said thus far turns on the overall badness of getting duped by others. We have claimed that argument matters because we all want to avoid being manipulated. But it is important to notice that not all duping comes from other people. We can dupe ourselves. Maybe that way of putting the point is a little too dramatic. But it is clear that when it comes to our cognitive health, we can be our own worst enemy. Recall from the previous chapter Aristotle's keen observation that humans are naturally sociable and desirous of knowledge. These two features can, in some contexts, come into conflict; and in other contexts, they can conspire against our cognitive aims. For example, our need for healthy social relations can sometimes render us especially vulnerable to peer-pressure; it can also prohibit us from speaking our mind in "mixed company," when we are not sure whether our views will meet with agreement. In these cases, we engage in self-censorship. In other cases, sociability and the desire to know work together to subvert our aim of believing what is true and rejecting what is false. Sometimes social pressures forcefully encourage one to speak one's mind, but only under the condition that one affirms a belief favored by the group. These are not cases of manipulation in the sense we identified above. Rather, they involve an *internal* short-circuiting of proper reasoning.

To get a sense of what we mean, consider what happened to Democratic pundits and other supporters a few months prior to the 2016 presidential election in the United States. They were all sure that the Democratic candidate, Hillary Clinton, was going to win the election by a landslide. They were so sure of this that they systematically discounted and dismissed all reports showing that Donald Trump's campaign was going well in many swing states. They repeatedly insisted that any polls showing an advantage for Mr. Trump represented statistical anomalies or flawed methodology.

Why would they say that? Perhaps because everyone they knew and talked with claimed to oppose Trump's election. Or maybe because they overestimated the impact of the fact that so many stars and talk show hosts were publicly denouncing Mr. Trump—they just figured that everyone thought that way. Consider the following predictions, all of which were made on the eve of the 2016 election:

- *Huffington Post*'s Natalie Jackson and Adam Hooper ran 10 million simulations of the electoral map with the very latest polling data and determined that Clinton was 98% likely (and Trump 1.7% likely) to win the Presidency.
- *Vox*'s Ezra Klein held that Clinton's win was "assured" and Trump's loss was "inevitable." He paused to note the strangeness of the situation: "We aren't used to this kind of victory.... Hillary Clinton has humbled Donald Trump, and she did it her way."
- *MSNBC*'s Joy Reid said that the Trump Campaign's plans on taking Michigan and Wisconsin were "weird," because she thought he had no chance in those states (which he won). And panelist Jamal Simmons said Trump was "being kind of a jerk" for campaigning in those states he was going to lose, because he should spend more time in states where his campaign could help senatorial candidates.

All of these experts were spectacularly wrong. Mr. Trump won the election with a substantial Electoral College win, despite Secretary Clinton garnering 3 million more popular votes. So what happened? For one thing, over the course of the 2016 campaign, it became more and more clear that polling for the election was unreliable for predicting results, and it was especially unreliable when it came to predicting how voters would swing for Mr. Trump. But these folks nevertheless made their predictions with what in hindsight seems appallingly disproportionate confidence. Importantly, this was not a case of *someone else* manipulating them, it was a case of them doing this *to themselves.* In these cases, in order to argue well, we need someone who can critically push back on our easy rationalizations. Again, argument is a social enterprise, and in these cases, the sociality of argument is that we don't just rely on each other for information, we need each other for critical pushback. If we're in an echo chamber of views we like, we are setting ourselves up for a fall.

We have presented a case for thinking that argument matters, and that it is important to try to argue well. But we have not yet said explicitly what proper argumentation is. Rest assured. We are on our way toward doing so. Before we turn to that issue, we must address a concern that one might raise with our account thus far.

A critic might claim that the views we have laid out are all well and good for those who do not know the truth. Such a critic might concede that the goods we have identified as attainable only by means of proper argumentation are indeed highly important. But she may then contend that the goods of argument pertain only to the processes of trying to *gain* knowledge. The critic might then claim that *once one has knowledge*, further argument is unnecessary. In fact, our critic could go further to say that for those who have knowledge, further argument is not only super-fluous, but also potentially dangerous, as it creates an occasion by which one might mistakenly exchange a true belief for a false one.

There is no denying that engaging in argument carries certain significant risks. When we argue, we exchange and examine reasons with a view toward believing what our best reasons say we should believe; sometimes we discover that our current reasons fall short, and that our beliefs are not well supported after all. Or sometimes we discover that a belief that we had dismissed as silly or obviously false in fact enjoys the support of highly compelling reasons. On other occasions, we discover that the reasons offered by those with whom we disagree measure up toe-to-toe with our own reasons and it seems as if the best reasons support equally two opposing beliefs. In any of these situations, an adjustment in our belief is called for; we must change what we believe, or revise it, or replace it, or suspend belief altogether. Typically we don't like having to make such adjustments, and in cases where the belief in question is one that is especially important to us, it pains us to admit that we are wrong. Indeed, with respect to certain especially important beliefs—such as moral, religious, and political beliefs—to come to realize that we are wrong is usually to invite a kind of cognitive turmoil. When we find that we must give up or change our beliefs of this kind, our lives change. In such cases, we often find ourselves wondering who we are.

Hence our envisioned critic is right to point out that argumentation is risky business. However, she seems to have overlooked the fact that risk assessment is always a *comparative* matter. That is to say, our estimation of the risks of engaging in argument must be informed by an assessment of the risks that are involved in resolutely *avoiding* argument or *declining* to engage in argument. The line of criticism we have been considering claims that once one has a true belief, there is no need to consider the reasons promoted by those with whom we disagree. After all, if you believe what is true and your neighbor holds an opposing belief, then it is clear that your neighbor is mistaken. So why should you bother listening to the reasons she can offer in support of her (false) belief? You know in advance that she believes what is false, and so the reasons she has for her belief are defective, incomplete, or misleading. As you already have the truth, engaging with those who oppose you promises no gain and can only occasion error. Better to just let it go, right?

It may seem that our critic is obviously correct here as well. But, as it turns out, she's not. There is overwhelming and continually growing evidence that shows that those who decline to engage with those with whom they disagree, and instead talk only with those who are like-minded, are prone to a phenomenon called *group polarization*. The phenomenon is this: *When one exchanges reasons about an issue only with those who agree, one's beliefs regarding that issue imperceptibly shift to more extreme versions of themselves.* For example, when pro-life activists discuss abortion only amongst themselves, over time each person involved in the discussion comes to adopt a more extreme version of the pro-life view than the one he or she held prior to the discussion. The same goes for those who hold the pro-choice view. That is, reason exchange among only like-minded believers produces a change in belief. Again, it doesn't matter what the view is (right or wrong). If you talk about the view only with people you agree with, you become more extreme. And as a consequence, you don't hold the view you started with in the first place.

Let's say that Alfred holds the belief that abortion is morally permissible only in cases of rape, incest, and where it is necessary to save the life of the pregnant woman. We can use the variable P to refer to Alfred's belief. It should be clear that P lies on a spectrum of pro-life views about abortion. One could, for example, hold a more permissive pro-life view, call it Q, according to which abortion is morally permissible in cases of rape, incest, or where it is necessary to avoid certain severe health risks to the pregnant woman (including but not restricted to her death). Or one could hold a more restrictive pro-life position, which we may call R, according to which abortion is morally permissible only in cases where it is necessary to save the life of the pregnant woman. There is of course the even more strict view, S, which holds that abortion is never morally permissible, but sometimes excusable; and there is the maximally restrictive view that abortion is under no circumstances allowable and never excusable. There are several other positions on the pro-life spectrum as well.

Now let us suppose that P is true. (Note that we are not claiming that P is true, we are only supposing that it is for the sake of argument.) The group polarization phenomenon means that if Alfred were to discuss his views about abortion only with others who hold views on the pro-life spectrum, over time his belief would shift from P to some more restrictive view on that spectrum (as would the beliefs of the others he discusses abortion with). He would come to hold R, or some such view. But recall that we have stipulated that P is true, and this entails that R is false. So, in declining to engage the issue of abortion with those on the pro-choice side of the debate and electing to discuss the matter only with those who are like-minded, Alfred loses the truth.

It may seem that our appeal to the group polarization phenomenon presupposes the claim that more extreme beliefs are always false beliefs, that a shift to a more restrictive view from a more moderate view is always a shift in the direction of falsehood. But our argument makes no such assumption. The important feature of group polarization is that the shift toward more extreme versions of one's pre-discussion belief is not caused by the introduction of new or better reasons. Group polarization is caused by group dynamics, not reasons. Accordingly, by discussing abortion only with those who share his general perspective, Alfred has not only lost his true belief, he has done so on the basis of something other than reasons. The group polarization phenomenon threatens our cognitive command, even if it may be that one reaches the truth by means of it.

Recall now the objection posed by our imagined critic. She claimed that when one has the truth, argumentation is unnecessary, superfluous, or even dangerous. We now see her error. Argumentation is not merely a process by which one forms and revises beliefs. Argumentation is also a process by which one maintains one's beliefs. Earlier, we analogized cognitive and bodily health. Like muscles and physical health in general, cognitive health requires us to engage in activities that exercise our capacities. Argumentation is the process of exercising our cognitive muscles, so to speak. Consequently, argumentation has value even to those who already have true beliefs. It is a way to inoculate oneself against group polarization. The group polarization phenomenon shows that by declining to exchange reasons with those who disagree, one runs the risk of losing the truth, *even when one already has true beliefs*. Argumentation is the way we should go about forming our beliefs and ridding ourselves of false beliefs; but it is also what we must do if we want to hold on to our true beliefs.

Thus far, our account of the importance of proper argument has been formulated primarily in individual terms. We have claimed that arguing well is important if one is to maintain control over one's beliefs and avoid being duped. Yet our discussions of manipulation and group polarization both point to the inherently social dimension of cognitive life. We want now to deepen this element of our account by picking up on a thought expressed at the close of our first chapter.

To put the point succinctly: Democracy is a mode of political association that significantly heightens the importance of argument. However much argument matters for our individual lives, it matters even more for those who are also citizens of a democratic society. It may be obvious why this is the case, but the point deserves to be stated explicitly. People living together under any political arrangement must rely upon each other in various ways, but in a democracy, citizens wield collective power over their lives together. Through familiar activities such as voting, campaigning, participating in political organizations, donating to social causes, volunteering in community initiatives, and attending local school board meetings, democratic citizens contribute to the processes by which our collective lives are managed. Laws are made, offices are filled, and policies are enacted by citizens. Just as we as individuals want to believe the true and avoid believing what is false, we collectively want to be governed by institutions and policies that can recognize good reasons and reject bad reasons. In fact, it could be said that democracy is precisely the attempt to live together according to our best reasons.

This is why democracy involves such a broad variety of collective activities. Although perhaps it is common to think of democracy simply in terms of elections and voting, it really is much more than this. To take a most obvious example, elections are preceded by campaigns. And, as we all know, candidates on the campaign trail do a lot of talking, and much of this talking is conducted in the mode of argument. Indeed, a lot of political talk in a democracy is explicitly presented as a debate, where candidates, pundits, journalists, and citizens speak more or less directly to each other in an attempt to exchange reasons. Yet democracy also involves more than campaigns. In addition to voting in regular and fair elections, democratic citizens are called upon to serve as jurors, to achieve a certain level of education, to uphold the laws, to hold public officials accountable, and to participate in the life of their communities. Indeed, many of the rights and entitlements that we most closely associate with democracy—free speech, a free press, due process, and much else—are directly tied to the social aspiration to have our collective lives managed according to our best reasons. It could be said, then, that democracy is the political and social expression of our aspiration to cognitive health and rational self-control; democracy is, as it is more commonly put, a system of *self-government*.

Given what the real world of democratic politics is like, our claim that democracy is committed to rational self-control will probably strike many readers as utterly incredible or as some kind of joke. Not so fast. Imagine a society in which collective decisions are made by an elaborate system of coin-tosses in which every option is given a fair chance of being selected as the group decision. Does such a system appeal to you? If not, why not? The imagined arrangement is defective because it does not allow collective decision making to be guided by what citizens believe; it rather decides on the basis of chance.

Imagine next a society which makes collective decisions by picking pieces of paper out of a bowl. Imagine that in this system, each citizen is allowed to write on a small sheet of paper his or her opinion about what the government should do, but imagine also that this system does not allow citizens to discuss their views with others. A question is put to the electorate, each citizen is asked simply to write down her opinion on the question, citizens are forbidden to share their views, and a decision is made according to whatever slip of paper is drawn.

Such a system is surely an improvement on the first in that it does allow collective decisions to be guided by what citizens believe, and, furthermore, it gives to each citizen equal input into the decision-making process. However, we suspect that this arrangement will strike our readers as ultimately defective. Why?

Here's the answer. What's missing in this imagined society is the connection between collective political decision making and our individual and collective reasons. A crucial part of democracy is the attempt to reason with each other about what we, collectively, should do. Democracy depends not simply on citizens voting on the issues of the day; it relies also upon citizens sharing their views and their reasons with others, prior to casting their votes. Again, democracy is the aspiration to conduct our collective lives according to our best reasons. And so, we think a *deliberative* conception of democracy is best.

At this point a serious problem for our account comes into view. We have identified democracy with the aspiration to be governed by our best reasons. However, we have yet to mention a central component of democracy, namely, majority rule. It seems there is a tension between the aspiration to be governed by our best reasons and the system in which collective decision making must track the beliefs of the majority. To explain, it has long been a favorite strategy among philosophers who oppose democracy to criticize the idea that majority opinion should determine collective decisions. Collective decisions are often focused on very complex questions, and finding rational answers to complicated questions often requires one to have a high degree of expertise. So why place the power to decide in the hands of the majority? Why not instead have experts rule?

This is the thought driving Plato's magisterial work of political philosophy, *The Republic*. In fact, the common interpretation of *The Republic* has Plato arguing that justice demands that political power be placed in the hands of those who are the most knowledgeable. Believing that philosophers are the only people who actually know anything, Plato draws the conclusion that philosophers should rule as kings. Hence Plato's famous idea of the idea of the *philosopher-king*.

The chutzpah manifest in Plato's view is often noted by his critics. However, one can feel the force of this argument against democracy by simply considering, first, that it matters what we collectively decide to do as a society. When a government acts, it can commit grave forms of injustice; it can waste precious resources, squander opportunities, unduly constrain freedom, and ruin lives. Most decisions made by a state are high error-cost decisions. They are the kind of things we don't want to get wrong. Next consider that we know that the majority of our fellow democratic citizens are not experts in matters of justice. In fact, it is common for democratic citizens to have an especially low regard for the cognitive capacities of their fellows. What then could possibly support the idea that collective political decision making should be determined by majority opinion? That's Plato's challenge, and it's serious.

This is admittedly a very difficult matter, and we cannot provide a full response to the challenge here. But we do have a two-part reply that will bring us back to the main topic of the importance of argument.

For starters, it is worth noting that history supplies a staggering number of examples of kingship gone terribly wrong, and few (if any) cases in which kingly political power has been exercised according to the best reasons concerning justice. To put the point in a philosophical way, Plato makes the mistake of comparing (what was in his day) real-world democracy with ideal-world kingship. You don't get to rig the comparison by saying: "my ideal version of kingship would do better than your real version of democracy." Of course it would! It's an *ideal version*, after all. A proper argument would have to compare either ideal-world kingship to ideal-world democracy, or real-world kingship with real-world democracy.

This occasions a further historical point about the real democracies Plato was looking at and the democracies in the world today. Democracy as Plato describes it is in many respects far removed from modern day democracy. Plato sees democracy as unconstrained and direct majority rule. In modern democracy, by contrast, the majority will is constrained by a constitution that identifies individual rights that constrain what even a vast majority can politically decide. Moreover, modern democracy is non-direct in that it involves a system of representation, where elected office-holders are largely charged with the task of reasoning about policy on behalf of those who they represent. Finally, in modern democracy, those who hold the greatest power are nevertheless constrained by a system of constitutional checks and balances. In short, although modern democracy has majority rule as one of its central elements, it is not merely rule by the majority.

Our second response to Plato's challenge is more philosophical than historical. Recall the distinction we drew earlier between the aspiration to believe the truth and the aspiration to possess the truth. We argued there that we aspire not only to have true beliefs, but also to see why they are true—we want not only cognitive success, but cognitive command. These two aspirations of our cognitive lives permit us to make a handful of replies to Plato.

A Platonic order where an expert makes all of the political decisions is one in which we could not see our collective and cognitive lives as ours. Such an arrangement would be the political analogue of the individual who takes Dr. Know's serum. Perhaps there could be a morally incorruptible expert who always decides political questions in a way that corresponds to what justice requires. A society in which such an individual possesses complete political power would no doubt be by some measure successful. But, like the beliefs of those who take Know's serum, it would fail to be a success attributable to the citizens of the society. In fact, it would be a society in which justice doesn't really matter to anyone except the expert ruler. Citizens would live according to rules required by justice, but could not *see* the justice of the rules, because all they would know is that they were decreed by the rulers. Consequently, they could not see their society as the product of their own collective efforts to reason together about their lives. They could live in a perfect society but not understand it as such. That seems a tragedy, a kind of shame. Or, if that's too dramatic an assessment, it's at least disappointing. And, remember, that's supposed to be an ideal society.

Perhaps most importantly, the Platonic arrangement causes us to see our cognitive lives as fundamentally disjointed. In a Platonic kingdom, citizens must rely on their individual and collective cognitive skills in order to form beliefs about the full range of non-political matters—from how to cook their dinners, clean their clothes, and fix their cars to what books to read and how to spend their free time—but they must nevertheless decline to apply those faculties to Big Questions about their social and political lives. They must see their social existence, along with their political beliefs and political activity, as *alien*. This seems to us a most severe kind of injustice, one that undoes whatever moral advantages the Platonic kingdom might seem to embody.

Here a critic might object in the following way. It seems that some good challenges to the idea of a Platonic kingship have been raised, but it is still not clear that majority rule can be defended. Even when constrained by the constitutional mechanisms of modern democracy, majority rule still seems to be in tension with the aspiration to believe what is true and avoid believing what is false. Moreover, majority rule is far too often the rule by those with little cognitive command, but who nevertheless want to give commands.

This is a worthy objection. Here's our response. Just as we must rely on others in our individual lives, our collective life in a democratic society involves a similar kind of reliance. Democratic self-government is rooted in a commitment to the cognitive soundness of a system in which individuals are permitted to freely exchange information, ideas, reasons, and arguments. The thought is that under such conditions, the belief that can win the assent of a majority is the best available guide to collective decision making that is consistent with the other values embodied by a modern democracy, including equality and liberty. This is of course not to say that in a democracy citizens must always regard the majority view as correct or even best given the available reasons. It means rather that over the full range of cases, a belief that has won the assent of a majority is the best guide to what our reasons say we should decide. It is important to emphasize that it is open to democratic citizens to hold that in a particular case, the democratic process has failed to track the best reasons and consequently has produced a seriously mistaken result.

This point about democratic error is why, in a modern democracy, collective decisions are understood to be revisable. In fact, many of the individual rights recognized by modern democracy are aimed at enabling those who object to a policy to challenge it, even after it has been validated or selected by properly democratic processes of collective decision making. That is, a basic commitment of modern democracy is that citizens must be permitted to engage in acts of critique, protest, resistance, and dissent. This provides an additional consideration that favors majority rule. Political majorities are not set in stone. Groups of dissenting individuals, even if they begin as a tiny minority, can continue to debate and criticize a given political decision, and at least in principle transform into a majority and bring about significant social change.

In our individual lives, we can do our best to believe in accordance with our reasons, and yet still fail. Similarly, even a properly functioning democracy composed of sincere and intelligent citizens can err. No method of collective decision making can guarantee correctness every time. Majority rule is simply the best decision procedure available, in that over the range of cases (even if not in every individual instance) it promises results that reflect our best reasons, while respecting the other values that democracy holds dear. The hope with democracy is that over time the truth will out, and when it does, we will not only have a truth, but we will possess it.

Although this response to Plato is incomplete, we think that it can be developed into a rather powerful defense of democracy. However, as with success of almost every kind, philosophical success comes at a price. As you probably noticed as the discussion developed, our defense of democracy places significant demands on democratic citizens. For example, our defense of majority rule—even the kind of majority rule that is constrained by the rights of individuals—calls for a democratic citizenry that is responsive to the ongoing arguments and criticisms presented by dissenting groups, even when such groups reflect tiny minorities. In addition, our entire discussion of democracy has presupposed that democratic citizens are fundamentally interested in reasons and arguments rather than raw power. That's pretty idealistic on our part. Some might call it dangerously optimistic.

We recognize that actual democracy is not so rosy. We realize that the politically powerful often dismiss the arguments of those less powerful without much thought. And we are not blind to the fact that democratic politics is most frequently driven by power in various forms—including money, class, status, pedigree, and so on—rather than reasons. But we also think that our account does not require us to deny any of these facts about real-world democratic politics. Here's why. The view that we have presented thus far identifies what we take to be the *aspirations* embodied in our individual and collective cognitive lives. We do not take ourselves to have been *describing* actual democracy any more than we took ourselves in our first chapter to have been describing how actual people go about forming and evaluating their beliefs. What we have been trying to do is present a model of cognitive hygiene—in both individual and social aspects—that is worth trying for.

Importantly, this model is not plucked from thin air by a couple of armchair academics. We have tried to identify and make explicit the aspirations that inhere in the everyday practices of people. It may be true that the proverbial man on the street often fails to believe what his best reasons say he should believe, but, crucially, the man on the street does not *take himself* to hold unfounded or otherwise defective beliefs. Rather, he takes himself to be successful in tracking his reasons. Otherwise, he would not believe as he does. Again, the man on the street may in fact believe on the basis of what barely could count as a reason, but he does not evaluate himself in this way. Instead, he sees his reasons as sufficient.

Consider again the political experts we mentioned earlier. They expressed unmistakable confidence in their predictions about the 2016 presidential election in the United States. Yet they were all wrong, and stunningly so.

But now notice that, even though it is clear to us in hindsight that they suffered from a form of group polarization driven by wishful thinking and social pressure, in offering their predictions, they were still talking about the reasons they had. Ezra Klein invokes his expertise, and the *Huffington Post* team insist they are looking at the available data objectively. Importantly, they do not say of themselves, in the midst of it all, "My views are all the product of a self-imposed intellectual echo chamber." Nobody ever says that kind of thing about his or her own beliefs. And here's why: in every case of belief, we take ourselves to have *not* been duped. To hold a belief is to take it to have been adequately formed. Even in the depths of profound error, people uphold the aspiration to proper cognitive hygiene. That's cause for modest optimism.

There is a further, more general consideration that is worth mentioning at this point. The prevalence of ongoing and persistent disagreement, of actual dispute among people over political and moral questions of the day, shows that people in general see themselves as beholden to the aspiration to believe on the basis of the best reasons they have. If this were not the case, it would be difficult to explain why the man on the street is in the least inclined to criticize those who disagree with him. It would similarly be difficult to make sense of many of the staple institutions and practices of our political lives, from newspapers, blogs, and political talk-shows to the hundreds of books published yearly by political commentators and pundits. In none of these cases do we allow people to assert that reasons do not matter. In fact, we demand that they provide us with reasons and are responsive to our objections.

In short, argument expresses our commitment to the aspiration to believe in accordance with the best reasons we can find. It reflects the pull we should feel for cognitive command. That argument so pervades our social and political lives demonstrates the widespread commitment to this aspiration. We have argued here that democracy is the political manifestation of the aspiration to conduct ourselves according to our reasons. As an aspiration, democracy requires us not to succeed always at rational self-government, but to sincerely and earnestly try to live individually and collectively according to our best reasons. We of course often fall short. But the fact that we fall short doesn't mean this aspiration is silly or worthless. We shouldn't give up on the aspiration of self-rule and autonomy so easily. That would be tantamount to seeing ourselves as deserving nothing better than to be ruled by others. It would be to resign ourselves to being subjects of a king or cabal of oligarchs whom we could at most hope are inclined to rule in accordance with the demands of justice. Rather, given what we have outlined here, we all have a deep aspiration to be individually and collectively rational. In this respect, we are all idealists about argument and about democracy.

Democracy is the project of self-government among free and equal citizens. Self-government among free and equal citizens inevitably involves collective decision making amidst ongoing disagreement among citizens about what should be done. In a democracy, we try collectively to decide on the policies and actions that enjoy the support of our best reasons. Accordingly, democracy calls for vibrant but reasoned public discourse and debate; the activity of trying to root out in dialogue what reasons one has to believe one thing or another is central to democracy. We may say, then, that democracy is self-government by means of public argumentation. Hence it matters how we argue, and that we argue well rather than poorly. Caring about arguing well about public matters is among the central duties of democratic citizenship. In our next chapter, we develop an account of what proper public argument involves.

For Further Thought

1   Early in the chapter, it is claimed that engaging in argument helps us to better understand our own commitments. Arguing helps us to gain a kind of command over our own beliefs. Is this plausible? Doesn't argument often result simply in greater uncertainty and doubt?
2   How might Plato respond to the defense of democracy offered in this chapter? Does the fact that anti-democrats feel compelled to provide arguments against democracy provide an unintended kind of support for democracy?
3   The conception of democracy defended here seems to place significant demands on ordinary citizens. The democratic citizens envisioned here are highly active participants in the political life of their communities. But surely there's more to life than democracy and the duties of a democratic citizen. Some people quite reasonably prefer to spend their time in other ways, including in more or less solitary pursuits. Can the view developed in this chapter accommodate this fact?
4   In the chapter, there were two kinds of manipulation proposed: diverting and distorting manipulation. Are there other ways arguments (or pseudoarguments) can manipulate?
5   Is the value of cognitive command undone by the fact that one can have command of an issue but still be wrong?
6   How could the phenomenon of group polarization create the illusion of cognitive command?

Key Terms

Deliberative democracy The attempt to collectively govern our shared lives according to our best reasons.

Group polarization The social phenomenon of intellectually homogenous groups to progressively hold more extreme versions of views.

3 Public Argument in a Democratic Society

We proposed in the preceding chapter that democracy is the social and political manifestation of our individual cognitive aspiration to be rational. The thought bears repeating: *Just as we individually aspire to believe in accordance with our best reasons, we collectively aspire to live together according to our best reasons.* Democracy is the social and political arrangement that enables us to pursue this cognitive goal. It is collective self-government by means of public argument among equal citizens. Consequently, democracy brings with it a duty of citizenship, specifically, a duty to try to argue well.

These sentiments may sound lofty, possibly even wholly detached from the real world of democracy. Indeed, thus far we have been talking about democracy in a way that is theoretical rather than descriptive. We have been trying to articulate a view of democracy in the abstract, or in the ideal. Sometimes it helps to talk in ideal terms because often it is by appeal to a sense of how things should be that we are able to critique how things are. That's what we have been doing. But now it is time to get real. We have spoken enough about the role of argument in an ideal democracy. What is the role of argument in actual democracy?

Giving arguments, articulating reasons, responding to criticism, and bearing the burden of having a command of information and its relevance are all important to politics. We note again that in the vast world of popular political commentary—from the daily transmissions of talk radio hosts like Rush Limbaugh and Amy Goodman, to the book-length analyses offered by best-selling authors such as Ann Coulter and Thomas Frank—argument reigns. In fact, not only do pundits and commentators engage in argument, *they claim that argument, reason, and truth are what matters.* Thus they profess to offer "no spin zones" and "straight talk." Moreover, they explicitly oppose "bias," "slant," and "fake news"; and they call out anyone who they perceive to be playing fast and loose with the facts. In short, the real world of democracy is saturated with argument. And this is precisely as it should be.

The previous paragraph might strike you as hopelessly naïve. You may think that democracy is saturated not with argument, but only with the appearance of argument. You may continue: Presidential hopefuls don't really *argue* with each other about the important political issues of the day, they merely try to *look like* they're arguing, while in fact they are simply jockeying for rhetorical points and clever catchphrases. Similarly, you may contend that the political punditry's self-professed commitment to truth, reason, and "no spin" is simply pretense, merely a marketing strategy to sell an audience on the idea that the commentator in question is to be trusted. In short, you might think that in a democracy everyone professes to be interested in argument, reason, and truth; but in fact, the only thing anyone really cares about is power. And it might strike you that in a democracy, one gets power only by convincing large numbers of people to cast votes and engage in other activities in your favor. Hence you might conclude that the real-world democracy is not about argument at all. Then maybe you'll go further to say that our book thus far has not only been naïve, but pernicious in that it has used the language of argument to give credibility to a political and social order that is fundamentally anti-rational and concerned only with power.

This is certainly a powerful line of critique, one that goes back ultimately to Plato and complements the Platonic criticisms of democracy that were explored in our previous chapter. You could expand Plato's thought with the observation that even those who are committed to democracy and actively participate in it nevertheless harbor Plato's critical attitude toward it. Witness the regularity of the complaint from parties that lose elections that the other party did not have the better argument, but only the better campaign. Political losers often claim that the citizens didn't see through the opposition's lies and cheap tricks, and so were duped. We call it the *Plato Principle*: Those who lose elections will more often blame the citizens for being credulous and the opposition party for pandering to their baser interests than take the election to rebut their own case. The mob wins, again, is the refrain. The irony is that those who win elections generally praise the wisdom of the populace.

Yet there is a crucial respect in which the argument sketched above is incomplete. Those who observe that democracy is saturated with only the appearance of argument rather than the real thing need to account for the pervasiveness of the pretense and appearances. Why must political candidates, commentators, and pundits constantly present themselves as motivated only by reason? Why must they always dress up their plays for power and influence in the garb of argument? Why are the images of "no spin" and "straight talk" so frequently employed as marketing tools?

Here's the short answer to these questions. The appeal to argument pervades *because it works*. Like most short answers, this one isn't much of an answer. It merely presses the further question: *Why does it work?*

In the wake of the first 2012 presidential debate between President Obama and Mitt Romney, two assessments came to be widely accepted. The first was that Mitt Romney handily won the debate. The second was that Mitt Romney's key claims in the debate were demonstrably inaccurate.[1] Neither assessment taken on its own looks particularly noteworthy. But when they are affirmed together, they sound dissonant.

Here's why. Debates are argumentative settings where one's performance should be assessed on the basis of the relative quality of the arguments one presents. The quality of an argument depends on the truth of the information presented as premises and the relevance of that information to its conclusion. So if we know that an arguer is employing premises containing important inaccuracies, we should not judge his or her arguments as successful. Therefore we should not think he or she did well in the debate. Yet this is precisely what the conjunction of the two prevalent assessments of the first presidential debate contends: Romney won the debate, but his central arguments were failures. There's the dissonance.

We can anticipate what our critics will say: "What Pollyannas these guys are!" They may then continue: "Academics are so naïve! Political debates aren't about arguments, but rather cutting a striking pose, displaying one's personality, connecting with an audience, and making one's opponents look dumb." The critics might then raise the example of the Nixon/Kennedy debates in 1960, where Nixon was considered the winner by those listening on the radio, but Kennedy won big with those who watched on television. Nixon looked tired, but Kennedy looked, well, like a Kennedy. This leads our imagined critics to conclude: "Winning over an audience, looking 'presidential,' taking a commanding tone—that's what political debate is really about. Everything else is just Ivory Tower chatter." And so goes a popular interpretation of democracy's deliberative moments. This is a resolutely cynical stance concerning democracy, and in fact it takes its cynicism to be a kind of virtue. Let's call it "just is" cynicism.

Now consider a more recent example of "just is" cynicism. In the 2016 presidential election cycle, Hillary Clinton was widely taken to have bested Donald Trump in all three debates. She had command of the issues, she responded to his reasons, and often she had surprising challenges to him and his policies. These results made measurable differences in the polls immediately after these debates, tilting thing significantly in her favor. But Donald Trump won the election. Let that sink in for a bit. A candidate who was widely taken to have lost all three debates still won the election. What does that say about the role that debates play? In this case, we have a divergence from the Romney–Obama phenomenon, since in this case, even the bad debate performance, even as a *debate* performance, did not negatively affect the outcome of the election. A regular thought was that in this case, the debates weren't really debates at all. Not even sham debates. Rather they were minimally civil (and sometimes not even that) confrontations, and to keep score on them as debates is to totally misunderstand the situation. Rather than attempts to offer reasons, they were more occasions for the airing of grievances. Once we see these events properly—that is, as confrontations—Donald Trump won them, and he won them handily. He was aggressive, disruptive, dismissive, and full of contempt. He enacted the disdain he and so many in his campaign had for Hillary Clinton, the Obama administration's representatives, and the entirety of the progressive Left in America. Once we fix our gaze on what the objectives were, so the reasoning goes, Trump's debate performances were not failures, but were exactly what they were supposed to be. The crucial thing is that you can't just come out and *say* that, since the "debates" must yet proceed as debates. So arguments under these cases are expressions of cultural confrontation, but they must maintain the illusion that they are more than that. Anyone who falls for the illusion and keeps score like they are high school debates deserves to lose in the world of real politics.

We sketched above a special version of "just is" cynicism, one that is popular among academics and beyond the academy. It begins just like the popular version: Politics *just is* the effective exercise of power. Democracy *just is* civil war by other means. Argument *just is* the process of eliciting assent. And so on. But then the academic version adds an additional layer of cynicism: saying non-cynical things—such as that politics is about *justice*, democracy is about *self-government*, and argument is about *rationality*—*just is* idealistic claptrap at best, and more likely just is one further exercise of power and manipulation. That is, the academic version of "just is" cynicism claims not merely that non-cynics are delusional. It claims in addition that in fact we're *all* cynics, with criticism of cynicism being the most cynical posture of all. The view alleges that any argument against cynicism *just is* cynicism, because it's just cynicism all the way down. Non-cynicism is false-consciousness. The academic version is popular "just is" cynicism gone global.

In the previous chapters, we gave reasons why we resist the cynical turn when it comes to democracy, and here we will explain why we resist it when it comes to argument and reason more generally. The short version of our case against global cynicism is simply this: *the view that argument and reasoning "just is" cynical manipulation must itself be the product of non-cynical argument and reasoning.* In other words, "just is" cynicism is self-refuting. The "just is" cynical view about reason and argument is parasitic upon an exercise of non-cynical reasoning and argument. After all, the academic cynic takes herself to be in a position to expose or reveal something about the true natures of reason and argument. Furthermore, she seeks to correct anti-cynics. Therefore, the cynic must admit that non-cynical argument and reasoning is possible, else there can't be a set of good reasons for being a cynic in the first place. Therefore global "just is" cynicism defeats itself because "just is" cynicism about reason and argument is something that, if you take the view on and then apply it to itself, can't see itself as any kind of cognitive success.

The self-defeat problem for cynical views of argument comes in two forms. Recall that argumentative cynics claim that argument *just is* rhetorical manipulation. One problem concerns the role that argument must play if there is going to be a case for adopting argumentative cynicism. The other has to do with the way one must see the reasons for the cynical view once one has come to adopt it.

First, if one believes that argument just is about getting others to believe one's conclusions, rather than about showing their truth or providing conditions for rational acceptance of a belief, then one must take it that this cynical view of argument itself is supported by good reasons, reasons that show—or at least sufficiently suggest—that the cynical view is correct. Accordingly, in assessing the reasons in favor of cynicism as strong enough to support the view, argumentative cynics supply killer counter-examples to their own view. They are "hoist with their own petard," as Shakespeare might have put it.

Second, if one believes that argument is just about getting others to accept one's preferred views, then one must view one's own arguments, even for that very position, as self-imposed verbal manipulation. But then the cynic must admit in her own case that she has no better reason to be a cynic than not, as there are no reasons to be had *for any view*. So the cynic must assess her own cynicism as no better founded than any opposing position. And this is not the worst of it. A consistent cynic can recognize no ground upon which to criticize non-cynical views of argument and reason. The cynic's charge that non-cynicism is *false* consciousness depends precisely on the idea that there is a *correct* view about things, one that acknowledges the evidence of the terrible truth of cynicism—namely, that nobody believes for good reasons, or anything like reasons at all. The trouble is that once "just is" cynicism has gone global, it must adopt a cynicism about argument and reason, and this in turn means that it must take a cynical posture on its own reasons. Hence it must admit that "just is" cynicism about argument and reason is also false consciousness. But then that admission would itself be subject to the cynical assessment: the evaluation of something as false consciousness is also false consciousness. Oh, the petards!

It doesn't make one a naïve professor to uphold the idea that debates are supposed to be about reasons, evidence, and truth. We all know that the election-time events that are called "debates" are actually carefully orchestrated national campaign-stops, where candidates compete on one stage by means of zingers and other rhetorical tactics for sound-bites, media coverage, and poll numbers. But *winning at a debate* is nonetheless distinct from *winning a debate*, and the world of high-stakes professional politics knows it, otherwise they would not invest so much time, effort, and energy into training candidates to achieve the former by appearing to achieve the latter. That's the reason why, despite the fact that we see that there's the merely rhetorical side to debates and so on, we have fact-checkers alongside those who announce a winner and a loser.

Imagine a political candidate giving a press conference in which she states the following:

> I am running for office because I am interested in gaining political power and the various other benefits that come from it. I have nothing to offer the electorate but catchy sound bites and flashy rebukes of my opponents. The things I say about public policy are intentionally vague and nonspecific, but always designed according to very carefully conducted marketing research aimed at discerning what you find most pleasing to hear. I look good while shaking hands and kissing babies, and I speak in a commanding tone of voice. But that's it. Now, vote for me.

Could a political campaign survive such a pronouncement? We think not. Were politicians to say this kind of thing, they would instantly undermine their chances for election. In order to maintain credibility and succeed politically, our politicians—and, in addition, our pundits, commentators, talk show hosts, journalists, activists, and fellow citizens—must present themselves as sincere and honest arguers, people who are interested in following where the best reasons lead. Why is that?

As we have already indicated, we think the answer lies in the fact that, no matter how cynical a view they might hold of the real world of democracy, democratic citizens whole-heartedly endorse the ideal of democracy that we have described. That is, politicians and others must uphold the ideals of reason and argument, and they must present themselves as committed to them, because democratic citizens endorse and insist upon those ideals. As citizens, we demand that our social and political world reflect and respect the norms and ideals that guide our cognitive lives more generally. To be sure, it is correct to think that the real world of democratic politics is most often little more than a rough-and-tumble contest for power in which the lofty ideals of proper argument are merely professed but not respected. Moreover, it is certainly more than likely that we will think all the things our hypothetical candidate is true of a large number of actual candidates. But as democratic citizens, we are bound to see all of this as lamentable, improper, and a symptom of democratic failure. The fact that we can make sense of the pair of dissonant claims from before—"Romney won the second 2012 debate" and "The things Romney said were false" and "Trump lost all the 2016 debates" but "Trump won the 2016 election"—means that we uphold the ideal, yet still recognize the ways in which the real world of politics falls short. Even if it is in fact most often mere posturing, those engaged in politics must make constant appeal to reason, truth, and argument because such appeals work; and they work because democratic citizens endorse the idea that democracy is the project of collective self-government by means of argument. Earlier, we said that you have to articulate the ideal in order to criticize the real. Now you can see how that goes.

We here confront both good news and bad news. The bad news is that our democracy regularly disappoints us. Abominable people win elections, despite ample evidence that they are incompetent and morally below standards for holding public office. And awful laws are passed, ones that no just state should even consider. It is not just bad from a theoretical perspective; it's often scaldingly painful to bear. For many, we've described their experience of seeing Donald J. Trump elected president in 2016, as they see him not only as someone not qualified for the office, but as someone whose policies distinctly harm them and their families. This is truly awful news.

But there's good news hidden in the bad. The good news is but a glimmer in the background, and it's this: it is still possible to think things should be and can be otherwise. And we can communicate that not only to each other, but we can do so even to those who may not yet know or even to those who disagree. That we can say to ourselves, as so many have in the wake of the Trump White House, "this is not normal." That the president, say, expresses contempt for the norms of reasonable exchange as vehemently as he has for women and immigrants does not make it *normal* in either case. This is because we yet expect better, hope for and hold out for those norms of exchange to again effectively bind us all. The good news is that the habits of public reason die hard. Even those who adopt a posture of hostility toward the Press and other fundamental institutions of democracy must nonetheless frame that hostility as driven by a deeper loyalty to those very institutions. To criticize *The New York Times* as "fake news" is still to present oneself as upholding the ideal of a free Press.

Yes, we know, this is cold comfort amidst a landscape as averse to progressive viewpoints as this, and with so many who refuse to abide the demands of public reason. But progress out of this situation, rectifying wrongs done, and addressing problems that linger is possible only if we deliberate together effectively. And what does that mean? Keeping those skills sharp is still important, even if the last election ran contrary to those norms. Because without them, there's no path out.

The insistence that our social and political worlds reflect the norms that govern our cognitive lives gives us a clue to how argument in democracy should proceed. Sometimes it helps to look first to breakdowns and failures in order to get a grip on what success is.

It might seem very strange to proceed in this way—to look to places where things aren't working in order to see how they should. But, in some ways, that's the way we come to understand many of the norms that run our lives. We don't often explicitly acknowledge the multitude of norms that govern our everyday knocking about in the world; only when they break down does it become clear to us that we follow them and rely on them. Consider etiquette. You can be a perfectly nice and considerate person in conversation, but if you stand too close to people (say, close enough for them to feel your breath on their face) you'll make them uncomfortable. So there's a rough appropriate distance you should stand from someone in conversation. We discover that when the rough rule is broken. Or consider another face-to-face conversational norm, namely, that of maintaining the right amount of eye-contact. Those who never look us in the eye make us feel uncomfortable, but not nearly as uncomfortable as those who stare us in the eyes the whole time. The former may be a sign of indifference to the conversation; the latter may be a gesture of hostility. Regardless, it becomes clearer to us that there is a rough norm with respect to eye contact (not too much, not too little) when we encounter cases where it is violated. One might say that this is characteristic of successful social norms: they're generally invisible to us until they're violated.

Now, recall our discussion from the previous chapter about manipulation. There we identified two broad categories of manipulation: *diversion* and *distortion*. The former kind of manipulation attempts to produce belief by diverting our attention away from the quality of the reasons that are available. The latter attempts to produce belief by distorting our sense of what reasons there are. If these two kinds of manipulation represent very general ways in which argument goes wrong, we can appeal to them in identifying two similarly broad argumentative norms, which we will call argumentative *earnestness* and argumentative *responsibility*.

In argument, we are called upon to assess reasons for belief. Manipulation that proceeds by way of diversion attempts to cause us to lose sight of the quality of the reasons that are being offered. Accordingly, argumentative *earnestness* is the norm associated with giving due attention to the quality of the reasons before us. Earnest arguers exhibit the resolve to focus on reasons and not be distracted by rhetoric, biases, prejudices, and other diversions. Moreover, earnest arguers follow where the reasons lead; they do not dogmatically cling to their beliefs in spite of compelling counterevidence, nor do they dismiss as irrelevant considerations that run counter to their beliefs.

But argumentative earnestness is not enough for overall cognitive success. In argument, we not only need to evaluate the reasons we happen to have before us, we also need to take steps aimed at bringing to our attention the full range of reasons there are. That is, in evaluating reasons for belief, we need to begin from a sufficiently broad set of reasons. In order to do this, we need to avail ourselves of the cognitive resources of other believers, especially those with whom we are likely to disagree. Argumentative *responsibility* hence is the norm that counteracts the distorting kind of manipulation. Instead of merely cherry-picking the facts that support their views, responsible arguers endeavor to bring into consideration *all* of the available reasons relevant to the issue at hand, and so seek them out.

These norms of argument have both internal and external aspects. That is to say, these norms operate both within an individual's own deliberations and in contexts of interpersonal argument. Argumentative earnestness operates internally as a set of cognitive habits that tend to keep our attention focused on reasons. Internally, the earnest arguer exhibits a kind of careful attention and perspicuity in assessing reasons. Moreover, earnestness involves a kind of intellectual courage; the earnest arguer does not succumb to peer-pressure, is aware of and can correct for her own biases, and knows how to separate reasons for belief from non-rational appeals. Externally, the earnest arguer both appeals to the reasons that count in favor of her views, and attends to the reasons others raise in support of theirs. Moreover, the earnest arguer is suspicious of bandwagons and groupthink. She appreciates skepticism in the face of consensus, and recognizes the value of dissenting views.

Argumentative responsibility manifests internally as a kind of intellectual patience and thoroughness. It is the habit of refusing to rush to judgment, of suspending belief until a sufficiently broad range of considerations has been evaluated. Externally, argumentative responsibility manifests in an eagerness to listen to and fully consider the reasons of the opposition. More importantly, the responsible arguer not only seeks out the reasons of those with whom she disagrees, she seeks out the best opposing reasons. In fact, the responsible arguer may even take it upon herself to imagine a better version of the opposition's case than the opposition, as constituted, actually give.

Admittedly, these characterizations of proper argument are very general. In fact, as an account of what it is to succeed at argument, they may seem positively mistaken. Some may charge that our dual norms of earnestness and responsibility are insufficient for the simple reason that it is possible for an individual arguer to manifest these qualities and yet fail to believe the truth and avoid believing what is false. Successful argument, a critic might hold, should be understood like a system of solid pipes—whatever you put in on the one end, you get out at the other. The critic might continue to say that our conception of argumentative success has no *truth preserving* mechanism. On our view, it is possible to succeed at argument and yet move from true belief to false belief. Our critic might wonder: If that's success, what does failure look like?

This line of objection is too hasty. Systems of logic aspire to articulate the formal rules for demonstrating the truth of one proposition given the truth of others. Although this is an important aspect of reasoning, our aim at present is different. Remember that in discussing argumentative success, we are attempting to identify the norms of cognitive hygiene. Our claim is not that those who embody argumentative earnestness and responsibility are guaranteed to arrive at the truth. Nor are we claiming that the earnest and responsible arguer will most likely arrive at true beliefs. The claim rather is that earnestness and responsibility are two especially salient virtues in managing our intellectual lives. Their importance lies in the fact that, by embodying these qualities, individuals gain a kind of intellectual self-control. The earnest and responsible arguer pursues the goal of believing the true and rejecting the false by employing a set of strategies for forming and evaluating beliefs that keep her on the trail of reasons. Argumentative success of the kind we are interested in examining in this book consists in gaining *command* of one's beliefs in the way we described in our introductory chapter. Cognitive command is not only a matter of believing what is true; one must also understand one's belief, see how it fits with other beliefs, and have a story to tell of the belief's significance.

On our view, this kind of intellectual self-control is the best means we have for pursuing the truth, even if in many individual instances it misses that mark. Again, the idea of cognitive *hygiene* is crucial. We are trying to identify belief-forming and belief-evaluating policies that are most likely to prove sound over time. And believing the truth and rejecting the false is, after all, not a one-off task. It is, like physical health, an ongoing project.

However, having said this, it also bears mention that the two argumentative norms that we have identified carry with them rather significant implications. Notice how earnest and responsible arguers are bound to insist on social and political arrangements that protect and enable the dissemination and sharing of information. That is, in order to argue earnestly and responsibly, we must be able to see ourselves as functioning within what we might call a *healthy social epistemic environment*. Such an environment is one that we can reasonably count on to provide and make accessible reliable information and a broad range of reasons pertaining to public and other matters. Think of it this way: In a highly propagandized society, where all forms of communication are carefully controlled by a central political body, and where dissent from official pronouncements is strongly discouraged, one cannot be an earnest and responsible arguer. The reason is simple. In order to follow the reasons where they lead, one must be free from the threat of political persecution for one's beliefs. Similarly, in order to try to bring under one's consideration all of the available reasons, one must have a reasonable expectation that with due effort, one can get access to a sufficiently broad representation of all of the reasons that are relevant to the question at hand.

We might say, then, that these basic norms of argument—earnestness and responsibility—can be exercised and satisfied only within a certain kind of social and political order. More specifically, one can argue well only within a social and political environment in which information can be openly exchanged, opinion can be freely expressed, inquiry and dialogue can be widely engaged, and dissent is strongly protected. In short, the familiar and central freedoms protected in a democratic society—free speech, a free press, freedom of association, freedom of conscience, and other constitutional guarantees of individual rights—not only reflect the cognitive norms that we already accept as appropriate for the conduct of our individual lives, they enable us to live by those norms. To put the point in a slogan, *one can argue well only in an intellectually open society*. And democracy is that political order in which intellectual openness is most explicitly encouraged and protected. Hence a surprising conclusion emerges. Despite all of the ways in which one might reasonably think that the real world of democracy is intellectually vicious, it also provides the social and political prerequisites for the proper conduct of our intellectual lives.

In making the case for thinking that democracy is so tightly connected to our aspiration to be successful arguers, we have emphasized the benefits that democracy confers upon individuals. To summarize, in a democratic society, there are official legal protections for individuals that enable them to engage in proper argument; moreover, those protections also enable what we above called a *healthy social epistemic environment* in which individuals share information, reasons, and arguments. It is important to realize that the cognitive benefits of democracy depend upon its social epistemic environment being healthy. That is, our claim is not that a social and political order that characterizes a democracy is sufficient for cognitive health. The claim, rather, is that the democracy *makes possible* the exercise of proper argument. Yet, to return to a point we raised in our introductory chapter about our mutual interdependence, a lot about our own individual success hangs on how others act. We cannot be successful arguers in isolation from others; similarly, we cannot be successful arguers in isolation from other successful arguers. This is because the basic norms of proper argument—earnestness and responsibility—can be satisfied only in the presence of others who are also trying to satisfy them.

From this it follows that we each have a responsibility to do our part in contributing to and maintaining the health of our social epistemic environment. Think again about the analogy between cognitive health and physical health. In order for you to maintain your physical health, the physical environment in which you live must be of a certain quality, and you depend upon others to do their share in helping to maintain the conditions under which physical health is possible. Moreover, you have a duty to do your own part as well. Just as you rely upon others to not poison the physical environment, you too have a duty to do the same. Things are similar with the cognitive environment. We must rely on others to be honest, to share relevant information with us, and to exercise the requisite care for accuracy and precision when they do so. One who is surrounded by liars, fabricators, or careless thinkers is severely hampered in the exercise of argumentative earnestness and responsibility. Likewise, one who routinely dissembles, misleads, misrepresents what she knows, and spreads unsubstantiated rumors as if they were known to be facts pollutes the cognitive environment, and thereby hinders the ability of others to sustain their cognitive health.

In this way, we each have a responsibility to others to try to argue well, and this involves trying to help others to argue well by sharing with them our reasons and information. But in addition, we have a responsibility to not simply contribute to the collective resources that compose the social epistemic environment. We must also attempt to draw contributions from others.

This is a significant implication of what has been said thus far. People tend to think that in a democratic society, our individual responsibilities consist exclusively in duties not to interfere with others when they are acting within their rights. And of course it is true that as democratic citizens, we do have such duties of non-interference. But on the view we have been developing, we have duties to positively contribute to the health of the shared social epistemic environment. And this requires us not only to not interfere with others, but also to help them exercise their capacities for argument.

An example might help clarify this point. On the account we have proposed, one of the reasons why democracies recognize freedom of speech is that this freedom is necessary if citizens are going to be able to share in self-government according to reason. A society in which the expression of certain views is forbidden is a society in which individuals cannot be earnest and responsible arguers. But notice that the cognitive benefit associated with free speech is not realized unless citizens listen to each other. That is, free speech requires more of us than to simply allow others to speak; if the policy of protecting free speech is to have the right impact on our social epistemic environment, free speakers need listeners. Perhaps they also need listeners who are ready to criticize, question, examine, and evaluate what is said. In short, if freedom of speech is going to deliver the cognitive benefits it promises, there must be *engagement* between speakers and an audience. With some freedoms, then, come some responsibilities.

This point about our responsibilities to listen and criticize seems especially apt in the cases of those who express unpopular, uncomfortable, or heretical ideas. Recall that argumentative responsibility requires us to seek to bring a sufficiently broad range of reasons into our evaluations of what to believe. In a way, then, proper argument involves trying to discover the reasons of those who hold opinions that are most unlike our own. That is, we contribute to the health of the social epistemic environment by expanding the breadth of our access to the cognitive resources of others, especially those who are unlike ourselves. In short, we have a responsibility to understand them, and if we continue to think they are wrong, we must find compelling criticisms of them.

These points can be encapsulated by thinking of three kinds of contributions to the social epistemic environment: *input, output,* and *uptake*. To argue well, we must be ready to express our reasons, to share our information with others, and to articulate our questions about and criticisms of the views of others. That is, we must provide certain kinds of *input* into the social epistemic environment. We must also draw resources out of the environment as well. That is, it is not enough to listen to the reasons of others; we must engage with and be responsive to them, we must be sensitive to the *output* of the environment. Finally, it is not enough to confine ourselves to argument with those with whom we know we have only minor disagreements, if any at all. We must seek to engage with unfamiliar others and those who possibly hold uncommon views. That is, we must seek to expand our *uptake* from the shared social epistemic environment.

One way of thinking about the interplay of input, output, and uptake is to imagine a society with the concept of disagreement and reasons, but not of argument. Individuals have their own reasons for their commitments and can make those commitments explicit to each other, but they don't have the vocabulary to put those reasons to public use in justifying their commitments. So when people disagree in this society, they don't have the tools to make explicit why they do so, only that they do so. So described, the only tools these have for managing disagreements will be either negotiating tactics (so, not addressing the disagreement, but mitigating its consequences) or in simply silencing what some part has to say. In this society, there are tools for input and output, in that disagreements can be registered, but both input and output are significantly diminished if reasons aren't part of the story told—because now we can't tell what quality of contributions are being made. Uptake, however, without reasons, is eradicated. If we don't see the *why* of a counterpoint, it comes across as noise at best. Uptake requires understanding a view and representing it as the product of rationality, and without that, our fellow citizens are little more than fair or foul weather.

Our view of proper argument in a democratic society should now appear rich and complex. It is also demanding. In fact, it may even strike you as overly demanding, requiring too much of citizens. To be sure, we concede that it is indeed a demanding view both of proper argument and democratic citizenship. But there's no reason to expect cognitive management to be easy. To again draw on the analogy with the body, the most effective exercise regimens test our physical endurance and capacity to tolerate pain. So too, the exercise of our cognitive capacities is not easy, and may be sometimes even uncomfortable. But it is what's required if we are going to maintain our cognitive health. Some exercises push us. Feel the burn.

If this seems too harsh, consider also that the demands of proper argument present us with requirements to try. Trying to believe according to the best reasons available is clearly consistent with failing to do so. Of course, the trying has to involve a sincere effort to argue earnestly and responsibly. One cannot merely "go through the motions" and discharge one's cognitive duties. But neither does one need to succeed across the board in doing everything one could do in evaluating one's reasons. As with life more generally, in our cognitive lives there are honest errors, and various other ways in which we fall short but nonetheless have behaved as we should. Furthermore, there are other legitimate goals in life besides those associated with gaining epistemological self-control, and these other worthy aims can place constraints on how far one must go in order to satisfy one's cognitive duties. So whereas proper argument is difficult, and the requirements to be earnest and responsible are not easily met, we think nonetheless that the aspiration to exercise proper cognitive hygiene is not overly demanding or all-consuming.

Finally, notice once again that argumentative earnestness and responsibility are norms we already hold ourselves to. Think back to the politician we imagined earlier who explicitly professed to have no concern for reasons and argument, but instead claimed to be simply hungry for power. Recall that we allowed that there may be some politicians who in fact satisfy this description. But we also noted that no politician could *express* a total lack of concern for reasons, and a single-minded interest in power, and still expect to succeed politically. This is because we insist that others try to argue properly, especially when they are attempting to gain political power over us. A similar point can be made in the more general case of our fellow citizens. We hold them to the norms of proper argument, especially in cases where they are expressing views about political matters. Correspondingly, when a fellow citizen speaks to public matters in the presence of others, she is likely to present her views as enjoying the full support of all the best reasons. She is also likely to present the opposing views as far less well-supported by reasons. And were a fellow citizen to claim to have no regard for reasons, and the comparative merits of the reasons for and against her views, we would rightly dismiss her as someone not worth listening to.

This brings us to a crucial point. We have claimed that the argumentative norms we have identified are in the everyday activities of ordinary people who are trying to figure out what to think about some matter or other. We have presented a case for thinking that democracy is that mode of social and political organization which enables us to respect these norms at the level of collective decision making. Yet there's an aspect of democracy that complicates this picture. To explain: When an individual is attempting to figure out what to believe about, say, how best to grow tomato plants in his garden, he would certainly do well to consult others, including others who know about gardens and tomato plants. However, if this individual were to dismiss the advice of successful gardeners and instead consult the local tarot-card reader, we would surely think him silly. But as the loss is his alone to bear, we would leave it at that.

Democracy is different. In a democracy, what people believe about public matters, and how they go about forming and evaluating those beliefs, is a matter that affects us all. This is because, in a democracy, what citizens believe about public matters helps to determine what our shared policies, laws, and institutions will look like. Unlike our gardener, when citizens decide what to believe about public matters, they contribute to a system of *collective decisions*, a system which makes decisions that typically we all must abide by. In fact, in a democracy, collective decisions often produce policies that are backed by the power of law. Consequently, democratic decisions often result in laws that force individuals—including those individuals who sincerely disagree with them—to act in certain ways.

Hence we see that there is a crucial difference between political argument and other argumentative contexts. In political matters the stakes are high, in that what we collectively decide will deeply affect others. This explains why most of the informing examples in this book make reference to *public* argument.

Argument is public when it is carried out in public and is about matters of public concern. On the view we have been developing, public argument is the core of democratic politics. Accordingly, the importance of arguing well in these public contexts is greatly intensified.

Public arguers must not only try to discern what the best reasons say they, as individuals, should believe; they must also consider what the best reasons recommend for us, the democratic polity. And this introduces complications. Often what our own best reasons say *we*, as individuals, should believe differs from what the best reasons for *us* recommend. This is because certain reasons might apply to us as individuals that do not apply to us as members of a democratic citizenry. The most obvious example of this phenomenon arises in the case of citizens who are also religious believers. To be a member of a religion is in large part to recognize certain kinds of reasons as salient or even decisive. Consider an obvious example. For certain denominations of Christianity, that the Bible forbids action X is a conclusive reason to refrain from Xing. Accordingly, individuals who belong to the relevant Christian sect must adopt a policy of refraining from doing X. The complication emerges once one realizes that not all of one's fellow citizens are members of that Christian sect, and thus the fact that the Bible forbids action X cannot act as a reason for *them* to refrain from Xing. Indeed, for many citizens in a modern democratic society, what the Bible says is irrelevant to questions about personal morality and public policy. And democratic citizens need to recognize this fact. If democracy is about collective self-government and collectively reasoning, the reasons should be accessible and acceptable to those who are party to the decisions.

This brings us back to a point we made in our Introduction about the *dialectical* demands of argument. When we are giving arguments, we are not merely presenting our own reasons for accepting some conclusion; we are also trying to present reasons to others so that they might come to rationally adopt our conclusion. As we noted at several points earlier, argument is most frequently engaged in as a response to disagreement. Argument aims to resolve disagreement by providing at least one party to the dispute with reasons to change his or her mind. In order to accomplish this, arguments must present disputants with the reasons that they can recognize as reasons. Accordingly, to argue against the permissibility of stem cell research strictly on the basis of papal authority in a dispute with non-Catholics is to fail at argument. "The Pope has decreed that stem cell research is forbidden" can be recognized as a reason only by Catholics. Consequently, an argument against stem cell research that draws exclusively from this kind of premise fails entirely to engage the dispute at hand. To put the point more generally, when offering public arguments, one must not only provide good reasons in favor of one's views; one must also attempt to supply one's fellow citizens with reasons that they could recognize as good reasons.

This means that public argument is different from the kind of argument that individuals might engage in when they are deciding for themselves the rules and policies by which they will live as individuals. When we engage in *public* argument, we are aiming to discern what the best *public* reasons say we should adopt. A public reason is a reason whose force does not depend upon one's acceptance of a religious or moral viewpoint that democratic citizens are at liberty to reject. To return to our example, being Catholic is not a requirement for democratic citizenship. Consequently, reasons whose force derives strictly from some element of the Catholic faith are not public reasons. Such reasons therefore are not reasons *for us* as democratic citizens, even though they might be especially strong reasons for those of us who are Catholic.

To put the matter in a nutshell, when we engage in public argument, we are looking to evaluate the reasons that *democratic citizens can share.* These are reasons whose force derives from the moral and political commitments of democracy as such, reasons that speak to the demands of equality, liberty, justice, and citizenship. Although religious citizens are certainly free to announce and profess reasons deriving from their religious convictions in public settings, they are bound as dutiful democratic citizens to look toward public reasons when arguing with their fellow citizens about public matters.

To conclude this chapter, we raise another critical thought owing to Plato. A critic might agree that perhaps individuals are indeed beholden to a certain set of norms that govern belief formation and evaluation. She might continue to argue that the fact that these norms have a grip on us does indeed require us to try to argue well, and even contribute to the health of the shared social epistemic environment. However, she might add, that these are duties to *try* to properly argue means that they are too easily satisfied. This is especially evident once it is noticed that it is easy to present oneself to others as if one were an expert, and it is easy to give the impression to others that one has properly evaluated all of the best reasons on offer from one's opposition. Expertise is as easily counterfeited as it is valuable. Consequently, the critic may allege that proper argument is easily mimicked. And democracy gives political power to those who are best at simulating proper argument. So democracy is ultimately self-undermining.

This is, once again, a powerful line of critique. So powerful, in fact, that we must concede much of it. It is true that in a democratic society political power is tied not to knowledge or expertise, but to the ability to convince others that one has knowledge or expertise. And it is also true that there are many highly effective ways in which clever speakers can convince large numbers of people to believe as they say. What's more, we concede that democratic politics very often proceeds by way of proper argument's mimics. That is, much of democratic politics is conducted with imposters of proper argument. When successfully deployed, these imposters allow a speaker to present himself to an onlooking crowd as fully compliant with the norms of proper argument, when in fact he has flouted them. We might say, then, that in placing argument at its center, democracy creates an opportunity for smooth talkers with handsome faces; it opens the possibility for rule by those who can best simulate argument.

That's a significant concession to our envisioned critic. However, we decline to follow the critic in drawing the conclusion that this much provides a knock-down objection to democracy or to the norms of public argument. The key to responding to this line of criticism, we hold, is to develop a systematic conception of the ways in which proper argument is mimicked. In turn, we think it is important to highlight some common errors in public argument and some techniques for their correction. We take ourselves to have thus far laid out in sufficient detail the conceptual apparatus driving our conception of argumentation. We will pause to consider a limit case for our conception of argument, that of deep disagreement, in the next chapter. Part II of the book is devoted to the identification and analysis of the ways in which argument is simulated, mimicked, and counterfeited. Each of the following short chapters is devoted to a single imposter. As it turns out, these are relatively easy to detect once their natures are identified and explained. The aim is to give our fellow citizens an easy way to detect them, avoid them, and criticize those who deploy them. Part III of the book is about the way forward, once we've seen the troubles—how do we repair arguments and the civic culture of argumentation, if it is so common that we have pathological arguments and they seem to be endemic to critical reflection?

For Further Thought

1 How might a cynic about argument and reason respond to the arguments presented at the beginning of this chapter? Does the claim that global cynicism is self-undermining support non-cynicism? Or might it be a further reason to be a cynic?

2 According to the view presented in this chapter, each of us is under an obligation to contribute to the overall health of our shared social epistemic environment. This requires us, in part, to seek out proponents of odd, unorthodox, and unpopular viewpoints so that we may listen to their views and feel the strength of the considerations in favor of them. Does this view entail that each of us is obliged to attend speeches given by racists, sexists, Holocaust-deniers, and the like? Must we, as democratic citizens, constantly expose ourselves to objectionable, offensive, and defamatory viewpoints?

3 In this chapter, it was argued that democratic citizens are required to present *public* reasons when arguing with their fellows about political

matters. This means that they must avoid presenting arguments that employ premises deriving from their own religious viewpoint. But doesn't this restriction constitute a violation of citizens' rights to freedom of expression, freedom of religious exercise, and freedom of conscience?

4   Is the "good news about the bad news" view just more academic idealism? If so, is there a form of "resistance" that does not rely on norms of reason and argument?

Key Terms

Argumentative cynicism	The view that argument just is the expression of political power (or cultural contempt or mere rhetorical manipulation).
Argumentative earnestness	The virtue of attending to the quality of the reasons given.
Argumentative responsibility	The virtue of searching for all the available reasons that bear on an issue, not being satisfied by a small sample of the reasons given.
Social epistemic input	The information we as arguers and speakers provide to an intellectual environment. Our testimony, arguments, objections, requests for reasons and clarifications.
Social epistemic output	The information others provide to an intellectual environment.
Social epistemic uptake	The attempts individuals and groups make to understand social epistemic input and output in ways that are productive of identifying issues and developing resources for rational resolution.
Public argument	Arguments carried out in public concerning matters of public interest that are constrained by the rule that reasons given must be publicly accessible.

Note

1   The *New York Times* fact-checker for the first debate is here: www.nytimes.com/interactive/2012/10/04/us/politics/20120804-denver-presidentialdebate-obama-romney.html

4   Deep Disagreements

We all have had moments when we feel that those with whom we disagree not only reject the point we are focused on at the moment, but also reject our values, general beliefs, modes of reasoning, and even our hopes. In such circumstances, productive critical conversation seems impossible. For the most part, in order to be successful, argument must proceed against a background of common commitments. Interlocutors must agree on some basic facts about the world, or they must share some source of reasons to which they can appeal, or they must value roughly the same sort of outcome. And so, if two parties disagree about who finished runners-up to the Hornblowers in their historic Sportsball League championship last year, they may agree to consult the league website, and that will resolve the issue. Or if two travelers disagree about which route home is better, one may say, "Yes, your way is *shorter*, but it runs though the traffic bottleneck at the mall, and that adds at least twenty minutes to the journey." And that may resolve the dispute, depending perhaps on whether time is what matters most.

But some disagreements invoke deeper disputes; disputes about what sources of information are authoritative, what counts as evidence, and what matters. Such disputes quickly become argumentatively abnormal. And so if someone does not recognize the authority of the Sportsball League's website about last year's standings, it is unclear how a dispute over last year's runners-up to the Hornblowers could be resolved. What might one *say* to a disputant of this kind? Does he trust news sites, television reporting, or Wikipedia entries concerning the SBL? Does he regard the news sites and the league website as reliable sources of information concerning *this* year's standings or when the games are played? What if our interlocutor in the route-home case doesn't see why the quickest route is preferable to the shortest? Maybe our traveling companion regards our hurry-scurry as a part of a larger social problem, or maybe wants to enjoy the Zen of a traffic jam. Sometimes a disagreement about one thing lies at the tip of a very large iceberg composed of many other, progressively deeper, disagreements.

The puzzle about deep disagreement is whether reasoned argument can work at all in them. There is a widely held view, perhaps at the core of deliberative views of democracy, and certainly central to educational programs emphasizing critical thinking, that well-run argument is at least never pointless, and often even productive. And many hold that it's important to practice good argumentation, especially in cases of deep disagreement. Call this view *argumentative optimism*. The trouble for this optimism is that as disagreements run progressively deeper, it grows increasingly difficult to see how argument could have any point at all. Again, in deep disagreements, there isn't enough shared commitment for there to be any place where arguments can resolve anything. This result, in turn, encourages us to regard interlocutors as targets of incredulity, bemusement, and perhaps even ridicule, contempt, or hatred. There's little, many think, one can *argue* or *say* that is going to rationally resolve certain disagreements. That's just how far gone the other side seems. In the end, it all may come down to who's got better propaganda, more money, or, perhaps, the better weapons. Call this view *argumentative pessimism*.

A famous argument for pessimism is given by Robert Fogelin in his essay, "The Logic of Deep Disagreements." The core of his case is as follows:

1 Successful argument is possible only if participants share a background of beliefs, values, and resolution procedures.
2 Deep disagreements are disagreements wherein participants have no such shared background.
3 *Therefore*: successful argument is not possible in deep disagreement cases.

Fogelin holds that "deep disagreements cannot be resolved through the use of argument, for they undercut the conditions essential to arguing" (1985: 5). And so, as Fogelin reasons, given that no rational procedures for resolution offer themselves for those in deep disagreement, we are in a difficult situation. He observes: "[I]f deep disagreements can arise, what rational procedures can be used for their resolution? The drift of this discussion leads to the answer NONE" (1985: 6). Presumably, when we face a deep disagreement and cannot argue any further (on Fogelin's reasoning), we must decide what to do next. Do we just give up the argument? Do we also give up the disagreement? If we can't give up the disagreement, what do we do? Could we use further means, non-argumentative and non-rational strategies? Fogelin approvingly quotes Ludwig Wittgenstein on this: "At the end of reasons comes *persuasion* (Think of what happens when missionaries convert natives.)" (1985: 6). What exactly is *persuasion* here, and how is the model of missionaries supposed to help? Fogelin's conclusion is that we need to look to persuasion, but he's not provided much beyond that. Here's how many have reasoned beyond Fogelin's conclusion.

4. In disagreements needing urgent resolutions that also do not admit of argumentative resolution, one should use non-argumentative means to resolve the dispute.

5. *Therefore*, in urgent deep disagreements, one should use non-argumentative means to resolve the dispute.

Fogelin did not explicitly endorse any particular non-argumentative means (beyond whatever missionaries use on "natives"), nor did he clarify how one might determine that a disagreement is deep (as opposed to merely hard) or urgent. But we can see that a form of argumentative pessimism can put us on the way to a more wide-ranging attitude toward argument, namely that it stands in the way of quickly and decisively resolving disagreements. The better option with deep disagreement, so says the more radical argumentative pessimist, is to make sure one's arsenal of rhetoric and propaganda is ready to hand in deep disagreements. Argument is, from the perspective of the pessimist, pretty much a waste of time. Persuasion is the key. Moreover, if the disagreements are deep, that usually means that there's a lot at stake. Best to win, even if it means that one has to bend the rules of argumentative exchange. Regardless, it is clear that argumentative optimists face a challenge in the face of deep disagreement and the radical pessimist's line of thought. How might they respond?

For starters, optimists should ask whether deep disagreements, so described as cases with *no* shared background, really exist. And so, an optimist could concede Fogelin's point, and yet contend that in fact *no actual disagreements are so deep that there are no shared background commitments*. One way the optimist could argue for this thought is as follows: In cases of persistent and hard disagreement, interlocutors seem not to share enough *meanings* in common to have their dispute count properly as disagreement. That is, in order for two parties to *disagree*, there must be a sufficient degree of other kinds of cognitive overlap, otherwise there is no disagreement at all, and the parties simply "talk past" each other. In other words, when one party asserts "Birds fly," and the other says "Birds don't fly," they apparently disagree. But if it is discovered that the two parties do not share in common a broad conception of what it is to fly, what things are birds, what authorities to consult, or whether one of them *really did see a seagull up in the air just the other day*, we should conclude that there is no *disagreement* after all, but rather a case of mutual unintelligibility. Perhaps it's worse to countenance the possibility of mutual unintelligibility than deep disagreement, but it's one way to retain argumentative optimism. The deeper the disagreement, the harder it is to see it as *a disagreement*.

This means that insofar as we see disagreements as *disagreements* at all, we must take the disputants to share enough in the background to allow them to talk about the same things; that is, in order to see parties as *disagreeing*, we must take them to inhabit the same world and talk about it in enough of a similar way that they can recognize that they have a disagreement. Consequently, we can never see disagreements as so deep that there's no shared commitment at all. Where we see disagreement, we see (at least in principle) resolvability.

A different optimistic strategy is to reject Fogelin's first premise. One might say that argument isn't *only* about resolving disagreements. An argument, as an exercise of manifesting our rationality, may improve our understanding of our own views and those of others. In an exchange, we may, in thinking about an issue, actually *create* common ground in developing a shared culture of reasoning together. Consequently, argument can be productive in deep disagreement cases, but it takes a longer-run view. But even if argument isn't productive of agreement in the end, there are other goods that argument can promote, and mutual understanding and the capacity to see the disagreement as the product of rational creatures who can reasonably disagree is a good, too.

Further, the optimist may reject even the fourth premise. She may deny that when argument gives out in urgent cases, one may resort to some form of non-argumentative persuasion. The optimist could insist that the fourth premise states a dangerous policy, since one may have misidentified merely difficult or hard cases as instances of deep disagreement. That, certainly, is a bad error to have taken what was a rationally resolvable disagreement to be rationally irresolvable. That's because you've missed an opportunity to reason with someone who may have something to say to you that's worthwhile, and you've treated someone you could have moved with reasons as someone who can only be moved by something other than reason. That's bad.

Additionally, the optimist might claim that resorting to propaganda, rhetoric, verbal coercion or other non-argumentative means gives up on the plausible thought that even in cases of severe and stubborn disagreement, parties still can learn from each other. The pessimist's policy presumes that when disputes seem irresolvable, the only alternative is to simply defeat or at least neutralize one's opponents. But notice that these tools, *were they used against us*, would strike us as objectionable.

It's worth pausing to let this last thought sink in. When we are thinking about rules for good argument, we should be thinking not only about rules that we would want us to be using *as arguers*, but we would also want there to be good rules for arguers to follow when they are *addressing arguments to us*. Our dialectical view of argument essentially takes argument as an interpersonal *process*, and that process is best considered as a *turn-taking* game of giving and asking for reasons. In argument, we take turns giving and receiving reasons. And we need the rules of argument to be straightforward enough as to not be too onerous for arguers, but also flexible enough so that we as hearers aren't forced to accept reasons that we can't see the point of. So the point is that as *hearers* of arguments, we wish that we be presented with cases that appeal to *our reason*, instead of manipulate us with fear or propaganda.

The dispute between argumentative pessimists and optimists is itself stubborn and unlikely to be soon resolved. But in light of the dangers of prematurely adopting pessimism, this tie, we think, goes to the optimist.

The problem concerning deep disagreement can be formulated in a different way. It is a common enough experience we've all had while arguing with those with whom we have serious disagreements: as a controversial view is supported, even more controversial reasons are given, to be followed by more and more controversial commitments. As we noted earlier, a regular strategy in what might be called *normal* argument is that arguing parties trace their reasons to a shared ground of agreed-upon premises and rules of support, and then they test which of their sides is favored by these reasons. But disagreements that are *deep* are those where shared reasons are not easily found. And consequently, it seems that under these conditions, argumentative exchange is doomed to failure.

Of late, our interest in deep disagreement has not been purely academic. With Donald J. Trump winning the 2016 U.S. presidential election and the rise of the alt-right movement in American politics, we found that we face very real cases of what had seemed a sheer theoretical posit. In particular, the intellectual movement of the self-styled "neo-reactionary right" and the "Dark Enlightenment" seemed to be exemplary. We have given an argument above for argumentative optimism in the face of deep disagreement, so our theory now has a real test case.

When we started reading around in the neo-reactionary corpus, we found ourselves in what felt like an upside-down world—all the dialectical elements of the argument were familiar, but none of the premises presented as truisms seemed remotely plausible. Liberal democracy was taken to be obviously wrong-headed, and the attitudes of totalitarian programs were presented as equally obviously right. The regular defaults that some measure of equality of consideration is required by justice and that peoples' voices matter are openly held in contempt. The journalist James Duesterberg captures his experience first reading the literature of the Dark Enlightenment:

> Wading in, one finds oneself quickly immersed, and soon unmoored. All the values that have guided center-left, post-war consensus ... are inverted. The moral landmarks by which we were accustomed to get our bearings aren't gone: they're on fire.[1]

This *Alice through the looking glass* experience is something that those on the neo-reactionary right anticipate in their reading audiences. But the writers in this genre have no plans of showing their readers the way back to the world they've left behind. In fact, this break with the world of purportedly liberal norms is one of the core commitments of the neo-reactionary program. Importantly, their view is that we all have been brainwashed by a quasi-religious political superstructural institution ruling the Western world—what those in the neo-reactionary movement call *The Cathedral*.

To start, the Cathedral is more a roughly ideologically confederated set of institutions: civil service, the university system, the media, and many religious movements. There are no legally binding or formal connections between these entities, but rather, they are all blind allies in a great, but unconscious, collaboration in illusion. It is a common strategy to analogize the Cathedral to religious commitment seen through naturalistic eyes. Religions aren't invented *as lies*, despite their being false. Rather, they arise as short-hands for why some norms are binding. Originally, this was simply religion *simpliciter*, but according to Mencius Moldbug, the Dark Enlightenment's prime mover on the blogosphere, the religious movement has morphed into a kind of secular religion of political idealism.

> You can go from religion to idealism and back simply by adding and subtracting gods, angels, demons, saints, ghosts, etc.[2]

The upshot is that contemporary progressivism, in the eyes of the neo-reactionaries, is a "nontheistic Christian sect." The worship of diversity and intersectionality, the insistence on political correctness, are all religious rites, ones where the meanings of the words do not really matter, but whether one chants them at the right times and at the proper cadence.

Consider the Cathedral, then, on analogy with some of the great philosophical set-pieces about grand-but-undetectable illusions. Plato's Analogy of the Cave in the *Republic* has the prisoners participating in games of shadow-image identification, and since they've never seen the real things the images are of, they cannot even fathom the idea of illusion. Of these sorry folks, Socrates has a dark aside, "They are like us" (*Republic* 515a). The movie trilogy *The Matrix* is premised on our lives taking place in a large-scale computer simulation, one about which one may have but only suspicions. And so, too, is the Cathedral—as Nick Land, the author of *The Dark Enlightenment Manifesto* notes, "the Cathedral has substituted its gospel for all we know."[3]

In order to fill in the Dark Enlightenment picture, a further trope from the literature of grand illusions needs to be mentioned. In Plato's *Republic*, one of the prisoners is released and is dragged out of the cave, to a blinding, painful light. In *The Matrix*, Neo is given a choice between a red pill and a blue pill. He chooses the red pill, which shows him what the Matrix is; the blue pill would have put him back deeper in the illusion. The neo-reactionaries, too, need a symbol for those who have foregone the comforting and tempting illusion of the Cathedral. They use a term from *The Matrix*, that of the *red pill*. Mencius Moldbug makes a contrast in selling his version of the red pill, because it turns out that there are *many* out there selling red pills.

> We've all seen *The Matrix*. We know about red pills. Many claim to sell them. You can go, for example, to any bookstore, and ask the guy behind the counter for some Noam Chomsky. What you'll get is blue pills soaked in Red #3... . [W]e provide the genuine article...

Seeing the Cathedral from the outside, neo-reactionaries feel they are shaken from an impossible but too comfortable dream. A similar vocabulary is necessary *internal* to the Cathedral—there are "woke" progressives, but this is more testament to the perverse incentives internal to the institution. That is, the best way to hide the illusion of the Cathedral is to acknowledge that there are illusions, but hold that they consist in not being aware of and committed to the core theses of Cathedralism.

Let's call the complex of all these elements of the grand-but-undetectable illusion line of argument (the commitment to the illusion, the prospects of being brought out of it, and that there are illusions of enlightenment within the illusion) *red pill rhetoric.* The basic program of those using red pill rhetoric is that those on the other side are so badly brainwashed, they, for the most part, are in a position where only the most invasive methods are capable of reaching them to turn them from the truth. The mode of engagement using red pill rhetoric is to start with the thought that one's intellectual opponents suffer from false consciousness, and so the failure of one's arguments shouldn't be evidence of them being bad, but rather evidence of how far gone the other side is.

Despite the depth of these disagreements between the progressive left in America and those on the neo-reactionary right, there are still prospects for productive argument here. One source of hope is the fact that so many neo-reactionaries already take themselves to engage in argument with the liberal progressive movement. As noted by Foseti, a reviewer of the Moldbug blog:

> It's important to remember this fact. The past year has seen an explosion of "reactionary" writing. And I'm left feeling … unsettled. The explosion of high-quality Rightist thought is fantastic and should be enthusiastically applauded by anyone outside of the Cathedral (or anyone that enjoys a good argument—is that redundant?).[4]

The thought that it is *redundant* to think that those outside the Cathedral enjoy good argument should be reason to hope that there are lines of argument that can be open between progressives and neo-reactionaries. How could they enjoy a good argument unless argument was not only possible but actual?

The main challenge to those using the trope of red pill rhetoric at this stage is a form of leveling skepticism. Recall that Moldbug had acknowledged other competing red pill narratives, which he'd said were really "blue pills soaked in Red #3." But doesn't the progressive left say the same of the reactionary right? That they are false enlightenments? Moreover, if we *really are under such circumstances of deep and internally undetectable illusion,* how can *they themselves* know they really are out of the purported illusion? Thousands of students every year are taught about Plato's allegory of the cave, and *The Matrix* is a piece of pop critique culture—hasn't the "it's all an illusion" narrative been coopted by the illusion itself? Think about it for a second: if you were designing an illusion to trap human minds, wouldn't you build into the illusion versions of those who say that it's all an illusion, but just push the deceived deeper into the illusion? Moldbug observes the skeptical scenario, but only looking at his competition:

> [Y]ou have no *rational reason* to trust anything coming out of the Cathedral—that is, the universities and the press. You have no reason to trust these institutions than you have to trust, say, the Vatican.

But under these conditions, we have no rational reason to trust Moldbug, either. The problem with high-grade skeptical tropes in red pill rhetoric is that once they are in place, they do not discriminate. The neo-reactionary narrative gets the same treatment as that of the most lefty social justice warrior—namely, that of the jaded eye of one suspicious that it's all overblown rationalization. The leveling skeptical consequence is that we are all returned to argumentative *status quo ante*. No one gets to claim to have genuine red pills any more than anyone else. Nobody gets to say, now, that the other side suffers from a false consciousness that they themselves have overcome. We are all on the same level, all with the burden of proof.

Now the leveling skeptical argument is both good news and bad news. The good news is that there are argumentative possibilities in these deep disagreement cases, and they are ones that both sides can see the consequences of. The bad news is that the consequences are skeptical, at least in the sense that when both sides use this rhetoric in these circumstances, the result is that the argument ends in stalemate. Now, that's bad news in the sense that we don't have a resolution that favors one side over the other at this stage, but there is more than one way to resolve an issue. Sometimes, the best answer to an issue is that we need more information— neither side, at this stage, has the better case. We need to keep talking, keep finding new evidence, new considerations. Just because we don't know *now* who has the better case, that doesn't mean we won't *ever*. And so, despite the skeptical conclusion of the leveling argument, there are some reasons still to be argumentatively optimistic.

Some further evidence for argumentative optimism arises from how we have outlined the dialectical state of play. Deep disagreement, from the theoretically optimistic perspective, is a mere theoretical posit, an antinomy of reason taken too far. Insofar as depth of disagreement is gradable and comparative, the theoretical worry about what one might call *Absolutely Deep Disagreement*, as disagreement with no in-principle overlap of premises to reason from and no disagreements possibly deeper, is purely a matter of conceptual possibility. *Actual* disagreements never reach this state, if only because in order for us to recognize disagreements *as disagreements* (where we share enough semantic overhead to contradict each other) we must share enough commitments in common to start to arbitrate the disagreements. Earlier, we gave a kind of purely theoretical argument for this thesis, but now, we have a case in point. In fact, the advent of the rhetoric of red pills is testament to this. For the rhetoric of the red pill to work, we need notions like the appearance/reality distinction, the idea of being duped, and the idea of there being someone who sees it all for what it is and arrives to perform some consciousness-raising. All those elements of what might be called the *dialectic of false consciousness and its correction* must be in place for any of those narratives to exist or to make sense to their audiences.

The truth of the matter is that we do share those concepts, and those shared concepts bespeak yet more in common, such as a love of truth, a desire to know what one's position in reality and society is, and a desire to have some measure of control over it. That is, the background agreement is on all those norms of cognitive hygiene, cognitive command, and rational self-control we've been going on about throughout this book. How about that?

With this broad class of background concepts in place, we can see that the disagreement between liberals and neo-reactionaries is perhaps *deep*, but it is not one that approaches *absolute depth*. The theoretical program with deep disagreement optimism is that many disagreements are deeper than others, in the sense that there are disagreements with more contested argumentative moves than others. In a word, as the disagreements get deeper, they become *philosophical*. This, of course, should come as no surprise, since philosophy arguably began and thrives in the spaces where we attempt to wrestle with the Big Questions that separate us. But we argue all the time about Big Questions—philosophy wouldn't be possible if we couldn't.

Our optimistic response here to deep disagreement does not guarantee that arguments will eventually resolve the disagreements; and given the leveling skeptical argument earlier, it may be that there are no solutions coming. But this does not imply that argument is impossible under such conditions. In fact, the skeptical *argument* itself shows that argument is possible. Let that point sink in for a bit.

We are aware that many will find our case for argumentative optimism out of tune in these politically dark days. In fact, we expect that some will see our line of thought as complicit with the objectionable politics of the powerful and the moral failures of those with the loudest voices, since the argumentative stance we advocate does not sufficiently *resist* their power. But the moral situation should make this point clearer, since if we find those who propose authoritarian policies morally blameworthy, we must think them rationally responsible for the policies they endorse and the thoughts and reasons they act on. But if we hold them rationally responsible, we must think that if they had different reasons manifest to them, they could and should act otherwise. If we, ourselves, have those reasons and the voice to get them out in argument, then we are obligated to do so. And so optimism about argumentative possibilities and prospects in deep disagreement is not pie-eyed Pollyanna-ism in the face of argumentative tragedy, but rather it is the view that well-run argument matters and is important to value, especially in the dark days.

For Further Thought

1   If depth of disagreement is gradable (some disagreements are deeper than others), then does it follow that argumentative optimism is only just a theoretical view?
2   The symmetry of dialectical norms requires that a rule for arguers should also be one that hearers of arguments can endorse. Notice that this now constrains what kind of reasons can be given. Does this amount to another version of the rule of public reason, or does this rule have a different outcome?
3   Can there be absolutely deep disagreements, only they are very hard to articulate?
4   Can members of the Dark Enlightenment reply to the skeptical challenge given? If they do, is their answer in the service of the democratic norms they say they reject?

Key Terms

Deep disagreement	A disagreement wherein the two parties do not share enough commitments or argumentative procedures to resolve the issue by argument.
Argumentative optimism	The view that either there are not deep disagreements or that argument is possible and worthwhile even when faced with deep disagreement.
Argumentative pessimism	The view that argument is either not possible or is pointless in cases of deep disagreement.
Dialecticality requirement	Arguments must be materially and logically successful in ways that their audience can recognize, and further, they must address concerns and challenges posed by the audience.
Red Pill Rhetoric	The argumentative technique of taking those with whom one has a deep disagreement to be deeply deluded and caught in a false-consciousness.

Notes

1   https://thepointmag.com/2017/politics/final-fantasy-neoreactionary-politics-liberal-imagination

2 http://unqualified-reservations.blogspot.com/2007/05/
3 http://www.thedarkenlightenment.com/the-dark-enlightenment-by-nick-land/
4 https://foseti.wordpress.com/2014/01/06/review-of-unqualified-reservations-part-1/

References

Fogelin, Robert (1985) "The Logic of Deep Disagreements." *Informal Logic* 7:1. 1–8.

Part II
Case Studies in Public Argument

5   The Simple Truth Thesis

In this and the following several chapters, we attempt to catalogue many of the most prevalent ways in which proper argument is *simulated* in popular public discussion. Well run argument is valuable, and as with other valuable things, there are counterfeits. Although many of the coming chapters will examine phenomena that are highly specific to particular kinds of argument, we begin with a most general form of simulated argument.

As we noted in Chapter 2, one common form of manipulation involves presenting an audience with a distorted view of the range of reasons that are relevant to an issue. Most typically, this kind of manipulation is deployed by a proponent of some view—let's call the view p—who endeavors to convince his audience to also adopt p on the basis of the claim that p *is simply and obviously true*. As it would be mad to reject a simple and obvious truth, the proponent uses his firm assertion that p is a *simple truth* as a winning argument for p.

This is obviously no argument at all. But it is a highly effective tactic in contexts where a speaker is addressing a group of people who see themselves as generally like-minded. In addition, an appeal to the Simple Truth is a way of outing those who may see themselves as part of the group, but in fact are outliers. It thus sends a strong signal to those in the audience that they must accept p, or else be regarded as an outsider, or worse yet, a poser. This is why Simple Truth is often accompanied by a kind of browbeating; the speaker affirms p as a Simple Truth, and then pauses to survey the audience for any signs of defection. Relying on group dynamics and a strong desire among people to be accepted by the groups they identify with, the Simple Truth tactic has a high success rate among speakers, even when they're not especially skilled in other respects. The rhetorical mantle of *common sense* and things that are *obviously right* is as powerful as it is easy to claim.

Although it is not a kind of argument in any respect, there is a sense in which the Simple Truth can be seen as an appropriate way to engage with an audience. After all, when one is speaking to an audience in order to make a case for some belief, one cannot begin from scratch. That is, there are contexts in which one must identify for one's audience the claims that will be assumed to be true or beyond dispute for the purpose of the argument at hand. And it seems perfectly reasonable for some speakers to present certain claims as beyond question for those who are members of their intended audience. So, in asserting that p is simply and obviously true, a speaker may merely be signaling that his remarks are intended only for those who already accept p. On this model of the phenomenon, the Simple Truth is not a mimic of argument; it is rather a strategy for identifying, or perhaps selecting, one's audience.

Were this the prevailing way in which Simple Truth appeals were made, there would be, indeed, no need to discuss the matter as a problem for argument. It would be simply a background phenomenon for argument overall. However, deployments of the Simple Truth are pervasive in contemporary political discourse, and they do not fit the rather innocent mold just described. Let us explain.

Political commentary proceeds by means of debate rather than report today. This is an understandable consequence of contemporary communications technology, which makes argumentative engagement easy. For example, news programs can feature panels of guests who disagree about some issue without needing to bring them all to the same television studio. People on opposite side of the globe are able to talk live and virtually in person to each other and to a large viewing audience. As should be obvious from our previous chapters, we think that this heightened reliance on public debate is a good thing, too. Open public debate is democracy's lifeblood. It is, as we argued earlier, the way in which we pursue the project of collective self-government by means of reasons.

Yet it is regularly noted that in the wake of vast advances in communications technology, popular political debate has taken on an odd hue. Rather than presenting facts, articulating reasons, and defending a view, commentators mostly present views concerning the views of their opponents. Despite heated disagreements over pressing Big Questions concerning health care, immigration, same-sex marriage, and what to do about global warming, there is a surprising consensus about the nature of political disagreement itself. Pundits and commentators seem to agree that, with respect to any Big Question, there is but one intelligent position, and all opposing positions are not merely wrong, but ignorant, stupid, naïve, self-serving, and dangerous. A minute in the public affairs or politics section of a local bookstore or the comments section of any political news site will confirm this. According to one popular conservative commentator, conservatives should talk to liberals "only if they must" because, as another observes, liberalism is a "mental disorder." Liberal commentators similarly dismiss their conservative opponents, since they are "lying liars" who use a "noise machine" to wage war on science, freedom, children, and many other good things.

Both camps betray a commitment to the Simple Truth Thesis, the claim that Big Questions always admit simple, obvious, undeniable, and easily stated answers. The Simple Truth Thesis encourages us to hold that a given truth is so simple and so obvious that only the ignorant, wicked, devious, or benighted could possibly deny it. On a recent occasion, an acquaintance of ours, in the midst of a political conversation, announced that opposing the flat tax was "stupid, evil, or both." With this statement, she affirmed that, in her opinion, there is no room for reasoned disagreement about the merits of a flat tax. In another recent discussion, a professor of philosophy asserted that there is not even one intelligent defense of the death penalty. *Not one*, he said.

It's an odd phenomenon. Part of what makes Big Questions so important and, well, *big*, is precisely the fact that reasonable, sincere, informed, and intelligent persons can disagree over their answers. That is, the Simple Truth Thesis has the effect of deflating Big Questions. But as it does so by casting aspersions on one's opposition, it deflates the questions by inflaming those with whom one disagrees. Consequently, as our popular political commentary accepts the Simple Truth Thesis, there is a great deal of inflammatory and defamatory rhetoric and righteous indignation, but in fact very little public *debate* over the issues that matter most. Thus the Big Questions over which we are divided remain unexamined, and our reasons for adopting our different answers are never brought to bear in public discussion. And, moreover, what passes for public argument is nothing like argument at all.

This should come as no surprise. It is clear that one of the direct corollaries to the Simple Truth Thesis is the *No Reasonable Opposition Thesis*. According to the No Reasonable Opposition Thesis, argument and debate with those with whom one disagrees is a pointless and futile endeavor. The reasoning driving No Reasonable Opposition is simple. If in fact the answer to a given Big Question is a Simple Truth, then there is no opponent of that answer who is not also woefully ignorant, misinformed, misguided, wicked, or worse. In other words, argument concerning a Big Question can be worthwhile only when there is more than one reasonable position regarding the question. And this is precisely what the Simple Truth Thesis denies.

One could argue that it would be a wonderful world were the Simple Truth Thesis true. Our political task would be simply to empower those who know the Simple Truths, and rebuke the fools who do not. But, alas, the Simple Truth Thesis is not true, and consequently, the No Reasonable Opposition Thesis must be dismissed as well. In fact, the Simple Truth Thesis is a fairy tale—soothing and satisfying, but ultimately unfit for a serious mind. We must recognize that for any Big Question, there are several defensible positions; indeed, as we said above, it is precisely this feature that makes them big questions rather than small or ordinary ones. Of course, to say that a position is defensible is not to say that it's true. One can acknowledge that there are multiple defensible positions in response to a Big Question, and still maintain that there is only one defensible position that is correct. We should be careful to add: to oppose the Simple Truth Thesis is not to embrace relativism, nor is it to give up on the idea that there are true answers to Big Questions. It is rather to give up on the view that the truth is always simple.

That last point about relativism is crucial. So let us take a moment to develop it further. We just said that denying the Simple Truth and No Reasonable Opposition theses does not commit one to relativism. Holding that there can be more than one reasonable answer to a question does not commit anyone to holding that all those answers are right. Nor does it prohibit anyone holding one of those reasonable views from criticizing another person holding another of those reasonable views.

Relativism is a claim about truth, about who is right. It is the view that everyone in a disagreement is right, or at least not wrong. In fact, it is not clear that we even need to appeal to disagreement in order to state relativism's main contention. It is that every view is correct for the person who holds it.

Now, relativism has its problems. First, relativism seems obviously self-defeating. If everyone is right and nobody is wrong, then it surely seems that those who hold that relativism is false must be wrong. But relativism says that everyone is right—so relativism must say that even relativism's deniers are right. But if relativism's deniers are right, then relativism must be wrong. It seems then that relativism is inconsistent with itself. Anyone who asserts relativism thereby refutes it. Maybe the only way to be a consistent relativist is to decline to affirm it. And that's good news for the anti-relativist, since the relativists now don't have anything to object. It's a cute argument against relativism; it's as old as the hills, too. Plato famously ran it against the relativists of his day, and it's still got a bite to it.

A second problem with relativism is that it seems to involve a mis-understanding of the role of truth in our cognitive lives. The mis-understanding turns on the idea of a belief being "true for" the person who holds it. To be sure, it is clear that to believe something is to hold it to be true. So there is a very weak sense in which everything you believe is "true for you." For any of your beliefs, it is "true for you" simply because you believe it. If Billy believes he can fly, it is "true for him" that he can. But, crucially, "true for him" in this case simply means "believed by him." When Billy believes that he can fly, he believes it is true that he can. After all, that's just what a belief is; belief is the attitude of taking a proposition to be true. So when Billy holds the belief "I can fly," he takes it to be true that he can fly. In only this weak sense can we say that the belief "I can fly" is "true for" Billy. But notice that we don't think that it is "true for him" in any stronger sense than this. That Billy believes he can fly doesn't mean that he can, indeed, fly. We all know that beliefs can be false. A belief is false when we take something to be true that is really not true. Relativism confuses the obviously correct observation that *believing is taking a proposition to be true* with the untenable and false view that *to take a proposition to be true is for it to be true.* If this distinction seems obscure to you, just ask yourself how it is possible for you to lose your keys. Losing your keys involves believing that your keys are in some location (and so *taking it to be true* that they are in that location), and finding out that they in fact are not there. If relativism is true, that can never happen. But it does.

The third problem with relativism is that it frequently comes with a promise it cannot fulfill. The appealing promise of relativism—holding that everyone's right about an issue in their own way and no one's wrong—is that it seems to encourage a significant measure of tolerance. If everyone's right and nobody's wrong, then it seems we should all just relax. We should leave others alone with their truths. We should live and let live. Call this relativism's *tolerance promise.*

Tolerance, within its proper limits, is indeed an important social virtue and practice that must be cultivated. But, alas, relativism can't make good on the tolerance promise. After all, relativism must hold that tolerance is good or important only if one believes it to be so. If, as the relativist alleges, it's *all* relative, then the principle that *if people have their own truths, then it's not worth fighting with them or forcing them to change their minds* is relative, too. According to the relativist, that principle is itself something that's true only for those who accept it; and, crucially, its rejection is true for those who reject it. So when the relativist confronts the opponent of toleration, it is not clear what he or she can say. Consider the bully coercing others to do his bidding, the cult leader brainwashing his followers, or the tyrant threatening the opposition. There is nothing the relativist can say in defense of toleration. If believing something makes it true, then anti-tolerance is true for bullies, cult-leaders, and tyrants, and the relativist has no means by which to critique their views. Again, if the relativist holds that everyone is right and no one is wrong, then the relativist cannot object to the views of those who hold that toleration is silly. Moreover, the relativist robs us of the resources by which we could *criticize* bullies, cult leaders, and tyrants. After all, to criticize another person is to affirm that he or she has made a mistake and needs to be corrected. But relativism is the view that there are no mistakes and no corrections. Relativism hence takes the bite out of moral judgment, reasoning, and critique. All of it.

That's the quick and dirty case against relativism. Now notice that none of these arguments bear on the view that there are multiple reasonable answers to Big Questions. In affirming that there are many defensible responses to each Big Question, one claims only that there is a difference between being wrong and being stupid. It is to acknowledge that even smart people, even people with real cognitive command, make mistakes. Take Plato. From the previous chapters, it should be pretty clear that we think Plato was wrong about a great many things. We already indicated that we think he was wrong about several matters concerning democracy, but that's just the beginning of the story. We think that Plato was wrong about almost everything from his theory of knowledge, to his theory of how the soul works, to his views about the nature of reality. But we also think it's obvious that Plato was a great philosopher. In fact, we think he was a genius. We admire him, wrestle with his thought, try to criticize his views, and in general take him very seriously. But, on nearly every philosophical issue, we believe he was wrong, wrong, wrong.

Holding that there is reasonable opposition, in fact, is a condition for thinking that criticism is possible. That's a big thought, so we'll have to give a pretty good argument for it. Here goes. Consider that if you think that those who you disagree with are simply stupid, benighted, or evil, you wouldn't have any arguments to give to them. Criticism of them and their views would be impossible. You would need only to state that they are wrong. But notice that it's only when you take your opponents to be reasonable—people who care about evidence, can see relevant issues, and are able to understand what's at stake in a debate—that you can actually criticize them. Criticism depends upon the background thought that the person you're engaging with has the capacity to reason in good faith. That is not to say that in order to criticize another person, one must endorse or accept their reasons. It means only that you must acknowledge that reasoning (perhaps flawed reasoning, or reasoning from false premises) is occurring, and that it's thus possible to assess and correct it. So to deny the Simple Truth and No Reasonable Opposition theses is not to capitulate to relativism at all. One can reject these theses and yet be committed to there being a single right answer to each Big Question; and one can still hold that those who deny what you believe are dead wrong. One who rejects these theses can still be committed to arguing earnestly with others, and to vigorously critiquing those who are wrong. In fact, you can even think that they have a level of command of an issue that's impressive, but still think they are wrong. But most importantly, the denial of the Simple Truth and No Reasonable Opposition theses actually delivers the kind of tolerance that relativism could only promise. Once you're committed to seeing your opponents as reasonable, intelligent, and sincere, but mistaken, you're less likely to use force or violence to correct them. You're more likely to use arguments to change their minds. That's where tolerance really lies.

Consequently, even if there is some Big Question whose true answer is p, there can nonetheless be formidable cases made in support of alternative, mistaken, answers. That's because when it comes to Big Questions, there are many different considerations that must be examined, and there will always be reasonable disagreements among intelligent and sincere people about the relative weight of considerations of different kinds. Again, Big Questions are *big* because they require that we take many, many kinds of considerations into account. Indeed, sometimes the answer to one Big Question depends on how we've answered other Big Questions. Things can get extremely complicated very quickly. Yet we are finite creatures with limited cognitive resources, and so it is sometimes hard for us to balance our philosophical checkbooks. Big Questions can dwarf our intelligence. Once we appreciate this, we must recognize that the No Reasonable Opposition Thesis must be abandoned. Even if we have the true answer to a Big Question, there will be room for intelligent, informed, and sincere people to disagree. In such cases, our opponents are mistaken or wrong, but not therefore unintelligent, wicked, untrustworthy, or ignorant. They deserve our attention, and we need to consider what they have to say.

In the context of real-world argument, appeals to "common sense" or "straight talk" are reliable indications that the Simple Truth strategy is being employed. Mike Huckabee, the ex-governor of Arkansas, a 2008 presidential candidate, and now Fox News commentator, describes most of his views as "common sense." When criticizing the Affordable Care Act's (Obamacare's) promise to prohibit insurers from declining coverage on the basis of an individual's preexisting conditions, Huckabee argued:

> I want to ask you something *from a common sense perspective* ... Suppose we applied that principle [to] our property insurance. And you can call your insurance agent and say, "I'd like to buy some insurance for my house." He'd say, "Tell me about your house." "Well sir, it burned down yesterday, but I'd like to insure it today."[1]

Now, regardless of what you make of Huckabee's analogy between health and home insurance, it is clear that his description of his view as one of a *common sense perspective* is intended to do additional argumentative work. In characterizing his view as common sense, Huckabee is communicating the thought that those who reject, for example, his analogy between housing and health insurance are lacking in common sense. To object that, perhaps, those whose houses have burned down deserve concern, too, would on Huckabee's reasoning be beyond the pale of reasonableness. (We'll return to this thought later in Chapter 9, on arguments by analogy and the particular difficulties they can have.) By Huckabee's lights, it's just obvious that he's right about this issue, and so he holds that those who oppose him are flatly, obviously wrong. Importantly, he seems to think that the best explanation of the fact that some people oppose his view is that some fail to see the truths right under their noses. Huckabee hence sees his opponents not as people who employ failed reasons or who fail to appreciate the full force of the available reasons, but rather as people who fail to be reasoners in the first place. Huckabee is especially fond of invoking common sense as the basis of his views, and he characterizes his opponents as people who are "waging a war against common sense."[2] Convenient, isn't it?

Let us look at another example. In a recent endorsement of Janice Hahn for a Congressional seat representing a Southern California district, President Bill Clinton invoked a version of Simple Truth conjoined with No Reasonable Opposition. Clinton said:

America is at a crossroads and we need to decide whether we are going to pursue a path of right-wing extremism or one of compromise and common sense solutions.[3]

Clinton presents a stark choice that we must make between extremists and common sense. And who would choose extremism? No reasonable person is an extremist. So Clinton, like Huckabee, has very conveniently described his opposition in a way that places them beyond the pale of reasonable debate. Independently of whether there are other options beyond the two that Clinton has identified, everything in his argument hangs on what is being labeled as common sense. It is of course no surprise that the solutions that count as common sense by Bill Clinton are the ones Bill Clinton favors.

The Simple Truth and No Reasonable Opposition strategies are so popular because often we feel deeply *invested* in our own Big Answers. But nonetheless it is a fantasy to think that the billions of people who reject our own answers have all simply failed to appreciate the obvious facts, are lacking in "common sense," or are just too dumb to know what's what. This fantasy is easily dissolved once we come to realize that those who reject our own Big Answers are often able to give good reasons for their views and against ours. We might not find ourselves convinced by the reasons our opponents propose, of course, but we will be no longer able to see them as ignorant or foolish. The lesson to draw, again, is that there is a difference between being stupid and being wrong. The most important truths are often the most difficult to discern, even by the most careful and sincere inquirers. This lesson dismantles the Simple Truth Thesis and leads us to acknowledge that although there may be but one correct answer to each Big Question, there are several defensible views concerning which of the going answers is, indeed, the correct one. So if the Big Questions matter to us, we should be most eager to hear the reasons of our opponents. We should pursue real argument, with real interlocutors, not the cooked-up arguments against caricatured opposition on offer from the political commentary industry.

That the Simple Truth Thesis is easily undermined once we actually engage with those with whom we disagree explains why those who deploy the Simple Truth and No Reasonable Opposition maneuvers so often insist on presenting their audiences with detailed portraits of those on the other side. It is important to the career prospects of conservative commentators that their audience gets its view of liberals not from the liberals themselves, but instead from the conservative commentators. The same goes for liberal commentators. They must ensure that they are the source of their audience's conception of what conservatives think. Were either audience to turn to their actual opponents to hear the reasons that actually drive those on the other side, they would be liable to see that the world of popular political punditry promotes a distorted and grossly oversimplified vision of our democracy.

And so we have come full circle. The Simple Truth Thesis and the resulting No Reasonable Opposition Thesis are employed as *audience cues*, indications of what one must think in order to be a member in good standing of some (in this case, political) group. But we also see now that in the context of democracy, this method of enforcing group identity and ideological discipline is pernicious. These tactics not only signal to group members what they must believe in order to be a proper member; they also cast aspersions on those who stand outside that group by portraying them as so deeply ignorant and stupid as to not be worth associating with, much less talking to.

The fragmentation of the citizenry into opposed political groups who have limited interaction with each other is an obvious boon to television news networks, talk radio channels, and book publishers. The fragmentation enables them better to identify the demographics of their audience, and thus it helps them to sell their products and those of their advertisers. And this in turn better enables them to attract advertisers. However, all of this comes at a high cost to democracy. As we have mentioned previously, democracy is the proposition that a just, peaceful, and morally decent society is possible among equals who disagree over Big Questions. Democracy tries to enable such a society by maintaining the conditions under which citizens can reason together, and, despite ongoing disagreement, come to see each other as reasonable. Citizens who see each other in this way can agree to share in the task of collective self-government despite ongoing discord over Big Questions. The Simple Truth Thesis repudiates this ideal. Accordingly, as our politics become more argumentative, they become less concerned with actual argument. Yet if we lose our capacity to argue with each other—to confront openly each other's reasons—we will lose our capacity to see each other as equal partners in self-government, and thus we will lose our democracy.

For Further Thought

1   Aren't there matters about which indeed the truth is simple and there are in fact no reasonable opponents? If so, how should we deal with those who unreasonably deny the simple truth?

2   Could relativists respond to the three problems raised with their view?

3   It seems plausible to think that sometimes strong group cohesion is necessary in order to motivate social activism. And this level of cohesion seems more easily achievable when one thinks that one's own side is obviously right and one's opponents are so obviously wrong that they must be insincere, deluded, uninformed, or worse. Does the view presented in this chapter run counter to the requirements for social action?

4   Is the view that there can be no reasonable opposition a different kind of relativism, not about *truth*, but instead about *reason*?

5 If we give up on the Simple Truth Thesis, does it follow that we must not debate all the Nazis, racists, and terrorists? Does it mean that we must now hold *them* reasonable?

6 Is it true that tolerance requires that you may think someone wrong about something? If one thought them *right*, would it still be *tolerance*?

Key Terms

Relativism about truth	All views in a disagreement are right, according to their own standards.
No Reasonable Opposition Thesis	All opposition to one's preferred answer to a Big Question is non-rational, and so undeserving of reasoned criticism.
Simple Truth Thesis	For any Big Question, there is only one answer, and all other answers are consequences either of blameworthy ignorance, wickedness, or outright deceit.

Notes

1 http://tpmdc.talkingpointsmemo.com/2010/09/huckabee-opposes-insurance-for-people-with-pre-existing-conditions.php
2 www.foxnews.com/on-air/huckabee/transcript/huckabee-war-commonsense
3 http://janicehahn.com/coverage/bill-clinton-endorses-janice-hahn-forcongress/

6   Pushovers

When we are exchanging reasons with interlocutors, it is important that the reasons we consider on the other side are the reasons actually given by those who oppose us. Yet when listening to someone else's reasons, it is easy not to feel their force. Sometimes we find it difficult to understand them (and so, we must ask for clarification), but on other occasions the reasons we consider most relevant are just not the ones given by our opponent. Consider the following exchange:

ALBERT: Wearing a seat belt makes it 60 percent more likely that you won't have major injuries in a serious car accident. It should be a law, because there's a public safety issue.
BETTY: Look, just because there's *a chance* that I might survive a car wreck if I wear my seat belt, that's no reason for you to force me to wear it.

Notice that Betty understands Albert's argument as one that makes use of the likelihood of avoiding injury, but in fact Albert's point is that (especially because the injuries avoided are serious) there is a *significant likelihood* that you can avoid these injuries. Betty's response acknowledges the fact that there is a possibility of avoiding a major injury by wearing a seat belt, but she fails to register the fact that Albert's argument claims that there is a high likelihood that wearing a seat belt will help one to avoid major injuries. When she criticizes Albert's argument, the significant likelihood mentioned by Albert becomes a mere unspecified *chance*. Betty has distorted Albert's argument in a way that makes his case for wearing seat belts (and thus laws mandating that they be worn) seem far less compelling. She accomplishes this by distorting the probabilities Albert cites.

There is a family of argument-imposters that involve the misrepresentation of one's opponent's view or reasons. The general strategy is to make one's favored view look good by making the opposition's position look flimsy or trivial. As they turn on a mischaracterization that makes one's opposition look frail or superfluous, we call them *pushover arguments*. The most familiar member of this family is widely known as the *straw man* fallacy. So that is where we begin.

The straw man fallacy proceeds in the following way. First, one misrepresents an opponent's view in a way that makes it far less defensible. Then one refutes that misrepresented view. And finally one draws the conclusion that the opponent's (actual) view has been defeated, shown to be wrong.

It is obvious why straw man arguments are violations of the norms of proper argument. They simply fail to hit their mark—the position that is criticized is not the opponent's actual view. Recall the distinction we drew earlier between formal and dialectical fallacies. Dialectical fallacies fail what we'd called in Chapter 4 the *dialecticality requirement*—that arguments (a) have recognizably good premises and support and (b) are responsive to arguments and objections of the opposition. The straw man is a dialectical fallacy *par excellence*. Here's why. First, engaging with a distorted and weakened version of an opponent's view doesn't address the reasons that must be addressed in the dialogue. And on top of that, it undoes the intellectual trust required for discussion in good faith. In the same way that you'd be disinclined to argue at all with someone who has no interest in giving reasons you can appreciate, you'd be less inclined to argue with someone who refuses to appreciate and reply to the reasons you give. Moreover, employing a straw man sets a bad intellectual example, as it misleads those listening to the exchange. So, in our example above, Betty not only gives onlookers conclusions that aren't supported by the evidence, she also confuses them about what the evidence is. Consequently she undermines her audience's ability to be responsible arguers themselves.

This much seems obvious. But it is worth going into greater detail in explaining what is wrong with straw man arguments. Proper argument requires a minimal background of cooperation between arguers, and one feature of that background is that in arguing, the discussants must be *exchanging* reasons. The exchange of reasons primarily involves someone making reasons explicit for another. But for two discussants to jointly examine and evaluate reasons, they must be considering the same reasons, and so it is important for arguers to get their opponents' arguments straight before evaluating them. Otherwise, they aren't really arguing with each other at all. Hence when we criticize or reject an interlocutor's argument, we must be criticizing the argument that was actually given. If we criticize distorted versions of the arguments of our interlocutors, as Betty does above, we haven't moved the discussion along. And we might have made a critical discussion more like a battle.

We may set down the following as a general requirement for proper argument: If one is going to criticize the case for some view, call it p, one must attend to the arguments actually given by those who support p. We think that this is about as uncontroversial a principle as could be found in all of philosophy. But just because it's an uncontroversial principle, that doesn't mean that everyone follows it. Returning to our example now, let us assume (what is certainly true) that there are many reasons and arguments offered by those who support laws enforcing seat belt use. And, naturally, the quality of these arguments varies. So consider the following arguments for enforced seat belt use. Imagine each of the following having "therefore, wearing a seat belt should be legally required" as their conclusion:

ALBERT: If you wear a seat belt, you reduce the likelihood of serious injury by 60 percent.
CHARLIE: If you wear a seat belt, you'll probably be safer.
DOPEY: If you wear a seat belt, you will feel safer.

Let us say that Dopey has heard Albert's and Charlie's arguments, but because he's dopey, he doesn't get them just right. He bungles the case for enforced seat belt use, but he means well and sincerely supports seat belt laws.

Now, remember our critic of enforced seat belt use, Betty. Let's suppose she endorses the requirement for proper argument we identified above, and so she holds that she must engage with the arguments *actually offered* by those who support seat belt laws. So she responds as follows to Dopey:

BETTY: Maybe wearing a seat belt makes you *feel* safer. But so what? That's no reason for having a law that requires people to wear them. All this seat belt law stuff is just about making people feel good. Sheesh!

Dopey gave a silly argument, and Betty correctly noted it and criticized it. She did not misrepresent Dopey's case. We might even say that Betty has refuted Dopey's argument. Yet if this is the totality of her case against seat belt laws, there's something amiss with her performance. Betty's distortion of the argument for seat belts does not lie in her representation of Dopey's reason; rather, Betty fails at proper argument because she has elected to focus *only on the worst case for the view she opposes.* Betty has left *the better arguments unaddressed.* In doing so, Betty gives the distinct impression that she has rebutted the case for seat belt laws as such, while in fact she has only knocked down an especially unsophisticated and weak version of the view she opposes.

In order to see this, imagine that Betty is now out with some friends, and out of the presence of Albert, Charlie, and Dopey. She is talking with them about the issue concerning whether seat belt use should be required by law. Imagine further that her friends are unaware of Albert's and Charlie's arguments. If she were to discuss only Dopey's argument, her friends would reasonably (but falsely) conclude not only that Dopey's case for seat belt laws is weak, but that the overall case for seat belt laws is weak. Unless Betty explicitly introduces the caveat that there are other, better, arguments in favor of seat belt laws, the argument she's responding to will be perceived as the dominant argument in favor of seat belt laws, and thus representative of the general quality of the arguments given by her opponents. But were Betty to make explicit note of the existence of these other more formidable arguments, her audience would rightly wonder why she bothered to respond to Dopey at all.

In replying only to Dopey, then, Betty has failed to argue properly. Her error consists not in misrepresenting Dopey's argument, but in presenting a distorted picture of the overall state of play in the debate. Not being followers of the seat belt debates, Betty's friends will come to think that the case for seat belt laws is notably weak. Thus Betty will have won support for her view on the basis of an implicit misrepresentation of the dialectical situation in the debate regarding seat belt laws.

Betty's strategy employs a second kind of pushover argument, what we call the *weak man* fallacy. Betty has selected the weakest of the opposing arguments and has responded only to that. She correctly represents the weak version, precisely because it is so weak, and she responds appropriately critically to it. Consequently, she has not committed the straw man fallacy. Her error, again, is that in taking up only with Dopey's argument, she implies that she has refuted an argument that is representative of her opposition generally. But Dopey's argument is not representative of her opposition. It is rather the weakest version of the opposition's case. She has failed at proper argument because she has misrepresented the dialectical situation that obtains among those who support and those who oppose seat belt laws. That is, she has selected and refuted a weak man.

A third member of the pushover family comes into view in cases of argument where there is no proponent of the opposition present to defend his or her view. In the absence of a real opponent, it is possible for a speaker to completely fabricate the entire argument the other side gives. So imagine, again, the following reasons for seat belts laws:

ALBERT: Wearing seat belts reduces likelihood of serious injury.
CHRISTINE: If you're in the habit of buckling your seat belt, you end up developing a habit of carefulness in the car. That's a good thing!Now imagine that Betty is again discussing seat belt laws with her friends. Recall that she's against such laws, and she says the following:
BETTY: The reason people favor seat belt laws is that they just need new rules so they can enforce them and feel good and superior when they follow them. *That's* their reason.

Betty here is responding to reasons *nobody* on the other side of the debate gives. Not even Dopey. In this case, it is not that she gave a weaker version of what's been given; that would be a straw man. Nor does she select the weakest argument among those given by her opposition; that would be a weak man. Rather, she creates an argument from whole cloth to represent the opposition's view. We call this tactic the *hollow man* fallacy.

Speakers commit the hollow man when they respond critically to arguments that nobody on the opposing side has ever made. The act of erecting a hollow man is an argumentative failure because it distracts attention away from the actual reasons and argument given by one's opposition. Furthermore, instances of the hollow man do a very serious disservice to the whole project of arguing. Hollow men misrepresent one's opponents by spinning a flat-out lie about what they say. It is a full-bore fabrication of the opposition.

Early in 2004, in the wake of the American invasion of Iraq, President George W. Bush was trying to manage the political fact that the entire operation was growing unpopular. Although in the lead-up to the invasion the CIA had professed to know that Iraq had weapons of mass destruction, there turned out to be no such weapons. Furthermore, as Iraq was becoming unstable under the coalition occupation, many Iraqis were becoming radicalized and growing increasingly suspicious of the U.S. effort and even began to express opposition to the U.S. as such. Many in the United States were concerned that the situation was not hopeful for the fledgling Iraqi democracy. In his 2004 State of the Union address, President Bush spoke to those worries as follows:

> We also hear doubts that democracy is a realistic goal in the Greater Middle East, where freedom is rare. Yet it is mistaken, and condescending, to assume that whole cultures and great religions are incompatible with liberty and self-government.

In case there was any doubt what Bush's implication in the State of the Union was, he followed up later with a statement in the Rose Garden of the White House:

> There's a lot of people in the world who don't believe that people whose skin color may not be the same as ours can be free and self-govern. I reject that. I reject that strongly.

Granted, it is unusual for presidents to respond in their speeches to specific criticisms offered by their political opponents, but it is unclear just who George W. Bush had in mind in delivering these remarks. And, importantly, Bush did nothing to identify anyone among his opposition. Instead, he suggested that the opponents of the Iraq invasion favor the following kind of view:

> The Iraq invasion should be opposed because Iraqi culture (or Arabic culture generally) and the local Shia and Sunni religious sects (or Islam generally) are incompatible with liberty and self-government. Therefore democracy is not a realistic goal in Iraq (or the Middle East generally).

Bush's suggestion is that his critics who express doubts about the feasibility of Iraqi democracy (and by extension, American support for those efforts promoting it) are actually cultural and religious bigots. The problem, however, was that *nobody among Bush's opponents had said anything like that*. Surely, no serious discussant would even think to hold that populations of people with skin darker in hue than George Bush's are therefore incapable of democracy, as it is widely known that India is the world's most populous democracy. The principal concern expressed by Bush's critics was that Iraqi institutions overtly sponsored by America could not stably govern Iraq, given the widespread anti-American sentiment that had grown among the Iraqi people. Other critics expressed doubts that the Americans had given the Iraqi government sufficient support in either troop numbers or administrative assistance.

Understandably, Bush's line was positively baffling to the critics of the invasion. Indeed, Edward Haley observed that Bush's strategy was to cast opposition to further occupying forces in Iraq as a "false dichotomy," so that "anyone who had even modest doubts about the democratization of Iraq was an unpatriotic bigot" (2006: 177).

Bush's casting of the opposition as racist was an effort not only to present the opposition as ridiculous, but to cast his critics as being motivated by views that nobody would want to publicly endorse. In other words, Bush's strategy was to impute an unexpressed and highly disreputable motive to his opposition. Those who supported Bush's views apparently were not troubled at all by the fact that no one among the opposition had said anything amounting to the expression of the kind of racism Bush had attributed to his critics. In fact, some celebrated Bush's response. For example, Jeffrey Lord claimed in the *American Spectator* that the Democratic Party as a whole is driven by unexpressed racist aims:

> [T]he party of race followed its support for subjugating millions of black Americans to slavery with support for a hundred years of segregation. After abandoning millions of people of color in their struggle against Communism, it now seeks to do the same as Iraqis struggle against Islamic fascists.
>
> (2007)

Consequently, even if those in the opposition were to press the president for an actual example of someone expressing racism-based doubts about the possibility of democracy in the Middle East, Bush's strategy would be to assert that even if none of Bush's opponents ever said such a thing, they nevertheless hold such views in private.

In his State of the Union address, Bush constructed a hollow man of his critics. He then decisively repudiated the argument he had constructed, thereby giving his supporters further grounds for their antecedent suspicions about liberals. In so doing, Bush mislead his supporters with respect to the actual criticisms of the Iraq invasion. In erecting a hollow man, he pushed the actual concerns of his real-world critics out of the debate. That's not only a failure of proper argument. It's also a failure of democracy.

Talk show host Jimmy Kimmel opened his show *Jimmy Kimmel Live* with a monologue about his newborn son's congenital heart defect and the medical treatment he needed to save his life. By all accounts, the story was very moving. And Kimmel then followed it with an observation that too many people without insurance coverage would not have had the medical access he had. It was, ultimately, a personal story about why the Affordable Care Act (Obamacare) is so important. Kimmel sums up his view about what we owe to each other:

> Before 2014, if you were born with congenital heart disease like my son was, there was a good chance you'd never be able to get health insurance because you had a pre-existing condition. [...] And if your parents didn't have medical insurance, you might not live long enough to even get denied because of a pre-existing condition. If your baby is going to die and it doesn't have to, it shouldn't matter how much money you make. I think that's something that whether you're a Republican or a Democrat or something else, we all agree on that, right? I mean, we do.[1]

Columnist Michelle Malkin responded critically at *The National Review*. She titled her piece, "A Thinking Mom's Message for Jimmy Kimmel."[2] First, she took issue with the fact that Kimmel "turned his personal plight into a political weapon" that so many were willing to re-tweet and like on social media. But then the argument, and not the opportunism, gets some critical attention:

> Kimmel doesn't need more maudlin Twitter suck-uppery. He needs a healthy fact-check. "Before 2014," he claimed, "if you were born with congenital heart disease like my son was, there was a good chance you'd never be able to get health insurance because you had a pre-existing condition, you were born with a pre-existing condition." This is false. If parents had health insurance, the child would have been covered under the parents' policy whether or not the child had a health problem.

This is a pretty uncharitable interpretation of Kimmel's sentence. Surely Kimmel's not saying that without the ACA *the babies* would need to have insurance coverage, but the baby's *parents*. In fact, note that Kimmel even clarifies the point not but a moment later by saying "If your parents don't have coverage..." But the second issue is not addressed at all—the point about pre-existing conditions. Sure, if the parents have coverage, no problem. But, without the rule that one cannot be denied coverage for pre-existing conditions, the parents can't apply for coverage *after* finding the condition without either huge penalties, going into a high-risk pool with sky-high premiums, or just not getting coverage. That's what Kimmel is focusing on. And that's not at all what Malkin's responding to.

This occasions an important theoretical point about how this fallacy works. Sometimes the straw man is constructed not in the *restatement or the explicit representation* of the opponent's view, but in the *indirect representation* in how one responds to the things they said. So when Malkin makes the picky point about parents and not the baby, she's painting a picture of Kimmel's view and argument by only stating the correction. And when she makes the point about health insurance already on the books, she obscures Kimmel's main point about the fact that the law is worth keeping by attacking something off stage. Again, Kimmel wants to highlight the fact that without medical coverage, he would not have been able to get the treatment his son needed. Since the ACA is a step toward providing that coverage for more than before, that's a good thing. None of Malkin's arguments touch that, but she proceeds as though she's demolished the case. Such is the false victory of pseudoreason.

We have introduced a family of pseudo-arguments that we call *pushover* arguments; we then identified three members of this broad family: the straw man fallacy, the weak man fallacy, and the hollow man fallacy. These fallacies are of a single family because they each involve a distortion of the dialectical situation between the speaker and his opposition that presents the opposition as feeble and thus enables the speaker to shut down further debate. In every one of these fallacies, the opposing side is portrayed as simply not having much of quality to offer to the discussion. The conclusion, then, is not simply that the opposition is wrong, but that there's no need to talk with them any further. They're pushovers. Accordingly, one needs simply to push them out of the way.

Although the general structure of these fallacies should be clear, some further detail is necessary in order to tell a more complete story about how they are all cases of argumentative failure. Things are about to get just a little bit technical.

On the standard account, the straw man occurs in an *adversarial* argumentative context between two speakers (A and B), where the proponent (A) represents her opponent's (B's) position in an inaccurate way which facilitates or strengthens A's case against B. Because the context is adversarial, A is out to win, and misrepresenting B is a means to that end. On this model, the straw man is a fallacy because it marks a failure of responsive argumentation. A's straw man argument against B undermines the goals of critical, even adversarial, discussion because the resolution of such critical exchange requires that parties argue responsively to one another. That is, A's setting up a straw man of B's view is a failure to actually engage with B and B's reasons. Even in adversarial cases, you still want to beat B's argument. Consequently, what makes the straw man a fallacy is that a speaker who erects a straw man advances an argument that misrepresents to her advantage the current dialectical situation. The crucial element of this misrepresentation that distinguishes the straw man from other misrepresentations is that the strength of the opponent's case is not reflected by the arguments the speaker attributes to the opposition. In erecting a straw man, a speaker misrepresents the dialectical situation that obtains between her and her opposition; she opportunistically misrepresents the argument given by her opponents.

Yet incorrectly representing a specific speaker's position or argument is not the only way to misrepresent the current dialectical situation. Remember from earlier: In arguing for her position, Betty surveys various arguments from the opposition. She takes up with an opponent, Dopey, she correctly recounts Dopey's argument, and then she legitimately refutes it. Betty then concludes that she has successfully defended her view. However, remember that Charlie had an argument that is far more formidable than Dopey's. In responding only to Dopey, and not to Charlie, Betty misrepresents the dialectical situation that obtains between her view and its opponents because *in taking up with only Dopey's arguments, Betty is implying that she is taking up with the best that her opposition has to offer.* Though Betty does not straw man Dopey's position or argument in the exchange, she nevertheless enfeebles her opposition more generally by refuting only her weakest opponent. Betty has presented a weak man by responding only to a relatively weak version of, or inept spokesman for, the opposition to her view. The weak man fallacy is vicious because it is posited on a misrepresentation of the variety and relative quality of one's opposition. It is a failure of what we earlier called argumentative responsibility.

We may ask how pushover arguments succeed in eliciting assent from their audiences. Generally, pushover arguments depend not only on a speaker's misrepresentation of her opponents' commitments and arguments, but also on her audience's inexperience or ignorance. In the case of the straw man, Betty's argument against Albert depends on her inaccurate presentation of Albert's view and case going undetected. Albert can correct this misrepresentation only if he keeps track of his own position and arguments for it, and if he can recognize and articulate the difference between them and Betty's corrupt versions. If Albert cannot, then Betty succeeds. Similarly, if Betty's audience cannot keep track of Albert's actual views, then Betty's straw man prevails. That is, straw man tactics work only when the distortions that run them are not detected and exposed.

By contrast, in the weak man, Betty correctly presents Dopey's argument and legitimately refutes it, yet she fails to countenance stronger opposing arguments from other sources. In so doing, Betty implicitly presents herself to her audience as having successfully defended her view against the going cases and as having thereby established her view. Unless her audience is familiar with the better arguments on offer by the opposition, Betty succeeds in winning their assent. In short, by earnestly responding only to Dopey, Betty shows herself to argue earnestly, but she fails at argumentative responsibility.

Now consider the hollow man. Betty simply fashions a terrible argument out of whole cloth and then presents it as capturing the view of her opposition. Recall that in our example above, neither Albert nor Christine ever gave anything resembling the argument that seat belt laws should be endorsed because it helps those who abide by laws to feel superior to others. Betty simply announced that as their reason for supporting seat belt laws. Hollow man arguments can work only when those listening know almost nothing about what actual opponents believe. It simply couldn't be the case that someone who knows Betty's opponents would agree that she's accurately identified their reasons. The reasons she's invoking don't look anything like what anyone on the other side actually says. Only someone who never has encountered someone on the other side of the issue could be moved by such an argument.

The three fallacies, then, take advantage of two different failings in their respective audiences. The straw man depends on the audience not detecting the misrepresentation of another speaker's argument or view. The audience must be inattentive in the sense that any nuance or sophistication of the criticized argument does not register or is deemed inconsequential. In the weak man, however, the argument depends on the audience being unaware of the variety and relative quality of opposition to the speaker's position. The audience can be very attentive to the details of the criticized position; however, if the audience is not knowledgeable about the range of arguments proposed by the opposition, the speaker sets the terms for argumentative success by default. Finally, the hollow man requires that the listening audience be wholly ignorant of what the opposition says, otherwise the game is up. In fact, because the hollow man depends on that ignorance, it functions as a way to mislead a listening audience about the issue under discussion. Of course when an audience knows only the hollow man representation of a view that opposes your own, winning their support is simple.

Donald Trump, in the midst of the 2016 election cycle, regularly claimed that "Hillary Clinton wants to abolish the Second Amendment. Hillary Clinton wants to take your guns away."[3] At an NRA rally, Trump claimed that Clinton's plan was to disarm single mothers and the elderly living in "tough neighborhoods." He said, "Hillary wants to take away any chance they have for survival. That's why they're gonna call her 'Heartless Hillary'."[4]

Seeing this line of argument as a hollow man of Clinton is not difficult. It most certainly is a misrepresentation of Clinton's expressed view, which was that she supported the Second Amendment, but she held that there needed to be more restrictions on gun purchases. That plan does not come to abolishing the Second Amendment, and it is not a case of coming to take guns that are already in people's possession. There's no evidence at all that Clinton planned to abolish the Second Amendment, so Trump has constructed a hollow opponent in this case. And it worked with his audiences mostly because they didn't have an accurate initial view of Clinton's policies beforehand. If your view of the opposition comes from how they are depicted by their critics, you're likely to have a view of them as intellectual pushovers.

How can one correct pushover arguments? First, showing that a speaker has ignored important opposing arguments is necessary. With the straw man, one has to be able to actually present the non-straw version of the opponent's argument. With the weak man, this may take the form of showing that though one opponent gives a weak argument, others give better. Crucially, you must make a case for thinking that the neglected arguments are superior to the ones criticized. And the same goes for the hollow man. In order to correct an instance of the hollow man, one must be able to identify what those who oppose a speaker actually say. This can be more difficult than might be thought, as hollow-manning sometimes involves the speaker trying to identify the opposition's real reasons, not just the ones they happen to give.

Accordingly, correcting straw, weak, and hollow men requires more than an analysis of what some speaker has said. One needs to be educated in the larger debate the speaker purports to be addressing. In these cases, the speaker relies on the ignorance of her audience; if she is to elicit their assent, her audience must be unfamiliar with the arguments made by the opposition. In this way, these tactics draw their success from the ignorance of their audiences. And, in the end, they reinforce it. In a nutshell, this is why pushover arguments are argumentative failures. They are in fact instances of simulated or mimicked argument.

Of course, a single person cannot master all of the debates and arguments afoot in contemporary public discourse. So a strategy might be to take to heart the view advocated by John Stuart Mill in his *On Liberty*. There, Mill argues that our understanding of our own position is directly proportionate to our understanding of those of our opponents. Mill writes, "He who knows only his own side of the case knows little of that" (1992: 42). It should be noted that the intuitive force of this Millian principle partially explains the success and prevalence of the fallacies we have been discussing. In order to convince, one must give one's audience the impression that they have adequately understood the opposition. The Millian thought, though, is that our conception of what our opponents think should come from our opponents rather than from those with whom we are in agreement.

It is troubling that the weak man seems to be among the most prevalent forms of fallacious argumentation at work in contemporary popular political discourse. In fact, we hold that the prevalence of this form of fallacy helps to explain the curious confluence of two seemingly inconsistent phenomena in contemporary popular politics: (1) high levels of public ignorance about fundamental political matters, and (2) heightened attention to sources of political analysis and commentary.

The fact of public ignorance is probably already familiar to you. We see it in spades in the simple fact that there is a television show with the title *So You Think You're Smarter than a Fifth Grader?* Late night talk shows feature humorous segments in which people on the street are asked perfunctory questions about contemporary politics, the basics of government, and simple facts about the world. And the people on the street typically prove stupendously ignorant.

The evidence for the claim that we pay a heightened degree of attention to political analysis and commentary consists simply in the fact that popular political commentary is now a billion-dollar industry. Even a cursory look through the politics section of a local bookstore will confirm the utter proliferation of books offering what professes to be detailed political commentary on the politics of the day, almost in real time. And this is to say nothing about the number of television programs, radio shows, and internet repositories devoted explicitly to current political affairs.

One would expect that greater attention to political analysts and commentators—even highly partisan analysts and commentators—would result in a *decrease* of political ignorance. But, alas, the trend does not work this way. In fact, a recent study has found that increased attention to the media forms that tend to feature more by way of real-time argumentation—namely, television and radio, as opposed to print sources—is *positively correlated with political ignorance.* [5] That is, the more you listen to people who just want to win an argument, the less you will know. But this positive correlation between exposure to sources of purported political analysis and political ignorance is precisely what should be expected from a mode of public discourse in which the weak man fallacy prevails. Again, it is the essence of this fallacy to cast the entirety of one's opposition in the terms adopted by one's weakest opponent. When the weak man prevails, one's audience is convinced that there is no intelligent opposition to one's view, and thus no forthcoming rejoinder from the opposition that could be worth attending to. Those who hear weak man arguments take themselves to have evidence for the stupidity of their opponents. Only a narrow and distorted view of contemporary political disputes can result.

Let's consider a few final examples. When President Barack Obama took office in 2009, he inherited a federal government with large deficits and an economy on the verge of disaster. His strategy was to stimulate the economy with government spending. The plan was that when the economy improved, the government's increased debt would later be recovered in taxes when private-sector spending increased. There was a good deal of concern about whether increased debt, especially in bad economic times, was a good idea for the United States government. In a speech to honor the 200th Anniversary of Abraham Lincoln's birth, President Obama defended his plan:

[I]n recent years, we've seen ... a philosophy that says every problem can be solved if only government would step out of the way; that if government were just dismantled, divvied up into tax breaks, and handed out to the wealthiest among us, it would somehow benefit us all. Such knee-jerk disdain for government—this constant rejection of any common endeavor—cannot rebuild our levees or our roads or our bridges. It cannot refurbish our schools or modernize our health care system; lead to the next medical discovery or yield the research and technology that will spark a clean energy economy.[6]

The trouble with Obama's statement is that his main opponents did *not* take the view that there should be no governmental response to the problems he mentions. Republican strategist Karl Rove responded forcefully in the *Wall Street Journal* as follows:

Whose philosophy is this? Many Americans justifiably believe that government is too big and often acts in counterproductive ways. But that's a far cry from believing that in "every" case government is the problem or that government should be "dismantled" root and branch. Who—other than an anarchist—"constantly rejects any common endeavor" like building levees, roads or bridges?[7]

President Obama weak-manned his opponents, as he selected the least defensible lines of argument to rebut and focused on them. He painted his opposition as all being anti-government extremists. This is no way to conduct political discussion in a democracy, since lumping those who counsel moderation in government spending are not equivalent to those who push for its abolition.

A regular complaint by President Donald Trump and his supporters is that coverage of his 2016 campaign and his current administration is unfair and often inaccurate. In many ways, their claim is that they are being straw-manned. When Michael Scherer and Zeke Miller of *Time* magazine ran a story about an extended interview with President Trump in the White House, an interesting detail about a shared dinner was included:

When the chicken comes, he is the only one given an extra dish of sauce. At the dessert course, he gets two scoops of vanilla ice cream with his chocolate cream pie, instead of one scoop for everyone else.

The reaction from Trump's supporters wasn't that this was a *false* claim, but that it was an irrelevant detail that now captured the attention of a media and populace hungry for anything nasty to say about the president. They were depicting the president as a glutton and a boor— slurping down two scoops of ice cream in front of others with just one.

When CNN ran a short review of this detail of the *Time* story, Sean Hannity of Fox News tweeted sarcastically, "Thanks for the hard-hitting news on your network." And Katherine Rodriguez at *Breitbart* took it that the real news was that *Time* and CNN thought that the detail was newsworthy.

In this case, really, we have a conflict between pushovers. On the one hand, Trump's supporters think that yet another defamatory picture of the president has been painted from the selective evidence of him getting another bowl of sauce and two scoops of ice cream. On the other hand, the news organizations are being cast as insipid machines of character-assassination on the basis of a short detail of a story that ran on a slow news day.

The lesson we take from the Trump's Two Scoops case is that when one expects the worst from one's interlocutors, one generally will be able to see it in anything they do. In many ways, the phenomenon of pushover interpretations of arguments of our fellow citizens has become akin to the ways that no statement or even pause can be interpreted charitably once a relationship has soured. Old friends who can't get along have no way of speaking that doesn't carry baggage, married couples who've had hard times now find that they can't hear the other even talk without hearing behind every phrase an ugly accusation, and siblings in the midst of rivalry can't hear even compliments without a hidden slight. And in the face of it, we are naturally inclined to dig in, prepare for battle. Cultures of antipathy not only produce more pushover arguments, but they prime us to hear most arguments as pushovers, too.

On any view about the ultimate purposes and nature of public political discourse in a democratic society, the prevalence of a fallacy that undermines argumentation and encourages irrational tenacity must be seen as a threat to a properly functioning system of self-government. In fact, it is very easy to see why weak-manning contributes to the patterns we noted earlier in Chapter 2, such as group polarization. That is, because the members of a group no longer have access to what a reasonable critic of their view would say, they not only take it that there is no reasonable opposition to their views, they become more and more entrenched in the views, and hence radicalized.

What's interesting about the pushover family is that in every case the arguments just by themselves are, in a way, perfectly fine. Remember the arguments about seat belt laws that we discussed earlier? Well, Betty was right to criticize the claim that because there's *merely a chance* of faring better in an accident, one should be required to wear a seat belt. Moreover, she was right to criticize the view that because seat belts make you feel safe, you should be required to wear them. The trouble with Betty is not with the *internal* workings of her arguments, but rather with the way in which her arguments represent something *external* to themselves, namely, the arguments that other people give. Betty's arguments fail because they fail to connect with what others have been saying. Her arguments fail to reflect properly the fact that they are given in a dialogue with an opposing side. That's why it is important to draw the distinction between *dialectical* and *formal* fallacies. Note that the same point goes for our presidential examples, too. President Bush's hollow man argument is a wholesale fabrication of what his opponents say, and President Obama's weak man is focused only on what the most extreme in his opposition has to offer. President (then candidate) Trump's claims about Hillary Clinton abolishing the Second Amendment were a misrepresentation of her explicit policy proposals. In all of these cases, the best reasons are left out of the debate.

Of course, these fallacies may make for dramatic intellectual theater. They mimic all the moves and elements of real, genuine argument between opposing sides, and there is something exhilarating about seeing a speaker decisively push over her opponents. But deployments of the straw, weak, and hollow men are in fact counterfeit argumentation, sham exchanges of reasons. A speaker who defends her views by these means in fact gives no defense at all. Or, perhaps better, she gives a defense that is more like a distraction. More importantly, as we have said, when these fallacies prevail in public discourse, the best reasons get shut out of the discussion, and the serious arguments raised by one's opposition are left unattended to. In a way, then, these fallacies are modes of simulated argumentation that not only fail to be argument; they at the same time undermine the aims of proper argument. Although they give us the feeling of satisfying our duties as arguers and as citizens, they in fact leave us less able to argue well. Accordingly, they undermine our aspirations to be in control of our cognitive lives.

For Further Thought

1   What should be done in cases where an especially weak argument in favor of a view that one opposes also happens to be the argument that is most popular among one's opposition?

2   Can the dialectical requirement to actually engage with one's opponent's reasons come into conflict with the requirement to seek out the best case that can be made for an opposing view?

3   Mill's principle says that "He who knows only his own side of the case knows little of that." Does this entail that one must give serious consideration to *all* opponents, no matter how bizarre, crazy, or offensive they might be?

4   Is it possible, as we held, in the Trump's Two Scoops case, that two sides can simultaneously straw man each other? Are there other cases? Can it happen with more than two arguers?

5   Could it ever be appropriate to interpret an interlocutor's argument in pushover fashion? Can straw men ever be useful for critical dialogue?

Key Terms

Pushover arguments	The general class of dialectically fallacious arguments that fail to represent the intellectual opponent's view and argument accurately.
Straw man	A distortion of a given argument so that it is represented as worse than it was.
Weak man	Picking out the weakest of the opposition's arguments and refuting it, and thereby implying that this is the final word.
Hollow man	Attributing a view to the opposition that not only none hold but that bears no resemblance to views they hold.

Notes

1 Full text at: https://thinkprogress.org/jimmy-kimmel-health-care-9219f83c4694/
2 http://www.nationalreview.com/article/447295/jimmy-kimmel-monologue-child-health-care-oversimplified
3 http://www.cnn.com/2016/05/07/politics/donald-trump-hillary-clinton-second-amendment/
4 https://www.politico.com/story/2016/05/donald-trump-nra-guns-223426
5 See the study by the PIPA organization, "Misperceptions, the Media, and the Iraq War," www.pipa.org/OnlineReports/Iraq/Media_10_02_03_Report.pdf
6 www.reobama.com/SpeechesFeb1209.htm
7 http://online.wsj.com/article/SB123561484923478287.html

References

Haley, Edward (2006) *Strategies of Dominance: The Misdirection of U.S. Foreign Policy.* Baltimore, MD: Johns Hopkins University Press.

Lord, Jeffrey (2007) "Iraq and the Party of Race." *The American Spectator*, February 16.

Mill, John Stuart (1992) *On Liberty and Other Essays.* John Gray, editor. New York: Oxford University Press.

7   Tone of Voice

It is a common enough occurrence. In the course of a conversation, someone says something that the other finds so outlandish, so preposterous, so absurd, so *unthinkable* that she can only incredulously restate what was said. In these exchanges, a good deal of argumentative work is done with the tone of one's voice. The speaker expresses her doubts about the other side's view, even if not her full commitment to its falsity. As such, incredulous restatement can be an informal way of opening a critical dialogue—one repeats the other's claim in a way that both confronts the claim with the fact that the view is rejected and challenges the person making the claim to provide reasons for it. Alternately, one restates another's claim in order to raise the possibility that she misspoke and to allow her the space to reformulate, clarify, or rethink what she has said. In this way, the speaker enables his interlocutor to save face in not having an explicit rejection of her view registered on record.

The problem is that tone of voice is frequently misused in argumentative contexts. Here, we want to provide an analysis of one category of such misuse, what we shall playfully call *modus tonens*.

Consider the following exchange. Two political experts are publicly debating gun control laws in the United States. Let us call the exchange "Gun Control":

ADAM: You see—if we allowed more people to carry handguns, then we would have fewer cases of gun violence. Arming people has a deterrent effect.

BRENDA: So, let me get this straight—*more* people with guns will *reduce* gun violence? (To the audience): *More people with guns will reduce gun violence?!?*

Brenda incredulously restates Adam's claim, and in so doing, she establishes a number of dialectical points. First, Brenda has expressed her rejection of Adam's view. Second, with the tone of her restatement, Brenda highlights what she takes to be the preposterousness of Adam's claim. This is more than mere rejection. With incredulous restatement, Brenda presents a surrogate for (or perhaps a promise of) a demonstration of how far off the mark

Adam's view is. Surely, she indicates, anyone can see the conflict between *more* people with guns and *less* violence. Third, as a consequence of these first two elements, Brenda has put an onus on Adam to clarify his claim, qualify it, or defend it. With rejection of this sort, Brenda has placed a burden of defense on Adam. So in restating Adam's view in the way she has, Brenda rejects Adam's proposal, expresses a commitment to a good deal of evidence contrary to his claim, and thereby requests defense, clarification, or qualification of the view. And all of this is accomplished merely by introducing a fluctuation in her voice.

Further, notice that Brenda is responding only to Adam's conclusion and not to his argument. Brenda's objection is to the view Adam holds, and she has said nothing to the case for it. Moreover, note that Brenda appeals to the audience after her initial response to Adam's claim. Tone of voice is used not only to mark out the dialectical terrain between two speakers; it may be used to mark it out for a third group of people, too. Here, Brenda's final sentence is addressed entirely to the audience, and with this there comes a further element. She not only communicates her rejection of and the preposterousness she sees in Adam's view, but she also implies that she expects the audience to share her assessments of Adam's claims. Use of tone of voice can, then, be *argumentatively averse* (with the avoidance of addressing Adam's case) and *manipulative of an audience* (as with the final sentence). It is on the one hand a diversion from the evidence by expressing outrage, and it is on the other hand a distortion of the evidence in expressing the clarity of the view's falsity.

Now, to be clear, there is nothing intrinsically vicious about expressing incredulity in response to claims that one sincerely takes to be inane. There are many silly and outrageous views out there, and we should be free to express our surprise at just how wild some views can be. The crucial thing is not to take the fact that one takes a view as outrageous or silly to be sufficient to change one's argumentative burdens in responding to it. This is where expressions of incredulity can destroy the goals of argument— they can be an instantiation of what we earlier called the No Reasonable Opposition Thesis.

As we have said, we will call the inappropriate use of incredulous restatement *modus tonens*. *Modus tonens* is vicious because it controverts the goals of argumentative exchange. We will sketch in the following the features that define it.

Modus tonens can be characterized by the interplay of two components, one *dialectical* and the other *pragmatic*. First, *modus tonens* involves the *dialectical* component of inappropriately shifting the argumentative burden. In this way, *modus tonens* resembles a common fallacy, the argument from outrage. This fallacy takes the basic form:

I am outraged by the things S said, therefore S is wrong.

Alternately the argument that *modus tonens* implies is:

I am incredulous at the things S said, therefore S is wrong.

Like arguments from outrage, *modus tonens* has the effect of shifting the burden of proof solely on the basis of the purported preposterousness of the opponent's claim. When one rejects an interlocutor's claim, one incurs an obligation to state the basis of one's rejection. That is what's called *listener responsiveness*—if you reject the things someone says, you're required to present some reasons. However, in cases of *modus tonens* and argument from outrage, one rejects an interlocutor's claim in a way that refuses to acknowledge the corresponding obligation to state the basis for the rejection. *Modus tonens*, like an argument from outrage, simply demands that the interlocutor reformulate or defend her claim on the basis of the fact that one emphatically rejects it. That's not a reason.

Despite this structural similarity, *modus tonens* is importantly different from arguments from outrage. An argument from outrage regularly expresses *moral* opposition to an interlocutor's view and hence *moral outrage* with the interlocutor. By contrast, *modus tonens* attributes a *cognitive deficiency* to one's interlocutor that in turn purports to explain the defectiveness of what she has said. Put otherwise, arguments from outrage begin from a negative moral assessment of the interlocutor's view and then draw an inference about the moral character of the interlocutor. But *modus tonens* begins from an expression of the purported stupidity or uninformedness of an interlocutor's view and then offers the interlocutor's alleged cognitive deficiency as an explanation of the fact that she holds her view. So, in "Gun Control," Brenda is implicating that Adam has not thought about his own proposal very carefully. If Adam cannot see how counter-intuitive it is to claim that having *more* people with guns leads to *less* violence, then he must be intellectually deficient in some important way. Brenda could just as well have said, "Seriously?" at the end of it.

Tone of voice communicates more than just how one feels about things that have been asserted. It also communicates how the speaker takes things to stand between her and her audience. Consider for a moment the way that a teacher responding incredulously to a student works. It is implied that the student perhaps has misspoken, or not thought things through, or may have made some error that she will see and correct, provided that she hears the view said back to her. Consider the case we call "Math Facts":

TEACHER: Billy, what's seventeen plus eight?
BILLY: Twenty four!
TEACHER: Twenty four?

In this case, the teacher's incredulous restatement is an indirect way of communicating to Billy that those who know what they are talking about would not say what he has just said. It is a way of inviting a student to take a moment to reflect, and this is sometimes entirely appropriate, even pedagogically sound. A teacher's role is in large part to guide and supervise the learning processes of students.

Among peers, however, incredulous restatement goes further. Again, in "Gun Control," Adam and Brenda are peers, and so there is no warrant for Brenda to treat Adam as her pupil. To be sure, in contexts of cognitive parity, one speaker may have a good deal to teach the other, but nevertheless, neither belongs in the other's tutelage, and neither is entitled to claim the role of the other's teacher.

This component of *modus tonens* enables us to identify the difference between acceptable and unacceptable uses of incredulous restatement. When acceptable, the restatement expresses non-acceptance in a way that requests further elaboration, thereby opening a dialogue. Or it invites rethinking that may allow restatement. That's what the teacher did for Billy in "Math Facts." When unacceptable, the restatement attempts to shift the dialectical burden while at the same time implying that the dialectical context is not one of intellectual parity. Accordingly, *modus tonens* rejects intellectual parity and threatens to dissolve argumentation into browbeating.

Yet we should be careful here. Expression of surprise at what has been said need not imply that one considers one's interlocutor intellectually subordinate. Asking for clarifications and arguments from one's interlocutors after one has been surprised by something they have said is part of the give and take of argument. Our point here is *that these elements of argumentative exchange can be abused*, and we are highlighting how these abuses may be captured *functionally*. So far, the functional elements have been dialectical, in that they are about distorting the roles that the two speakers are playing as the discussion unfolds. However, there are two further functional abuses of tone of voice in restating an interlocutor's view.

Modus tonens may be introduced at two different stages in argument. On the one hand, a *modus tonens* may be issued at the opening stage, when premises or presuppositions are being announced. On the other hand, one may introduce a *modus tonens* in the concluding/evaluative stages of an argumentative exchange. In the former case, *modus tonens* is objectionable because it, without justification, claims the default status for the rejection of the interlocutor's view on the basis of both the speaker's rejection of the view and the alleged cognitive asymmetry between the speaker and interlocutor. That is, it functions not just as registering rejection, but it amounts to calling the opposition's view absurd. In the latter case, incredulous restatement occurring in the evaluation of an argument still registers non-acceptance, but its vice is that it does not provide any reason for rejecting the conclusion beyond its purported implausibility. We will treat these two features of the misuse of *modus tonens* separately. To put the matter simply, one can be incredulous before the argument or after the argument. How and why incredulous restatement can be unacceptable depends on those circumstances.

Think, again, of arguments from outrage. They are predicated on *shifting and increasing the burden of proof* by invoking the supposed outrageousness of the opponent's view. Arguments from outrage are considered arguments from emotion, which generally suffer from problems of relevance. That certain claims outrage you doesn't mean they are false. After all, many truths are outrageous. So it seems as if outrage is not relevant to the evaluation of an opponent's view.

Nonetheless, it does seem that expressing outrage is not always out of bounds. If the opposition's view *is outrageous*, it should not only be allowable but may even be required that one express outrage. This, precisely, points to the main problem with arguments from outrage. Expressions of outrage themselves are not sufficient to demonstrate that the claim criticized is itself actually outrageous. With such expressions, one merely substitutes sincerity for argument. Further, with outrage, one is taking on a significant commitment—namely, that what one is expressing outrage about is not only something worthy of criticism, but something so egregiously wrong that it should cause right-minded people to feel indignant. Surely it is this view that requires an argument, since outrage is not only an expression of non-acceptance but the vehement denial that the interlocutor's claim is even a contender for truth. In taking on this attitude, one should shoulder a measure of the burden of proof in the dialogue. However, expressions of outrage usually stand less as openings for further arguments, but more as surrogates for them.

The same is true for *modus tonens*, since what is doing the argumentative work resides entirely behind the scenes—namely, the implication regarding the alleged intellectual asymmetry between the two speakers. You can talk to someone as if you think he is stupid, but that does not mean that he is stupid. Nor does it mean that you're smart.

If the interlocutor's claim is the conclusion of an argument, *modus tonens* is a failure of argumentative exchange. Remember, negative responses to argument carry the burden of responsive reasons—reasons that articulate why either the premises or their support are not sufficient to elicit assent to the conclusion. That's the duty of responsiveness. If someone gives you an argument for a conclusion you still don't like, your problem now is with the argument, and you have to address it, too. Given that arguments are designed not only to gain the truth about some matter but to resolve disagreements, both parties should contribute responsively to the discussion in ways that promote those ends. Surprised or incredulous restatement, as an invitation to deliberation and argument (a qualified invitation, as noted earlier), can help us to pursue those ends. However, as a response to argument, it stands in the way of those ends. This is because with *modus tonens* an argument is rejected without giving an account of how it has gone wrong. It is utterly unresponsive to the argument.

As such, those on the receiving end of a *modus tonens* do not have enough information about what the criticism is of their view for them to reformulate it in a way that resolves the disagreement, or even respond to the criticism. Just as incredulous stares cannot be refuted, one cannot refute a *modus tonens*. That is, with *modus tonens*, a disputant disagrees, and vigorously so, but offers no actual criticism of the other's position beyond the emphatic expression of rejection and implication that those who hold the position need to be educated. How the other party in the dispute should proceed, then, is left mysterious, since if the problem is with the view, it is unclear how to either clarify the view, or reformulate the argument, or weaken the claim to make it acceptable.

Remember that in "Gun Control," Adam provided an argument for more gun ownership from deterrence, but Brenda's response does not address the case for deterrence; it only registers the alleged pre-posterousness of the claim that expanded gun ownership would result in less gun violence and crime. As such, the disagreement not only persists, but it persists with no indication as to how it may be resolved. Additionally, given that Brenda's tone suggests that Adam needs to rethink his view, it is suggested that now Adam must respond. But in light of the lack of specific details of what is wrong with the view or the case against it, there is little for Adam to go on in fashioning his reply. All Adam has is Brenda's snarky tone. Brenda has not made any case as to why Adam's deterrence argument fails, and as such, it seems that the only proper response to an incredulous restatement of a view is a confident or matter-of-fact restatement. But the aim was to exchange reasons, not cop attitudes. Not only does *modus tonens* fail to help with reason-exchange, but it also entrenches the disagreement and further polarizes the discussants.

Thus far we have focused on the use of *modus tonens* from the point of view of the argumentative relationship between two speakers. However, *modus tonens* is frequently employed as a rhetorical tool for engaging an interlocutor in front of an audience. Note that in "Gun Control," Brenda restates Adam's claims for those observing their debate.

Employed as a rhetorical tool, *modus tonens* can take the form of a subtle threat. When used in this setting, *modus tonens* not only implies that the opponent belongs in the speaker's tutelage, but also threatens ostracism or lowered group status for members of the audience who side with the opponent. By promising both a refutation and embarrassment or humiliation if the interlocutor does not revise her view, *modus tonens* provides a cue to the audience of where their loyalty should lie. In this way, *modus tonens* is not only an attempt to alter the argumentative situation by redescribing it to one's advantage, it is also an attempt to alter the *social dynamic* of the situation by suggesting to one's audience that they must adopt the implied description of the argumentative situation, namely, that the interlocutor is ignorant and should not be believed.

As we noted earlier, many of the reasons given in arguments, instead of being addressed to the interlocutor, actually are addressed to an onlooking audience. In extreme instances, the appeal to the audience via *modus tonens* serves a purely rhetorical purpose, in which the speaker is actually making a gesture wholly for the sake of the onlooking audience. That is, the speech act may be introduced not for the sake of challenging the interlocutor or even for putting her on the defensive, but instead as a reminder to an audience of what their core commitments are (or ought to be). Because the speech act of *modus tonens* describes the circumstance as one that is intellectually asymmetric, the message it communicates to the audience is that only the stupid, benighted, or positively vicious would articulate or hold fast to the opponent's view. And as such, the speech act serves as a gesture of solidarity within the group (the speaker and audience) against those who reject their core commitments (namely, the interlocutor). Incredulous tone of voice is a signal for in-grouping and out-grouping.

In both its modest and extreme instances, the oratorical use of *modus tonens* serves the decidedly *anti*-argumentative purpose of attempting to turn the audience's attention away from reasons and towards non-argumentative features of discourse. It is thus an instance of the *diverting* kind of manipulation we identified earlier, and hence it marks a failure of argumentative earnestness. In the short run, *modus tonens* is simply one of the many tools of deception available to a wily speaker, who must sustain the perception that he is concerned above all else with reasons and argument while in fact engaging in tactics designed to obstruct actual argumentation. But the long-run consequence of the oratorical feature of *modus tonens* is more troubling, since it encourages the group to which it appeals to become increasingly cognitively insular. If critics of the group's commitments are deemed too uninformed or thoughtless to merit substantive response, then the group will never take any form of substantive criticism seriously. This encourages the idea that all opponents are undeserving of argument, but rather in need of education, or perhaps a scolding. All that with the tone of voice, but that's why it's so important to think about how tone works with arguments.

We have noted earlier the deleterious effect of the kind of cognitive insularity on cognitively homogeneous groups that is encouraged by *modus tonens*. The chief problem is *group polarization*, which is the phenomenon in which like-minded members of a deliberating group eventually come to adopt a more extreme version of the belief they had at the beginning of the deliberation. This tendency of groups with similar beliefs to polarize— that is, to move together towards a more extreme version of their pre-deliberation views—is exacerbated in contexts in which the group is exposed to a constrained set of arguments and reasons. Again, the remedy for group polarization is dissent that is taken as presumptively possibly well-founded and correct. That is, when exposed regularly to dissenting views and internally encouraged to take such challenges seriously, groups tend to not polarize, and polarized groups tend to de-polarize.

To repeat, the claim that group polarization is to be avoided does not rely on some presumption that more extreme views are more likely to be false than moderate ones. Rather, the problem is that when groups polarize, they do so without regard to the strength of the arguments and reasons in favor of their preferred view. More importantly, as groups polarize, they grow increasingly unwilling to and incapable of seeing dissenting views as anything but irrational, ill-informed, and silly. Put otherwise, members of polarized groups are unable to engage in proper argument. Insofar as *modus tonens* encourages individuals to identify with a cognitive "in group" which sees its opponents as hapless and benighted, it is not merely a corrupt move within an argument. It is in addition an attempt to corrupt the process of argument itself.

Modus tonens has been our main point of focus for this chapter, but it is but one instance of a larger point to be made about the role that one's tone of voice plays in argument. We all know that tone of voice can communicate a good deal of information. One clear example is sarcasm. When you say to a waiter at a restaurant, "Yes, this soup is very good" in a normal tone of voice, you're complimenting the chef. When you say it with the sarcastic tone, you're not. Tone makes all the difference.

Notice also that tone is used often to signal group membership. Sarcasm certainly works this way. When employing sarcasm, one is often appealing to a group that is cued to hear the message that is being communicated by the sarcastic remark. Think again of the sarcasm about the soup. Such a remark is made typically in the presence of other diners that one suspects are similarly dissatisfied. And if the waiter fails to catch the sarcasm of the remark, so much the worse for him; in an odd way, his failure simply adds to the criticism. Not hearing or misunderstanding the tone just makes everything worse for the waiter and restaurant staff.

Consider next other kinds of tone. We are all familiar with cases in which one speaker adopts the tactic of speaking very slowly and deliberately, as one would normally speak to a confused child. There is also the closely related phenomenon where one speaker takes the tone that expresses an excessive degree of patience. These tonal affectations are employed in order to signal something—usually, they attempt to express the idea that we are engaged in an exchange in which, despite appearances, our partners in discussion are not our cognitive equals, but rather our inferiors or our pupils. And all of that gets communicated simply with our tone.

President Obama serially employs tone in order to portray himself relative to his detractors as the only real grownup in the discussion. One particularly clear case of this occurred in his second presidential debate with Mitt Romney in 2012. This debate was widely taken to be the most contentious of Obama and Romney's interactions, and the exchange was described in the *Economist* as a "verbal brawl." For sure, the debate contained several unpleasant exchanges between President Obama and Governor Romney, but one exchange is of particular relevance at present. In the lead-up to the debate, there had been concerns raised about the Romney tax plan. Particularly, there was a question about whether under Romney's plan the middle class would be financially pinched in order to bankroll ongoing tax breaks for the wealthy. Romney was asked about the plan in the debate, and he provided a detailed answer. But when President Obama was then asked whether Governor Romney's answer was sufficient, whether it settled the questions regarding the tax plan, President Obama responded as follows (from NPR's transcript):

> No, it's not settled. (Chuckles.) Look, the cost of lowering rates for everybody across the board 20 percent, along with what he also wants to do in terms of eliminating the estate tax, along [with] what he wants to do in terms of corporate changes in the tax code—it costs about $5 trillion.

Of course, the transcript does not capture Obama's tone of voice. But it's worth taking the time to find an audio recording of this moment in the debate. You'll find that Obama sharply said, "No." Then he overtly and dismissively guffawed. Then he adopted the tone that one might take when attempting to teach basic arithmetic to very young children.

Now, here is what's *not* wrong with Obama's response. Some ideas (including some tax plans) are laughable, and it's okay to laugh at them when they are earnestly proposed. After all, we are not robots, and it is sometimes not only acceptable but appropriate to respond with emotion to a question that has been posed to you. The guffaw was not wrong. But it was the lead-in to something that is wrong. The guffaw communicated that Obama at that point took himself to have to switch his dialectical gears; it expressed that he took himself no longer to be addressing his peers, but suddenly saw himself as being forced to address a simple error, one that a mere collection of basic facts would correct. And his tone expressed his exasperation at having to correct a beginner's error.

Throughout the 2008 and 2012 presidential debates, President Obama's opponents increasingly adopted the view that they were being talked down to. And much of the subsequent criticism of Obama cited his elitism, his distance, and his alleged tendency to talk like a professor. He may take what conservatives say seriously, but the way he speaks to and about conservatives often suggests that he sees them as intellectual lightweights, immature minds. Accordingly, Obama's now infamous remark at a 2008 San Francisco fundraiser about residents of rural communities clinging to "guns and religion" is regularly cited by his critics as an unintentional articulation of his true self.

But, again, note that these deployments of tone only get in the way of argument. They divert attention away from substantive reasons and turn the discussion toward ephemeral matters concerning supposedly hidden attitudes and disguised worldviews. All the while, real and pressing matters of public policy are left hanging.

President Donald Trump would hardly be taken to be professorial in his delivery, but he, too, uses tone to change the argumentative ground with his interlocutors. To start, President Trump regularly will pause and announce with a deep and authoritative voice a number of surprising and controversial claims. Here are a few:

> Nobody loves the Bible more than I do.
> Nobody has more respect for women than I do. Nobody.
> Number one, I am the least anti-Semitic person you've ever seen in your entire life. Number two, racism. I am the least racist person.
> Nobody is more pro-Israel than I am.
> There is nobody bigger or better at the military than I am.
> Nobody builds walls better than me.
> There's nobody that's done so much for equality as I have.
> Nobody would be tougher on ISIS than Donald Trump.
> There's nobody that understands the horror of nuclear than me.
> Nobody knows more about trade than me.
> Nobody knows the system better than me.

There are many more instances of the same, each with the claim that he is the best at or most knowledgeable about something, and each delivered with a frank and commanding tone. The puzzle with so many of these is how one deals with the hyperbole, and how the tone makes it difficult to determine how one might ask for support or clarification of the claims. Take the first, Trump's claim that nobody loves the Bible more than he does. How does he know this? How is this comparison made? Does Vice President Pence, a very publicly devout Christian, agree? Or is this an emphatic way of just claiming that he really loves the Bible? But on top of these critical questions, the delivery, given that it's a confident and categorical assertion, makes it hard to see how to ask those questions *to him*. Tone matters, since *the way* we make claims influences not just what they mean (as we saw with sarcasm earlier), but it also directs how we interpret whether it's appropriate to ask further questions.

Imagine that you ask your neighbor whether they think the new highway going in nearby will be good for the neighborhood. The neighbor answers, "Most certainly, it will." How they say it matters, though. For sure, the statement has a whiff of No Reasonable Opposition with the qualifier "most certainly," but that may just be a way of making clear that they think they've got good evidence. The question, however, is whether this person is open to hearing some pushback and some requests for those reasons. On the one hand, imagine further that they say it with an uptalk on *will*. On the other hand, imagine them say it with a very distinct and heavy stress on *certainly* and *will*. Delivery matters, and the first, as we take it, is best read as a controversial claim the speaker is confident in, but is willing to hear pushback on. That's what the uptalk at the end often signals—that you make an assertion with the intonation of a question, so you let your listeners know you're open to them saying something back. The second is one delivered with the objective of letting listeners know they will have a very rough time with a critical conversation. A strident answer doesn't invite follow-up questions. Tone matters.

Now, return to President Trump's claims above. Every one of those are delivered with the emphases that communicate the challenge to those who doubt the claims. His pronouncements are designed to communicate power and authority. *They are claims that are delivered like orders.* In fact, President Trump frequently adds to such statements the coda, "Believe me." Consequently, critical questions are received as insubordination rather than dialogue. And the best way to lay claim to power is to display and expect others to defer to your exercise of it. Act like you own the place, and next thing you know, you're in charge. And so, with President Trump, categorical, authoritative, and strident hyperbolic claims on controversial issues are ways he exhibits how powerful he is. He makes wild claims in a tone of voice that lets people know he's in charge. Nobody challenges him on them, and that just shows everybody what? That he *really is* in charge.

Accordingly, it is important to notice how President Trump reacts when he actually is challenged. When John Dickerson of CBS News interviewed Trump in the Oval Office, he challenged Trump's claim that then-President Obama's White House had tapped the phones in Trump Tower during the campaign. Trump had brought it up in the interview when talking about Obama, and Dickerson took the opportunity to ask for some clarity on the issue.

JOHN DICKERSON: You stand by that claim? [....] You're President of the United States. You said he was "sick and bad" because he tapped you. I just—
PRESIDENT D.J. TRUMP: You can take—any way. You can take it any way you want.
JD: But I'm asking *you*. Because you don't want it to be fake news. I want to hear it from Donald Trump.
DT: You don't have to ask me.
JD: Why not?
DT: Because I have my own opinions. You can have your own opinions.
JD: But I want to know your opinions. You're President of the United States.
DT: Okay. That's enough. (Walks away) Thank you. Thank you very much.[1]

Notice two important features of this exchange. First, if one announces something controversial from a position of authority, one should be willing to take on the burden of proof—to provide evidence or to clarify exactly what the claim is. But President Trump does not do that. Instead, he simply ends the interview and dismisses Dickerson. This leads us to the second point, which is that the authoritative tone of Trump's claim was not about announcing how well supported his view is. Rather, it is a claim to his being in charge, not whether he knows anything. And since he's in charge, he's not to be questioned. Why? Because the claim is delivered not as an assertion to be considered, but as an order to be embraced. So asking questions is hence treated as an act of defiance. And so, as is seen in the interview, asking a question is really just a way of ending the exchange.

That President Trump's tone is both a claim to and evidence of what he sees as significant power was on clear display in his 2016 campaign debates with Secretary Hillary Clinton. In the first debate, he interrupted Clinton 51 times to her 17.[2] And in the second debate, he interrupted Clinton six times in less than 45 seconds.[3]

Interrupting a speaker is a way of insisting that your remark is so important that it cannot wait for the interlocutor to finish speaking. And so, in interrupting, a speaker claims for himself a significant contribution to the dialogue—that the statement is introduced as an interruption communicates the interrupting speaker's view that the comment he wishes to make is important enough to override a rule of well-run critical exchange. But when the interruptions are so constant and disruptive (and not positive contributions), they communicate something else—namely that the speaker is exercising their power over the other person by silencing them, derailing them, and (especially in the case of Trump interrupting Clinton in the second debate), not even allowing them to complete a statement.

We noted earlier that one's tone communicates one's attitude regarding the dialogue not only to one's interlocutor, but also to one's onlooking audience. And so an incredulous tone lets an interlocutor know that you reject their claim, but it simultaneously lets the onlooking audience know that you find the interlocutor in need of education. The same goes for authoritative and strident tones of voice. They announce a confidence, but they also let interlocutors and onlooking audiences know that you take yourself to be the one in the exchange who is entitled to make proclamations. And how you treat your interlocutors in dialogue, too, communicates your view of them both to them and to those looking on. Hence dismissing someone who asks a question, or consistently interrupting someone who you are supposed to be debating, also communicates more than what is said with one's words.

What can be done? People use demeaning tones of voice all the time. People regularly talk down to each other. And moreover, to explicitly point out when someone's doing that kind of thing is often counterproductive in an argumentative exchange. To say to an interlocutor something like, "Don't talk down to me," or "Your tone suggests that you think it's obvious that you're right" makes you sound touchy and thin-skinned. It's certainly not a way to make a disagreement less hostile.

The added trouble is that tone of voice, because it communicates asymmetry, can also be code for additional assumptions and stereotypes that lie beyond the discussion. For example, it is not uncommon even these days to hear men taking patronizing tones when arguing with women. Those tones communicate the acceptance of ugly stereotypes that not only downplay the concerns of women, but even take their voices away, sometimes leaving them without dialectical recourse. The "don't worry your pretty little head about that, sweetie" tone is still around, and it's pernicious. Tone of voice in these cases is not just something that corrupts argumentation, it is a unique form of social injustice that makes it so that people's arguments don't count or cannot even be heard as arguments in the first place.

So, again, what can be done? We admit that we don't have a silver bullet for combating these sorts of rhetorical strategies. As suggested earlier, straw-manning can be undone simply by stating the opposition's side in a way that doesn't fall to the way it has been portrayed. That's still difficult to achieve, but it nevertheless is something that is effective once it has been done. But inappropriate deployments of one's tone of voice are less easy to combat. Again, it seems strange to criticize someone for the tone they take, and it is difficult to make this kind of criticism stick because the evidence upon which it is based is so fleeting. One can't typically stop a debate to replay the audio evidence of an inappropriate deployment of tone! Consider our example above about President Obama's reply to Mitt Romney's tax plan. We noted that the transcript only records the words he uttered and that he chuckled. We indicated that we think that Obama's chuckle is better characterized as a guffaw, since it communicated not amusement but a dismissive kind of frustration. That the chuckle was mentioned in the transcript itself is significant, but what couldn't be recorded is the tone he took in replying. Evidence of abusive tone is hard to come by.

In President Trump's case, he uses this authoritatively strident tone regularly, and it's an argumentative abuse of tone. Yet it's unclear what the solution is. The reprimands of the moderators in the debates failed to rein him in or diminish the force of his usage. And it seems that comic and parodic commentary (whether it be from the late night talk shows or famous sketch comedic sendups) was also ineffective, at least in the short run. Some have proposed that Democrats run another blowhard against him for the next election, to fight abusive tone with abusive tone. That may win an election, but it's worse for argument, and also worse for the country. Maybe that's a tradeoff some are happy to make. In Trump's case, the abusive tone is tolerated because it expresses contempt for those who many of Trump's supporters condemn: progressives, feminists, those in the Black Lives Matter movement, liberals, immigrants. Abuse of tone for the onlooking audience really rides piggyback to a broader culture of contempt. We will have a few thoughts on that later, but for now, it's only something to highlight.

There is an old skit by the comedy troupe The Kids in the Hall about a man who cannot speak in any other way than sarcastically. Everyone misunderstands what he's saying. In one instance, someone tells him something, and he says "That's interesting." But because of the sarcastic way in which he delivers his reply, they take him to actually be saying that he's not interested in the least. He is asked why he's talking that way, and he says he can't say anything except in a sarcastic tone. But, as that statement is presented in a sarcastic tone, his interlocutors don't believe him. He then says he's lonely, but all everyone hears is that he wants to be alone. Ultimately, he is left alone, and he says (again, in a sarcastic tone) that his life is miserable and he wants to die. And even we, the audience, tragically, have a hard time taking him at his word.

A few lessons emerge. First, it is important to note that tone can be invisible to the one employing it. The habit, say, of talking down to people is not always acquired intentionally. Someone may have tried that tactic a few times in the past, gotten what he or she wanted, and now almost involuntarily speaks that way all the time. We're academics. Believe us when we say that we know more people than we'd like to admit who "talk down" as a matter of course. And with those folks, putting up with their tone is like putting up with bad weather—one simply must endure it. The point is to figure out ways to prevent such communicative habits from undermining the possibility of sincere argument. Recognizing that the tone of one's voice is not always something one is aware of or in direct control of is a good start.

But adopting an inappropriate tone of voice isn't always merely a matter of being grating or presumptuous. As we noted above, sometimes it is a face of injustice, a way of infantilizing, dismissing, and defaming others. Again, we don't know of any perfectly effective strategy in responding to such abusive communicative actions. Of course, one may simply confront the fact that a demeaning tone is being employed. We've seen that strategy succeed, but we've also seen it fail. Alternatively, one may allow the demeaning tone to stand, but try all the more vigorously to set a good example in dialogue oneself. That is, in response to a demeaning tone, one can begin to speak even more calmly, deliberately, and judiciously. Sometimes that works to settle things down, but we've also seen it yield further abuse. What's troubling is that *modus tonens* and abusive authoritative tones draw their power from demeaning stereotypes and contempt between groups that prevail in the cultural context that provides the background for the exchange. Accordingly, it is the worst and most abusive deployment of *modus tonens* and other tones that are the most destructive for public argument, but they are also the most difficult to disarm.

Perhaps one way forward would be to recalibrate the criteria for effective response to abuse of tone of voice. Winning the argument is too high. Even successfully pointing out the abuse is too high, given how difficult that can be. But perhaps making sure that the use of incredulous or condescending tone doesn't insulate audiences from your message is sufficient for dialectical success in response to *modus tonens*. And so when confronted with patronizing tone or incredulous restatement, perhaps the best response is to even be concessive: "I understand that I'm proposing something that is counter-intuitive right now. But you need to hear me out ... " If you then keep getting the dismissive tone or continue to get interrupted, it may be appropriate to note that the other side is hearing your *conclusions* but not your *reasons*. You can even take advantage of the fact that in employing *modus tonens*, the interlocutor has implied that you are his pupil—you can ask him to help you see where you've gone wrong. He *must*, then, attend to your reasons. If you keep this up (and if you have a pretty good argument in the first place), it will start to become clear that you're getting the tone because of something other than the argument. And that's a start.

For Further Thought

1   Could there be virtuous deployments of *modus tonens*? Suppose one is arguing with someone before an audience that largely agrees with your opponent. Perhaps you're confident that the audience does not have a firm grasp of why you reject your opponent's view. Might it be virtuous to engage in exaggerated and incredulous restatement of the opponent's commitment that strikes you as most questionable?

2   Sadly, not all argumentative situations are calm and casual. In fact, most are highly constrained in various ways. Most often, we simply do not have the time to see an argument through to its proper conclusion. Does *modus tonens* help expedite an argument?

3   Let us suppose that for the most part *modus tonens* is indeed vicious. Could an interlocutor behave in such a way as to *deserve* a *modus tonens*?

4   Is there anything really wrong with stating something with an authoritative tone, especially if one really is an authority? Where is the abuse of strident authoritative tone if one, perhaps, is just looking to be a firebrand? Or stand up for something?

5   Ask a friend a question and keep interrupting them as they try to answer. After a few minutes, see how you and they feel. Are you still friends? Why the stress, if it's just interruption?

Key Terms

Burden of proof   When it is a disputant's responsibility to provide the argument—so, for example, if you say p and

	your audience has no view on the matter, you have the burden of proof.
Shifting the burden	When one has the burden of proof, but finds a way to make it so that other disputants must provide the reasons. This is a fallacy. So, if you say that p, and your audience asks why p?, you to shift the burden of proof, may ask back, well, why not p?
Modus tonens	By restating the conclusion of an opponent's argument with an incredulous tone, one rejects the conclusion and shifts the burden of proof back on the other.
Listener responsiveness	If a listener to an argument rejects its conclusion, the listener must explain what has gone wrong in the argument, either in how the premises are not acceptable, how they do not support the conclusion, or how the argument does not address a standing worry.
Argument from outrage	By expressing outrage at the conclusion of an opponent's argument, one rejects the argument's conclusion and shifts and increases the burden of proof.
Onlooking audience	Often in exchanges between two arguers, the reasons the arguers give to each other (and the other communicative actions they perform in light of each other's contributions) are not just to address each other, but to move an audience who is watching the exchange.

Notes

1 Transcript and video: https://www.cbsnews.com/news/president-trump-oval-office-interview-cbs-this-morning-full-transcript/
2 https://www.vox.com/policy-and-politics/2016/9/27/13017666/presidential-debate-trump-clinton-sexism-interruptions. Others put the number at 56.
3 The transcript is available here: https://splinternews.com/donald-trump-interrupted-hillary-clinton-6-times-during-1793862638

8   The Surprising Truth about Hypocrisy

Al Gore urges us all to reduce our carbon footprint, yet he regularly flies in a private jet. William Bennett extols the importance of temperance, but he is a habitual gambler. Pastor Ted Haggard preached the virtues of "the clean life" until allegations of methamphetamine use and a taste for male prostitutes arose. Mother Teresa ran a hospital for the dying and destitute of Calcutta, but she went to only the best European hospitals when she was ill. When he was a senator representing Idaho, Larry Craig voted against equal rights for homosexuals, but he was charged with soliciting gay sex in an airport bathroom. Eliot Spitzer prosecuted prostitutes as Attorney General in New York, but it was revealed that he was a regular client of a prostitution service.

These famous failings of public figures all involve hypocrisy. In its standard form, hypocrisy occurs when an individual does not live according to the precepts he or she seeks to impose on (or strongly recommend to) others. Charges of hypocrisy are common in debates because they are highly effective. We feel compelled to reject the views of hypocrites. We rightly see hypocrisy as a vice, specifically a symptom of incompetence or insincerity. Yet we should be exceedingly careful about letting our moral and emotional reactions to apparent hypocrisy color our judgments of substantive issues.

In fact, one general truth about hypocrisy is that it is often totally irrelevant to what's at issue. The fact that someone is a hypocrite does not have anything to do with whether his or her position on an issue is false. Environmentalists who litter do not thereby disprove the claims of environmentalism. The fact that a pro-life activist once sought an abortion for her daughter does not mean that abortion is acceptable. Even if every animal rights activist is exposed as a covert meat-eater, it still might be wrong to eat meat. In short, just because someone's a hypocrite doesn't mean that what they say is false.

Allegations of hypocrisy are treacherous because they can function as argumentative diversions, drawing our attention away from the task of assessing the strength of a position and toward the character of the position's advocate. Such accusations trigger emotional reflexes that dominate our capacity to see the matter clearly. It is for this reason that arguments from hypocrisy are often called *tu quoque* (Latin for "you, too") fallacies. "You do it, too!" is a regular retort to critique, and we admit that it feels emotionally satisfying to score a point like that. The trouble is that it is precisely in the hard and pressing cases that our emotional reflexes of rejection are most often inadequate. Thus, listeners should temper such knee-jerk reactions toward the messenger and instead independently consider the character of the message itself. It also pays to closely examine what the duplicitous deeds really mean. For sure, there are times when the fact that someone can't keep their story straight or can't walk their own talk is a relevant consideration. Surely, if you are making a decision about having a reliable and sincere person in some position of authority, whether they are a hypocrite is a worthy matter of concern. And from some vantage points, such behavior may actually support a hypocrite's point of view. That's right. Hypocrisy can sometimes *support* the hypocrite's view. That's a surprising truth about hypocrisy. We'll say more about it in due course.

In the second presidential debate of 1988 (October 13), moderator and CNN correspondent Bernard Shaw asked Michael Dukakis, the Democratic candidate, the following hypothetical question: "If Kitty Dukakis [Dukakis' wife] were raped and murdered, would you favor an irrevocable death penalty for the killer?" Unsurprisingly, Dukakis, a known death penalty opponent, answered that he would not. Nonetheless, Shaw's line of reasoning was clear enough: Though Dukakis does not think so *now*, were some crucial things different, he *would* think differently. By Shaw's standards, Dukakis was a hypocrite.[1]

The implication underlying Bernard Shaw's hypothetical question is a special instance of a *tu quoque* argument. In its most general sense, a *tu quoque* argument alleges that someone is wrong because her words and actions conflict, and in this case with Dukakis, it is not Dukakis' *actual* actions, but actions he *would take*, at least as far as Shaw sees it.

The argument Shaw seems to have employed is captured roughly along the following lines:

> You are against capital punishment *now*, but what if your wife were taken, beaten, sexually abused, and then murdered? Ten to one, you'd change your tune.

The core of the argument is that were critics of capital punishment to experience the grief and horror consequent of certain crimes, their vengeful inclinations would be sparked. They would see the value in giving others the full measure of retribution. Schematized:

P1: *Now*, you say capital punishment is wrong.

P2: Under special conditions X (namely, conditions under which someone you love had been victimized), you would say it is right.

The crucial thing about the assumption behind this line of argument is that it seems that Shaw and many proponents of the death penalty accept the following additional premise and conclusion:

P3: Special conditions X are the appropriate conditions under which to make a judgment regarding the death penalty, and the normal conditions that prevail now are inappropriate conditions.

C: Therefore, the death penalty is right and you (Michael Dukakis) are not only wrong, but hypocritical, to oppose it.

If P3 were true, then the premises would become relevant to the conclusion and the argument could be saved. The problem is that P3 is false.[2] Being a victim (and even an *indirect* victim) of a crime tends to distort one's judgments concerning the requirements of retributive justice. That's a pretty heavy thought, so let's break it down a bit.

First, victims maximize assessments of their suffering and perpetrators minimize the suffering they cause, and so if a victim is then placed in the position of determining a proportionate punishment for a perpetrator, there will be a *magnitude gap* between the harms (see Baumeister 1999: 160 and Mandel 2002: 186). Think about it this way: Everybody who's ever had the chance to "get back" at another has faced the serious temptation to give back more than they got. When you were a kid, if your brother hit you, you hit him back harder. When your sister said something mean to you, you tried to think of something even meaner to say in response. There's a reason why that's the case. It's the magnitude gap, and it distorts the way we can evaluate what the appropriate punishment is for those who've wronged us.

Imagine that your neighbor has a really nice mug, and it just broke. He's now throwing a meltdown tantrum about it. It's disappointing for him, to be sure, but we may say that ultimately he's just got to deal with the loss. Next imagine your grandmother's precious china sugar bowl, the one that you've prized since she gave it to you, just broke. Sure, you've got to deal with it just like your neighbor, but when the loss is *yours*, it becomes much more difficult to react appropriately. Our point is that in both cases the loss is roughly the same, but when the loss is *yours*, you can very easily blow it out of proportion. That's the magnitude gap, and that's why victims shouldn't determine the punishment for the crimes they have suffered. They will opt for a punishment that is more severe than the crime.

What's wrong with making punishments more severe than the crimes? Well, for one thing, perpetrators deserve only as much punishment as the crime is bad. To punish someone more severely than the damage that was done by their crime is to commit a moral error. For sure, people who commit crimes deserve punishments, but those punishments must be proportionate to the crime committed. That's what it is for punishments to *fit* the crime. Remember some moral error you may have committed as a child. You may have been rude to a relative or you may have told a lie to your parents. That was wrong.

Now imagine that you were caught in the rude moment, your lie is detected. And next imagine that as a punishment you were beaten to within an inch of your life. And once you got better from that beating, you were given another beating. And then another. And then another. You get the picture. Sure, rude children may deserve punishment and lying kids need correction. But a series of severe beatings is excessive, no matter how rude the kid was to her aunt or how big the lie was. To punish excessively is morally wrong.

Now let us put these two points together. First, victims have a magnitude gap when they assess the damage done to them and what the perpetrators deserve. They will regularly function so as to give back much more punishment than the harm they suffered. Second, it is unjust to punish anyone more than they deserve. Putting these two facts together, we see something important. If victims determine the punishment, they will likely opt to punish excessively and thus unjustly. That's a sad fact, but it nevertheless is a fact. And that's the heavy thought broken down.

Return to the Dukakis case. That Michael Dukakis, an opponent of the death penalty, would burn with murderous vendetta under the conditions of knowing his wife was brutally murdered is irrelevant to the question of what the proper punishment for the murder is. We now know why—the magnitude gap. Of course, one could hold that the victim's perspective is relevant to deciding the degree of punishment that is appropriate; however, we know that that victim's perspective cannot be definitive of what the appropriate punishment is. So even if Michael Dukakis would indeed burn with murderous rage upon hearing that his wife was brutally murdered (which, by the way, he denied he would), it wouldn't be relevant to his principled stance against the death penalty. Sometimes hypocrisy is totally irrelevant to determining the truth of a belief. However, even when they are raised within the context of a hypothetical example (as in the Dukakis case), charges of hypocrisy can move people. Dukakis was roundly taken to have lost that debate, primarily because of how he answered Shaw's question. Yet the exchange with Shaw over the death penalty was completely devoid of proper argumentative content.

Let's take a step back. For our purposes, we will understand that *tu quoque* arguments, broadly speaking, hinge on speaker inconsistencies. Such inconsistencies are manifested in two ways: inconsistencies between a speaker's claims—what can be called *cognitive* inconsistency—and inconsistencies between a speaker's claims and his or her deeds—what can be called *practical* inconsistency. Practical inconsistencies are instances of hypocrisy.

The basic schema for *tu quoque* arguments is as follows:

Tu Quoque

1   Speaker S advocates X.
2   S fails to X.
3   *Therefore*: S is cognitively or practically inconsistent.
4   *Therefore*: S's claim X is false or unacceptable.

Textbooks of logic and critical thinking usually include the *tu quoque* in their lists of fallacies of relevance, because, as we have noted, facts about the speaker's inconsistency do not necessarily bear on the truth or falsity of the speaker's claims. So when someone alleges that Al Gore's claims about global warming are false because he drives a gas-guzzling car and lives in a big house, she is guilty of the fallacious variety of *ad hominem tu quoque*.

More Latin. *Ad hominem* arguments are generally arguments against the person, instead of what the person said. So the general *ad hominem* tactic is to say something like:

He's a drunk, so his views on politics are false.

In this case, we're substituting an evaluation of the person for an evaluation of what the person says. The trouble is that it's often the case that whether the person has some vice or other is irrelevant to an assessment of what the person says. And in our example, the fact that the person drinks too much doesn't mean he has false views about politics. In fact, *it may be because he knows too much about politics that he drinks so much.* (That joke kills in our logic classes.)

Tu quoque arguments are of the *ad hominem* family, because they are cases of where a speaker is criticized for some vice (specifically hypocrisy) and then taken to be wrong about what she's been talking about. And so, they generally have the form:

She's a hypocrite, so her views are false.

It seems strange to note that this, actually, is all there is to hypocrisy charges when deployed as refutations. They seem simply and obviously silly.

Sometimes, however, one does not intend a *tu quoque* to allege that a speaker's claims are false. One's argument, in fact, might be *formally* similar to the fallacious variety of *ad hominem tu quoque* in that it rebuts a speaker's argument on grounds of inconsistency between thought and action. Such arguments may not be intended to demonstrate the falsity of a speaker's claim that *p*, rather, they may rightly shift the burden of argument back onto the speaker to explain the inconsistency between claims that *p* and actions that seem inconsistent with it.

Direct use of the *tu quoque*, then, is to the falsity of the view in question. Indirect use of *tu quoque* opens a wider discussion of the issue. So, to put things formally:

Direct: S is a hypocrite, so S's claims are false.
Indirect: S is a hypocrite, so S must explain the apparent contradiction between his claims and his actions.

Thus, while their direct use is fallacious, their indirect use might serve an important dialectical role. That is, if a speaker has been inconsistently claiming that we should do X, that is a relevant consideration for a full discussion of the matter. The reasoning may go: *You say that we should do X, but you, yourself, don't do that. What gives? Perhaps things are more complicated than we had assumed?* Or maybe the speaker has recently changed his or her mind based on some new information. Consider, for example, a child who objects to an early bedtime and asks the parents why they get to stay up late. Or imagine someone who objects to driving the speed limit when ambulances, police cars, and fire trucks get to drive over the speed limit and run red lights. These are occasions to clarify the situation, so that one can say that, in fact, there is no real inconsistency. Parents can stay up later because they need less sleep than children. Emergency vehicles get to speed because they are responding to emergencies. Insofar as one has posed a challenge of inconsistency as an occasion for clarifying a complex phenomenon, it's not a fallacy *per se*. It, really, pushes critical dialogue along, in that we now have an occasion to make some distinctions. The indirect *tu quoque* posed here functions as a directive for the speaker to further clarify his/her position or elaborate on her evidence. We call the use of *tu quoque* to open further discussion of the issue *dialectical tu quoque*.

We believe the familiar charge of flip-flopping is a form of *tu quoque* argument. The core of that kind of charge is that at one time, a person thought X was a good idea, but now does not. The charge is that the flip-flopper can't make up his mind, perhaps isn't sincere, or maybe is confused about the issue. Once the charge sticks, it doesn't matter much which diagnosis is correct, since any one of the charges impugns the person's character, and that is then taken as a case against the person's views. But this is often too quick. Why? Because reasonable people change their minds about things all the time! New information can come to light, new experiences can be had, the facts may change, or one's assessment of what the facts mean can shift. Only a blinkered dogmatist would be opposed to changing his mind as new evidence arises. And so, we think that sometimes flip-flopping on an issue shows that a person is really thinking about things, that he is attending to the issue.

Consider a charge that was often brought against Mitt Romney in the run-up to the 2012 presidential election. It was frequently claimed that Romney is a flip-flopper on abortion and state-mandated health insurance. When running for Senate in Massachusetts in the 1990s, Romney said he would support abortion rights. When later seeking the Republican nomination for president and as the nominee, he stood firmly against abortion. While governor of Massachusetts, Romney enacted a large-scale state governmental health care mandate. But as the Republican nominee for president, Romney stood against a very-similarly structured federal mandate introduced by President Obama. He seems to have flip-flopped on two highly important issues.

But consider that Mitt Romney's later views may be the results of his experiences, what he has come to learn, and what he has seen since adopting his former views. In fact, this is how Romney explains the changes to his positions. He says he changed his mind about abortion in 2007 when he was discussing stem cell research with a group of scientists. They described how the stem cells are harvested from embryos, and Romney found himself reacting. Here is Romney's account:

> It hit me very hard that we had so cheapened the value of human life in a *Roe v. Wade* environment that it was important to stand for the dignity of human life. ... We learn with experience. We gain perspective over time, but the principles remain the same. I have a number of principles, and the principles remain the same.[3]

Mitt Romney changed his mind, and he says that it was because he came to see the moral relevance of unborn babies. It took the experience of discussing stem cells and how they are harvested with scientists for him to rethink his position on abortion.

And that's how it should be. We, the authors, regularly teach courses in ethics, and we very often see people's minds change about important moral issues. A good conversation can change your perspective. Sometimes in the course of a conversation we hear a good argument, one we'd never heard before or even thought of. That's why college classes are good for us—they limber up our minds. Regardless of whether we're right about the value of ethics classes in college, one thing is clear: Some questions are hard, and it takes a long time to think them all the way through. Indeed, one who never changes his or her mind about such matters is very short-sighted. More importantly, adopting the policy of never changing one's mind is cognitively unhealthy, especially when the policy is motivated by social pressures to avoid flip-flopping.

Let's pause for a moment to consider another element of hypocrisy charges. Sometimes, they aren't about what the person says or does at all, but they are entirely about the person, full stop. Consider how flip-flopping charges are sometimes deployed entirely for the sake of impugning the person's character, showing that someone simply has no judgment or will just say what is most convenient at the time. An example of this line of argument is how people have criticized President Donald Trump's character. In the lead-up to the 2016 election, *Time* magazine ran a story titled, "How Donald Trump Flip-Flopped on Three Major Issues." Here's the core charge:

> Before he became a candidate, Trump reversed course on several issues. He used to be pro-choice; now that he's running in the Republican primary, he's pro-life. He used to support assault weapons bans; now he is against them. He told Howard Stern in 2002 that he supported the invasion of Iraq; now he calls it a mistake.

Further, the story details other changes of course on the status of Syrian refugees, allowing worker visas, and the use of torture for interrogation. After the election, there was the question of how well now President Trump kept the promises he made as a candidate. He did not label China a currency manipulator (which he promised to do "on day one"), he played more golf than his predecessor (despite having criticized him for almost every round he played), and his promise to "drain the swamp" in Washington yielded a cabinet of executives from Goldman Sachs. And there were many, many, more cases to consider.

The objective with hypocrisy charges along these lines, again, is not to show that the target—in this case, President Trump—is wrong in any of these cases, but only that he is a *hypocrite*, and that is it. These are una-bashed *ad hominem* arguments—their objective is to make the case that he has bad character, and that is all. Sometimes, in the midst of thinking about the issue, you can't help but think about the people at the center of the issue. And when we do that, it's hard not to assess their character as honest arbiters or as cheaters and manipulators. It's not wrong to do that, but it is important to make it clear how the reasoning proceeds.

The standard way to read *ad hominem* arguments is to take them as falla-cies of relevance. If we are to make an inference about what the person being evaluated is saying, they regularly have no bearing on the conclusion. So whether Alice drinks too much isn't relevant to the conclusion of her argu-ment, and whether Barry has an annoying voice doesn't have much to do with whether what he says with that voice is true or false. But in the case of deliberating about who should be president of the United States, character counts. And so if the fact that a presidential candidate will say anything or has no core beliefs can be revealed by a record of flip-flopping, then it is a relevant consideration. Consequently, it is clear that hypocrisy can be rele-vant in at least the cases where it's important to have a clear picture of someone's intellectual character. In particular, it's important to know the difference between a case of hypocrisy and an instance where someone has simply updated their beliefs and actions in light of new evidence. As we showed earlier, the only way to defend against these sorts of charges is to give an account of how one changed one's mind by attending to the evidence.

President Trump has taken care to explain his apparent flip-flopping. In his 2016 campaign, candidate Trump promised to "repeal and replace Obamacare" (the Affordable Care Act). However, upon taking office, the new president found that this was a more challenging task than he realized. He famously complained:

> Now, I have to tell you, it's an unbelievably complex subject. Nobody knew health care could be so complicated.

That's an explanation for the change, of course, but notice something important. It's simply not true that *nobody* knew health care laws are complicated. That there is a whole specialization among lawyers—and entire departments in law firms—devoted to health care law should suffice to confirm this. Further, there's a reason why the Affordable Care Act was as long as it was (approximately 20,000 pages of regulations): designing, funding, and regulating healthcare for a large country is complicated. So, yes, the president updated his views in light of evidence, and that's a good thing. However, this also reveals that his previously held views (and explicit campaign promises) were not based on any evidence or reflection whatsoever. That's a bad thing.

So far, our general point has been this: Just because a person does not have the fortitude to live up to his or her professed convictions, it does not mean that those convictions are false or dismissible. Moreover, a person can change their mind in light of new evidence. Thus, it seems obvious that charges that a speaker is a hypocrite prove nothing about the truth of the speaker's beliefs. So we must ask: Why are charges of hypocrisy so potent?

The answer is that allegations of hypocrisy summon emotional, and frequently unconscious, reactions to the speaker that undermine his or her credibility, and thus undermine his or her views. Put otherwise, charges of hypocrisy serve as attacks on the cognitive authority of their targets. When we label a person a hypocrite, we verbally punish him or her. The punishment not only comes in the form of overtly chastising the person, but we also strip that person of the moral standing to speak to the issue about which he or she has been inconsistent. Pointing out hypocrisy is a way of saying: *Don't lecture me about how to live—just look at how you're living!* And, as we've argued, sometimes people don't have the moral authority to speak to things, and hypocrisy charges make that clear.

From this point about moral authority and hypocrisy, we think an interesting and surprising consequence can arise. Once a speaker's clout is undermined in this way, the stage is set for dismissal of the speaker's position. Consider the following two cases:

Smoking Dad

DAD: You shouldn't smoke, son. It's bad for your health and it's addictive.
SON: But, Dad! You smoke a pack a day!

Gore's Airplane

AMY: Have you seen Al Gore's *An Inconvenient Truth*? We need to reduce our carbon footprint right away.
JIM: Al Gore? You know he leaves a huge footprint with all his private jet flights!

In "Smoking Dad," the son feels that his father is not an appropriate source of information on smoking because Dad, being himself a smoker, is a hypocrite. The accusation of hypocrisy does not so much defeat Dad's position as nullify it, leaving the situation almost as if Dad had never spoken. The same holds in "Gore's Airplane," although the speaker, Amy, is not the alleged hypocrite but rather it is Gore, the authority to which she appeals. In both cases, hypocrisy is proffered as evidence of the insincerity or incompetence of a source, providing justification for ignoring his or her advice or instruction. That's how charges of hypocrisy work.

Now, let's take another look at those arguments. Further examination reveals that Son and Jim would be foolish to dismiss Dad and Gore—and not only because their alleged hypocrisy is not pertinent to the perils of smoking or the human contribution to global warming. Consider what Dad's persistent smoking suggests. Dad believes smoking is bad for him, *yet he continues to smoke.* He continues, of course, because he's addicted to smoking. Thus, Dad's behavior—his hypocrisy—actually supports his point that smoking is addictive. That's interesting and surely worth noting. Sometimes a speaker's hypocrisy is not only relevant to the issue, but counts in favor of what the person says. As we mentioned above, that's a surprising truth about hypocrisy.

Consider that Gore's behavior also bolsters one of his arguments for a change in energy policy. Our national systems of energy use require that active members of society leave a large carbon footprint, *no matter how hard they try to be environmentally responsible.* Gore purchases offsets, he works to reduce (not eliminate) his footprint, but he, nevertheless, lives as a member of our society, and *even he* cannot manage to live in an ecologically responsible way. That's troubling, isn't it? Think of this: Gore should be highly motivated not to be a hypocrite. He's criticized for hypocrisy all the time. But still he cannot eliminate his carbon footprint. That's not evidence that Gore is stupid, insincere, or incompetent. That's evidence that he's right! He is correct to urge that there needs to be a massive revamping of our energy and transportation systems. That *Al Gore* is a hypocrite shows that one can't live in our society without doing significant environmental damage. And that's a crucial element of Gore's position. Again, that's a surprising truth about hypocrisy.

Of course, hypocrisy cannot always be parlayed into support for the hypocrite's view. Eliot Spitzer's repeated visits to an escort service do nothing to reinforce his official opposition to prostitution. Neither do Ted Haggard's dalliances with illegal drugs and male prostitutes support his recommendations to live the clean life. That is, not all hypocrisy arguments are created equal. So it is important to examine each instance individually. In some cases, hypocrisy has precisely the significance that Son and Jim assign to it. In other cases, however, hypocrisy is either irrelevant or actually constitutes evidence in favor of the hypocrite's position.

The trouble is that what determines the significance of hypocrisy is often our judgment concerning the truth of the position proposed by the hypocrite. For those who reject Gore's views about global warming, his hypocrisy has the significance that Son attributes to Dad's: that is, it cancels his position. For those who agree with Gore about global warming, his hypocrisy only strengthens his case. Consequently, the significance of hypocrisy sometimes depends on whether the hypocrite's position is true. But a person should assess that question by considering the strength of the evidence and arguments that support this position versus an opposing view. So, once again, whether any particular individual is a hypocrite is argumentatively irrelevant.

Now we see more clearly the danger of charges of hypocrisy. People often present them as sufficient for dismissing the views of their targets. But as we have seen, hypocrisy is not sufficient for dismissing the hypocrite's view. At best, they are only cases against their authority to speak on an issue. In any case, since whether the hypocrisy is relevant or not depends on whether the view espoused by the hypocrite is correct or not, dwelling too long on hypocrisy is an argumentative distraction.

There's a difference between dwelling excessively on hypocrisy and seeing how hypocrisy charges can clarify an issue. Recall our distinction between *direct* and *indirect* versions of inconsistency arguments. Direct inconsistency clearly suffers from relevance issues, but indirect arguments present occasions for clarification. It is important to highlight the dialectical role that inconsistency charges play in reasoning about a point of controversy. Philosophers often invoke the methodological principle: *When faced with a contradiction, make a distinction.* A charge of inconsistency often leads to the introduction of further nuance and precision. Consider the following exchange about bedtimes we mentioned earlier:

DADDY: Time for bed, little one. It's 8:00. It's bedtime.
DAUGHTER: Alright, Daddy. But ... how come you get to stay up? That doesn't seem fair that I have to go to bed but you get to stay up. If bedtime's at 8:00, you should go to bed, too.

Of course, this could be a case in which Daughter is merely stalling before bed; asking Daddy to clarify a rule delays bedtime. But it nonetheless is a perfectly legitimate question. Daughter is pointing out what looks to her like an inconsistency. If Daddy says bedtime is at 8:00, then why is it that *he* gets to stay up? And if he says that only after 8:00 do the good shows come on, that doesn't seem fair. But the rule has some inexplicit nuance—8:00 is the bedtime for children, adults can stay up later. Now Daughter can ask: Why the different treatment? And Daddy can respond: Because children need lots and lots of sleep, because their brains are still growing; without the sleep, the brains don't get the rest they need. He can continue: Adults don't need the same amount of sleep, because their brains are grown. He could then say something like the following: Moreover, adults, if they don't get enough rest the night before can drink coffee; kids don't like that stuff. And so it goes.

Dialectical *tu quoque*, then, occasions a discussion, one where clarifying distinctions are made, justifications given, and explanations provided. Sometimes they work out, as with the bedtime case above. But sometimes they don't. For example, imagine one of Ted Haggard's parishioners asking him the question: *You preach the clean life for us but turn around and use methamphetamines and sleep with male prostitutes ... what gives?* Haggard obviously couldn't introduce the kind of distinction Daddy gave to Daughter in the case above. Imagine him saying: *You see, preachers are different from those in the congregation ... you live the clean life, we preachers need the speed and prostitutes.* That just won't work.

And imagine, further, all these questions being posed to President Trump about his "flip-flopping" on a variety of issues. Imagine him saying about these cases something similar to what he has said about healthcare ("nobody knew healthcare is so complicated"):

> Look, I said that when I was running for office. Then, I only needed to act like I knew what I was talking about. And I thought then that being president just meant that I gave orders and they happened. Now that I'm really president, it turns out, I didn't really know what I was talking about. Nobody knew that being president is so complicated. Live and learn!

Again, given what Trump regularly said, it turns out that this statement is accurate with respect to many issues. He didn't expect the judicial branch of government to exercise any of its checks or balances, and it turns out that he also has to cooperate with Congress, too. Who knew that being president is so complicated?

Tu quoque arguments come in a variety of forms and they are deployed for a number of different purposes. The key to replying to them, then, depends on first identifying the forms and purposes they have. For the most part, we've seen that the *tu quoque* argument form has the regular trouble that comes with attacking the person instead of the person's claims. *Ad hominem* arguments that are merely abusive name-calling are clear failures. So if the point of an argument from inconsistency is just to score the point that someone's a hypocrite, then it's little more than pointless name-calling. Again, because we seem to naturally react so negatively to hypocrisy in others, it's a pretty effective rhetorical tool. But it is not a good means of argument. However, replying to arguments of this kind takes some judgment.

The reality is that we are not perfect, and it is likely that even if you're right about some moral principle or some political proposal, you haven't consistently lived in accord with it. Vegetarians regularly have this trouble, as they may eat the odd burger here and there. Or they may wear a leather belt, or have a pair of horn-rimmed glasses. In these cases, it is best, when charged with hypocrisy, to admit it. A vegetarian could say something like: *Look, meat is delicious and things made from the bodies of animals are often cool and really nice. That doesn't make using them right, and when I'm saying that we should be consistent vegetarians, I'm also addressing myself. I admit that I need to work harder at it, too.* That's honest, and it's probably exactly how to handle the situation. It turns the matter back to the principle, focuses on why the principle needs an argument, and then even acknowledges that if we live with the principle it may have costs, costs that even someone making the case for vegetarianism can acknowledge.

The same admission could be made in the Ted Haggard case, too. He says that we should live the clean life, but he fails pretty spectacularly at doing so. That's not a surprise, as most demanding moral perspectives are hard to live by. After all, that's what makes them demanding. It's not as if Haggard or any Christian would want to hold that the life of righteousness is free of tests and trials. Temptation wouldn't be temptation if it weren't hard to resist. To be sure, the Haggard case is galling for other reasons, as most of us are able to resist the temptation to binge on drugs with prostitutes. But, hey, maybe we're just lucky to have that kind of self-control.

Things are somewhat similar with the indirect forms of *tu quoque* argument. Most often the best response is to begin by acknowledging the apparent inconsistency. But then the task is to find some relevant difference in the apparently inconsistent cases. In the bedtime example, the father presents reasons for the difference in the policies governing adults and children. If the distinction is indeed relevant, then we've acknowledged the apparent inconsistency, but resolved it by means of the new distinction. Of course, everything turns on whether the proposed distinction can actually serve as a good basis for the difference between the seemingly contradictory cases. Consider the following exchange:

MOLLY: Hey Mike. You pay men $10 an hour, but women only $8 an hour for the same work. What gives?
MIKE: Molly, that may seem inconsistent, but, you see, men are the breadwinners for their households. They need to be paid more than women.

Here Molly has posed a dialectical *tu quoque*, and Mike has provided an answer. But Mike's answer fails on two important criteria. First, it is just not true that only men are the breadwinners in their households. The easiest counter-examples are single-parent households where the parent is a woman, but there are of course others. Second, Mike's reason, even were it true, doesn't support his policy of unequal pay. As an employer, Mike pays his employees for their work; if the women and men are doing the same job, they deserve equal pay. Mike is being inconsistent, and Molly is right to challenge it. Mike's response is inadequate, and so there's an important fact that has been brought to light—there are unequal, and unfair, pay practices in Mike's business.

The upshot is that charges of inconsistency are not always irrelevant. Sometimes, they are relevant, but actually help the hypocrite's case. And sometimes, they show deep problems with the views and practices of those who are inconsistent. That's why, even given the regular troubles with hypocrisy charges, it is important to consider them and respond to them. Sometimes, in examining alleged hypocrisy, we uncover something significant.

For Further Thought

1   Suppose Gore is a hypocrite. Suppose also, as has been suggested, that Gore's hypocrisy provides further evidence of the truth of his views about climate change. Does this make him any less blame-worthy for the hypocrisy?
2   Does the significance of hypocrisy charges change when they are directed at arguments that have in their conclusions not statements about what's right (or wrong), but rather commands to do (or refrain from doing) something?
3   Are there cases in which it is appropriate to dismiss what someone says simply on the basis of the fact that he or she is a hypocrite?
4   Notice that both arguments by analogy and *tu quoque* arguments rely on a background principle of treating similar cases similarly. Analogy requests consistent treatment, and *tu quoque* charges inconsistency. But if argument by analogy is open to backfire problems, could *tu quoque*?
5   What exactly is it for someone to have moral authority to speak to an issue, and why does hypocrisy seem to attack that?

Key Terms

Tu quoque arguments	Arguments that conclude that a speaker is wrong or has no authority on an issue because they have been inconsistent (either in word or deed) on it.
Ad hominem arguments	Arguments that attack the person for some perceived vice and thereby conclude that the person's claims are unacceptable.
Magnitude gap	The tendency for those suffering a loss to judge the loss greater than impartial viewers.
Fallacy of relevance	A particular kind of fallacy wherein the truth of the premises has no bearing on the truth or acceptability of the conclusion.
Dialectical *tu quoque*	A challenge of inconsistency that is posed as a request to clarify an issue.

Notes

1   See an excerpt of the debate at www.youtube.com/watch?v=DF9gSyku-fc
2   Of course, we can imagine some moral theories which would deny this, but would hold that one's emotive state in making moral judgments is relevant to which moral judgments one should accept. If Critic C were to hold such a view of moral judgments then it might be the case that P3 would be defended and this argument might not be fallacious. Whether the relevance condition is

granted may in part be a result of the dialectical context within which the argument is being deployed.

3 *Time,* Tuesday, May 10, 2007: www.time.com/time/magazine/article/ 0,9171,1619536,00.html#ixzz1oNKAJfDW

References

Baumeister, R. (1999) *Evil: Inside Human Violence and Cruelty.* New York: Barnes and Noble.

Mandel, D. R. (2002) "Evil and the Instigation of Collective Violence." *Analyses of Social Issues and Public Policy* 2(1): 101–108.

9   Arguments by Analogy

Argument by analogy is like a powerful chainsaw. If you know how to use it, you can do some nice work. But if you aren't careful, you can make a big mess, and maybe hurt yourself as well.

The core form of argument by analogy is to infer from two things' acknowledged similarities that those things have further, as yet unacknowledged, similarities. One begins with a generally familiar phenomenon (the *proximal object* of the analogy), and then attributes salient features of the proximal object to another, less familiar matter (the *distal object* of the analogy). On the basis of the analogy, it is established that what is true of the proximal object is also true of the distal object.

Argument by analogy is a particularly widely used tool throughout philosophy. Plato's analysis in *The Republic* of the good person runs on an analogy between justice in the soul and justice in the city. Plato's argument is that, as justice in the city consists of a certain kind of hierarchical order of those who know being in charge, the just person's soul manifests the same structure, with reason in charge. This way, harmony and health are maintained.

As an additional example, consider that Judith Jarvis Thomson's famous defense of abortion runs on an analogy. Thomson analogizes unplanned pregnancy to being kidnapped, taken to a hospital, and hooked up to a famous violinist who needs use of your kidneys for nine months in order to stay alive. Thomson's reasoning is that since it is not immoral to refuse to remain hooked up to the violinist, it is not impermissible for a woman to end a pregnancy.

And William Paley's notorious argument for God's existence starts with the hypothesis that the world's functions (and those of many bodies within the world and parts of the body, too, like eyes) are similar to those of a watch, whose very existence suffices to demonstrate the existence of a watchmaker who designed and created the watch. Since watches manifest a level of complexity that cannot be explained without appeal to a watchmaker, it stands to reason that the world, with all of its complexity, stands in need of its own explanatory designer-creator. According to Paley, that's God.

It is not difficult to see how arguments by analogy may be challenged. They depend on there being good reason for accepting the proposed analogy in the first place, so an obvious strategy for challenging an argument by analogy is to attack the alleged analogy asserted as a premise. Accordingly, many of those who reject the conclusions of Plato's, Thomson's, and Paley's arguments contend that the analogies themselves are at least as controversial as the conclusions they are supposed to support. Consider Paley's watchmaker argument. The premise that the world is analogous to an artefact (such as a watch) goes a long way toward reaching the conclusion that there must be a God who designed and created the universe. However, if you think the conclusion unacceptable, then the initial analogy just won't look right. And many who've rejected Thomson's and Plato's arguments have taken similar lines of critique: pregnancy is *not at all* like being hooked up to the violinist; the justice of a city is *fundamentally different from* what makes an individual person just.

Hence arguments by analogy face a particular dialectical obstacle. Only those already roughly in agreement with the desired conclusion will readily grant the initial analogy. And so it seems as if the analogies are either unnecessary or they are proxies for arguments that establish the appropriateness of the analogies. Arguments by analogy, then, are either otiose or insufficient.

The arguments by analogy that are commonly deployed in debates concerning same-sex marriage demonstrate the difficulty. Analogizing laws against same-sex marriage to anti-miscegenation laws telegraphs the conclusion that laws of the former kind are obviously and unambiguously unjust; and arguments that begin from an analogy between same-sex marriage and bestiality similarly contain the desired conclusion within the initial analogy. That is, the proximal analogue chosen regularly tells us how the distal is to be judged. So when an argument opens with the observation that any law preventing citizens from marrying those they love is like a law that forbids interracial marriage, the proximal analogue is the (we assume to be clearly taken) unjust anti-miscegenation law, and the distal analogue is a law against same-sex marriage. And if the proximal analogue, alternately, is a law prohibiting bestiality, then it becomes clear how the line of argument is going to bear on same-sex marriages. So, Texas Senator John Cornryn has argued that holding that same-sex marriages were on par with legalized bestiality:

> It does not affect your daily life very much if your neighbor marries a box turtle. But that does not mean it is right... . Now you must raise your children up in a world where that union of man and box turtle is on the same legal footing as man and wife.[1]

In both cases, in announcing the analogy, one is less arguing for a conclusion than situating one's conclusion within a broader worldview. How one challenges the analogy, then, takes on a particular form. So, for example, challenging the analogy between same-sex marriage and bestiality should start with the observation that the analogy isn't particularly apt, since it is clear there's a moral difference between relations between humans and those between humans and animals. The first is a simple moral difference: there is no established frame of injustice associated with same-sex marriages. They are, like modern heterosexual marriages, a relationship between equals. Not so with animals. The second disanalogy between same-sex relationships and bestiality simply concerns consent. Adult humans can give consent and enter into contracts, turtles, dogs (or what have you) can't. Thus the argument by analogy against same-sex marriage fails. See? It's not so hard, is it?

But what's also necessary to see here is that the argument by analogy with bestiality is not really an argument aiming to *establish* the conclusion that same-sex marriage should not be legally permitted; it is more like an *expression* of a speaker's moral perspective. That is, arguments by analogy are best understood as *heuristic devices* that take argumentative form. Again, they do not supply reasons for adopting a conclusion, but rather reveal or make manifest the way the person wielding the analogy represents an issue more broadly. By attending to an interlocutor's argument by analogy, we do not expose ourselves to new reasons concerning the matter in dispute, we rather come to see how the interlocutor understands what's fundamentally at issue. In the case of same-sex marriage, those who deploy the argument by analogy with bestiality are using the analogy to *express* or *signal* the perspective that same-sex relationships violate a natural order, or involve the coupling of things that do not belong together. Note, however, that this is precisely the *conclusion* that the argument by analogy is supposed to establish; but in the proposed argument by analogy, it functions as a premise.

Arguments by analogy confront a second dialectical complication, one that arises from the background presumption that beliefs about the proximal phenomenon are more settled or obvious than those about the distal. Consider the ancient philosopher Lucretius's famous parity-of-reasons argument that one should not fear death. Lucretius acknowledges that we fear death. But, he asks, why should we? Consider the following: you don't fear or feel bad about the time before you were born. You just weren't. Well, Lucretius reasons, the same goes for the time after you are alive. You just aren't. Lucretius contends that if two things are alike, we should have the same attitude toward them. Since being dead is just like the time before you were born, and you don't normally feel bad about the time prior to your birth, you shouldn't have bad feelings about the time after your death. And that's why, according to Lucretius's argument by analogy, we shouldn't fear death.

It's a nifty argument. But imagine someone responding to Lucretius as follows:

Yeah, I accept that the time before my birth is analogous to the time after my death. So I should have the same attitude toward both. But my more stable reaction is feeling really fearful of my death, so instead of changing my attitudes about the time after my death, I'll change my attitudes about the time before my birth. So I'll remain afraid of death, but now I'll also feel bad about the time before I was born. Thanks a lot!

Call this the *backfire effect*, and it is a challenge for anyone who runs an argument by analogy. Arguments by analogy depend on our attitudes about the proximal phenomenon being stable, and this stability is what allows one to extend them to the distal phenomenon. But if those proximal attitudes are not stable, the argument backfires. And note how this backfire effect has begun to bear fruit in ways in the political realm. Analogizing President Trump's behavior in obstructing investigations into his campaign to that of President Nixon's famous Watergate corruption relies on stable anti-Nixon sentiments. But if for a particular interlocutor those anti-Nixon sentiments aren't that stable (and the more robust attitudes are pro-Trump) the analogy backfires; the interlocutor is simply encouraged to adopt more sympathetic thoughts about Nixon, and the argument ends.

Let's pause a moment to make clear how the background parity-of-reasons thought should be working for arguments by analogy. Initially, we said that arguments by analogy start with a proximal analogue with its properties and then makes an inference about a distal analogue and its properties. The argument, generally, works according to the following form:

> X (the proximal analogue) has properties a, b, and c.
> Y (the distal analogue) has properties a, b, and c.
> X also has property d.
> *So*, Y has property d as well.

The key to most arguments by analogy is that they depend on the two items uncontestably sharing some set of properties (a, b, c) and the proximal analogue having some target property (d). But there needs to be some connecting principle between these, and the entire argument depends on that connecting principle. The principle needs to be something along the following lines:

> It is because X has a, b, and c that X has d

That is, the connection between X's properties a, b, and c and its property d cannot be merely coincidental; the having of properties a, b, and c must be asserted to *indicate* the having of property d. And so, we see that it's in the connecting (but often unexpressed) principle that arguments by analogy work.

Now we can understand *how* being hooked up to a violinist is supposed to be a guide to the ethics bearing on unplanned pregnancies, *why* watches are a model for how to think about the world and bodies in it, and *how* our attitude about marriage to box turtles is supposed to direct our thoughts on same-sex marriage. Only if those connecting principles are right are the analogies proposed in the arguments effective. And once we see this, the argument by analogy's logical force is that, given the principle, is really *a matter of ensuring that we have consistent judgments*, that we judge similar things similarly.

Hence arguments by analogy use the parity of reasons as a way to point out that we have inconsistent commitments — we are treating things that are alike in ways that aren't alike. So we need to restore consistency. And this parity of reasons feature of argument by analogy is why the backfire effect works the way it does. When we have an inconsistent set of commitments, logic doesn't tell us what to do in order to resolve the inconsistency. We may eliminate one of the inconsistent beliefs, or we may eliminate some other. Alternately, we can eliminate both, or we could reject the principle that connects them. Backfire happens because logic doesn't dictate what we do, and so when we find that an analogy shows that we must make an alteration in order to restore consistency, there will be no guarantee that our audience will establish consistency in the way we expected.

Return to Lucretius's famous analogy between the period before our birth and the time after we die. He affirms that we should judge those times in the same way, and as we do not fear the former, we have no reason to fear the latter. But if aversion to non-being is a very stable inclination, it's perfectly consistent to regret not existing before one's birth and continue fearing death. This is not an uncommon phenomenon. In fact, taking a negative attitude toward the period before one's birth is familiar: some people regularly lament having been "born in the wrong decade." The same goes for all the other analogies that demand consistency; they are all open to backfire. So, with Thomson's violinist case, students in our ethics classes insist that because abortion is murder, disconnecting from the violinist is murder, too. With popular analogies between President Trump and Hitler, some have taken this to be a reason to consider a more sympathetic view of National Socialism. And in light of the analogies between same-sex marriages and bestiality, some have agreed that this is a reason to decriminalize sex with animals. Again, arguments by analogy show that we must be consistent, and the backfire effect shows that consistency can be achieved in many (sometimes surprising) ways.

Our overall result is that, despite their pervasiveness in dialectical exchange, arguments by analogy rarely cut much argumentative ice. The reasons why one regards the initial analogy as salient are often drawn from the same cloth that supplies the reasons why one embraces the conclusion. From the perspective of one's interlocutor, however, one's argument by analogy will appear simply to beg the question. Alternatively, one's argument by analogy simply occasions a backfire counter-argument. Although they may be useful ways to signal or express one's general viewpoint, arguments by analogy most frequently offer one's interlocutor no reason whatsoever to change her position. In fact, in many of the contexts where arguments by analogy are most pervasive, they are also most prone to occasion backfire. In these cases, those wielding the argument saw off the limb they're standing on.

We need next to turn to how one may criticize a proposed analogy. That is, we should make it clear what it takes to establish that an argument by analogy runs on a *false analogy*. Let us start with an example, and then we'll draw some lessons.

In the 2016 presidential election, candidate Donald Trump's son, Donald Trump Jr., made an analogical argument against admitting refugees from Syria (which at the time was in the midst of a bloody civil war, forcing much of the civilian population out of the country, creating a significant humanitarian crisis and also widespread worry that the immigrants were also disguised terrorists). Given the humanitarian crisis for countries accepting the war refugees and the concerns about whether Islamic terrorists were using the crisis as a means to send their agents abroad, there was discussion in the United States about whether any Syrian refugees should be admitted. The Trump campaign was decidedly set against admitting any refugees. Trump Jr. supported the policy of prohibiting refugees. He tweeted the following argument by analogy:

> If I had a bowl of Skittles and I told you that just three would kill you. Would you take a handful?

Along with this hypothetical question, he presented an image of a bowl of Skittles candy and the message:

> This image says it all. Let's end the politically correct agenda that doesn't put America first. #trump2016

The reaction to Trump Jr.'s tweet was swift. Some praised the analogy as apt, as the point of the argument was to show how reasoning about allowing in refugees was a matter of risk management. However, a good deal of replies to Trump Jr.'s tweet were critical. Many of the critics claimed that the argument ran on a *false analogy*. These criticisms came in two forms: the first challenged the appropriateness of an analogy between refugees and candy; the second alleged that the candy bowl grossly exaggerated the risks of admitting Syrian refugees into the United States.

The first critics claimed that (in the words of a spokesperson for the manufacturer of Skittles), "Skittles are candy. Refugees are people." This is not much of a criticism, since analogies are not identities. The issue regarding the appropriateness of a proposed analogy is whether the items analogized are dissimilar in a way that renders the analogical reasoning no longer properly analogical. Pointing out differences among the analogized items is at most the *beginning* of a criticism of an argument by analogy; the key is to break the analogy by explaining what makes the differences more salient than the alleged similarity. Accordingly, those who insisted that Trump Jr.'s analogy was inappropriate pointed out how "taking a handful" of Skittles is merely an act of eating candy, whereas saving a handful of refugees from a war-torn country saves human lives. The thought is that we take the Skittles for our own pleasure, but we take in refugees because we owe something to our fellow humans. The criticism continues that as there is a significant moral obligation to help people, we are required to assume a greater risk if that is necessary in order to meet the obligation. Not eating candy because of a chance of harm seems wise, but not helping those in desperate need because there is a chance they may be harmful is immoral. Hence many replied to Trump Jr.'s tweet by posting photographs of refugees with the tag #notaskittle, emphasizing the moral difference between the purported analogues.

The second line of criticism challenged the accuracy of the representation of the risk. The "bowl of Skittles" with the three poisoned Skittles was a vague representation of the probabilities, and it inflated the likelihood of eating a piece of poisoned candy to a point where it should seem positively reckless to take a handful. Many took the representation of the probabilities to heart, and responded that, given the data on the occurrence of refugee-related-terrorism, for Trump Jr.'s analogy to be apt, the bowl of Skittles would need to be about the size of one and a half Olympic-sized swimming pools. That's a lot of Skittles, and so taking several handfuls would be not particularly risky. For some perspective, consider that, according to the U.S. Safety Council, the chance of being killed by a refugee in a terror attack is 1 in 3,640,000. There, in fact, is a much greater likelihood of choking on a Skittle.

The lesson is that the analogies deployed in arguments by analogy can be criticized as being inappropriately framed, as *false analogies*. To show this requires not just pointing out differences between the analogized items, but giving reasons for thinking that the differences are both relevant and sufficient to override the connecting principle driving the argument.

We close with a few observations about how analogical reasoning, despite being weak in resolving disagreements, is nevertheless a useful heuristic and explanatory tool. As we noted earlier, arguments by analogy work best as ways of making a viewpoint clearer, more fecund and explicit. One way to see this is to notice that so many wisdom traditions work with fables, parables, and exemplary stories. They are, at their core, analogies about living well and reflectively.

Jesus of Nazareth communicated his ethical view most effectively with parables. He analogizes his love for humanity to a shepherd who searches all night for one lost sheep and to a poor widow who finds a lost silver coin (Luke 15:3–10). One of Jesus' most famous parables involves a Samaritan traveler who is exemplary of those who love their neighbors as themselves. A man traveling from Jerusalem to Jericho was set upon by thieves, and he was left for dead. Many who were taken to be holy passed him by, but the Samaritan cared for the injured man and covered the expenses of his convalescence. Jesus tells his followers to "go and do likewise" (Luke 10:25–42). That is, he enjoins us to see the core principle behind the story and apply it to the particular cases we see in our lives. The core of this tradition's wisdom is being able to reason analogically.

Aesop's fables were widely considered a source of wisdom in ancient Greece and Rome, and their wisdom came only by our capacity to see them as proximal analogues for distal application in our lives. And so, when a farmer's wagon gets stuck in the mud, he calls out to Hercules and the gods for help. A voice from the heavens thunders back: "Try getting out of the wagon and giving it a push first." This story is a regular touchstone for similar wisdom, such as Benjamin Franklin's aphorism, "God helps those who help themselves." Further, Aesop's famous fable of the Tortoise and the Hare, too, became a source of inspiration for the dicta that "haste makes waste," and "slow and steady wins the race." The tortoise and the hare were to race, and the hare got out to a quick lead. Once ahead, the hare took a nap, only to be overtaken and beaten by the tortoise. We take the lesson now to be a rebuke to arrogance and a celebration of persistence and earnestness.

Religious and philosophical traditions are thick with literary arguments by analogy, and this is no surprise. What function these stories have is that they, in the breadth of their application, become distillations of core cultural values. They are less demonstrative and more instructional of the ways of life that bind a group of people together. And they are additionally reminders of the aspirations that people share. Literature plays this role in a culture, too. We expand our moral understanding by imagining the complications and challenges of a different life, but when we do so, analogies arise, and we can see how what had seemed so dissimilar is not.

For Further Thought

1   Is it possible to run a backfire argument on *all* arguments by analogy, or only just some?
2   If arguments by analogy are not as argumentatively productive as is regularly thought, then why are they so prevalent?
3   Aristotle famously demonstrated argument by analogy with the following reasoning: The Athenian leader Pisistratus asked for bodyguards, and when he got them, he made himself tyrant of Athens. And so did Theagenes in Megara, and many others in other cities. Dionysus now asks for bodyguards, so he must be scheming to be a tyrant

(*Rhetoric* 1.2.1357b.25–35). How might a defender of Dionysus (or any other modern day politician targeted with this argument) reply?

4   Why should we judge similar cases similarly? Can't we judge according to the particularities of the various situations?

5   Are literary arguments really analogical arguments?

Key Terms

Argument by analogy	Assuming analogy between two analogues, an arguer holds that the property of a proximal analogue is also a property of a distal analogue.
Proximal analogue	The more familiar (and presumably less controversial) analogue, which also has the property in question to be attributed to the distal analogue.
Distal analogue	The less familiar (and presumably more controversial) analogue, which has a property in question.
Parity of reasons	On the assumption that we should treat similar cases similarly, if similar reasons bear on two cases, they should yield similar conclusions.
Backfire effect	When attitudes about the distal analogue are more stable than those about the proximal, and so controversy about the distal analogue is inherited from the proximal.

Note

1   http://www.washingtonpost.com/wp-dyn/articles/A43048-2004Jul11.html

10 Argumentation Between the Ads

In the real world of political talk, getting the last word is often what counts most. This is especially the case where political talk is conducted in the limited space between commercial breaks on television news programs. In such a forum, "getting the last word" does not mean what it means in more typical dialectical settings. Normally, one gets the last word in an argument when one articulates a *decisive* point, a point to which not even one's smartest and best informed opponents could object. The "last word" in this sense does not merely *conclude* an argument, it rationally *settles* it. In popular political talk, by contrast, "getting the last word" means *being the last speaker to utter a coherent and self-contained thought*. Statements of this self-contained variety tend to be received by one's audience as the "take away" from the exchange, and hence they are most likely to be remembered. Again, the "getting last word" in this political sense is especially valuable in settings where argumentative exchanges are subject to the constraints of television programming. When political opponents face off on an evening news program, their exchange is *necessarily* subject to the constraints of network time and viewers' attention spans. There isn't time for the careful referencing of complicated data, of the drawing of subtle distinctions. The clock is ticking, and for news networks, time is money. Of course, the setting is far from ideal for those who wish to engage in proper argumentation. Recall our discussion in Chapter 5 of the Simple Truth Thesis. Any issue worth arguing about is bound to be too complex to be settled within the short period between television advertising breaks. And yet, the "panel discussion" has become the prevalent format for delivering news on television. Accordingly, the value of "getting the last word" in a televised exchange has correspondingly skyrocketed.

One obvious strategy for speaking last in an exchange is simple and direct: Do not stop speaking; just continue uttering words until the time is up. Call this tactic argumentative *steamrolling*. Steamrolling is the strategy of simply running out the clock on the argument by *disallowing* discussion. Although it is sometimes attempted in mass media venues, steamrolling rarely succeeds at delivering the last word to the steamroller. The most natural response to an interlocutor's steamrolling effort is simply to fight fire with fire, and when multiple speakers are engaging in steamrolling, hosts and moderators simply can shut off speakers' microphones, or cut to commercial earlier than necessary. More than this, steamrolling is dialectically risky. Remember that the overarching aim is to get the last word, to be the last person to formulate a clear, coherent, and self-contained thought. But it is not easy to speak coherently over other voices that are trying to break into the discussion; and so attempts at steamrolling frequently result in crosstalk at best, but more often flustered babbling. Moreover, when one refuses to yield to others who wish to speak, one begins to look like a blowhard or bully. The attempt to get the last word by steamrolling hence can set one up to be the butt of late night comedians' jokes. Thus the steamrolling strategy not only can fail, it can backfire.

These risks aside, there are occasions where steamrolling is still a choiceworthy strategy for some speakers. Even though steamrolling is unlikely to secure the opportunity to have the last word, it might yet be an effective way for an interlocutor to *prevent* her opponent from getting the last word. That is, steamrolling is often an effective method for *escalating* conflict among disputants. In this case, steamrolling is deployed not as a tactic for getting the last word, but rather as a way of aborting all pretense of earnest argument. By escalating hostility, the steamroller incites a shouting match. This means that she will not get the last word in the exchange, but it also means that her opponent won't get the last word, either. When there is no pretense to earnest argument, no one gets the last word. And in some contexts, that is the best result available to a speaker embroiled in a political debate on television. We see, then, that steamrolling is ultimately an expression of cynicism about argumentation; deploying it indicates that one sees argument as merely a cover for bald assertion and the exercise of power.

We explored this "just is" cynical stance toward argument in Chapter 3. For now, it is worth repeating that overtly expressing cynicism about argument is *itself* a losing strategy in politics. As we noted earlier, our public political discourse is organized around the idea that earnest argument is not only possible, but worthwhile. Our news media would not be structured the way it is unless the prevailing attitude about political argumentation were decidedly non-cynical.

The arena of national politics is high-stakes and highly public, and it is driven by argumentation. Speakers' interest in getting the last word creates a strong incentive for devising strategies other than steamrolling. Hence a distinctive kind of conversational distortion aimed at enabling a speaker to get the last word has arisen. Whereas the steamroller seeks to disallow argumentative exchange, a more recent alternative attempts to *derail* it.

One derails an exchange when one speaks for the sake of creating a conversational rupture that substitutes the topic previously under consideration with some ambiguous, contentious, and unwieldy alternative. Once derailed in this sense, an argumentative exchange loses focus, and the disorientation can render one's interlocutors momentarily incapacitated; the person deploying the derailment then can swoop in and communicate his or her predesignated message, calmly and clearly, just in time for the commercial break. Derailing of course takes many forms. But one derailing tactic has become so prevalent in contemporary political discourse that it deserves analysis.

The derailing strategy we have in mind may be called *spitballing*. At its core, spitballing works as follows: One makes multiple contributions to a discussion, often as fast as one can think them up (and certainly faster than one can think them through). Some contributions may be insightful, others less so, but all are overtly controversial and thus provocative. What is most important, though, is that each installment express a single, self-contained and memorable thought. Accordingly, *slogans* are the spitballer's dialectical currency. As the metaphor of the spitball goes, one keeps tossing slogans until something sticks. Thus it helps if one's slogans are ambiguously tinged with something disagreeable or beyond the pale. As the spitballer's interlocutors attempt to reply to what he has said, the spitballer resolutely continues spitballing. That is, instead of defending his claims against the interlocutor's pushback, he simply introduces an entirely new topic, usually by voicing another slogan that is even more outrageous than its predecessor.

As a result, the spitballer's interlocutors are compelled to handle multiple disparate claims, and simply cannot keep up. In the process of reacting to so many rapid-fire provocations, they never have the chance to fully *respond* to any of them. Thus, by the time the commercial break arrives, the spitballer will have voiced multiple memorable slogans, and none of them will appear to have been adequately challenged. To many in the viewing audience, the spitballer will appear uniquely reasonable, informed, collected, and decisive, while the interlocutors will seem scattered, irrational, flailing, and frantic. In the world of national politics, that's a considerable win for the spitballer.

As we have said, spitballing is understandably effective in formats where discussion is shoehorned into 12-minute segments in between commercial advertisements. But as spitballing trades in slogans, it brings correlate advantages as well. Slogans are intrinsically vague and suggestive, and they thereby admit of multiple interpretations. Accordingly, when a spitballer's pronouncement is subjected to critical analysis in, say, print media, the spitballer's response is simply to return to the confines of the television studio to denounce the interpretation of the slogan that was scrutinized. The denouncement begins with an indignant "what I *actually* said was …" and is followed with the introduction of a new slogan—hence a new provocation—which is no more precise or transparent than the original. Thus the process begins anew. All the while, the spitballer derails the discussion by ensuring that no one else actually gets to speak about anything other than the spitballs. And yet, as the spitballer trades only in vague but provocative slogans, there can be no real argument about his claims. Any attempt to examine a spitballer's pronouncements must proceed from an *interpretation* of what the spitballer's slogan *means*; but those slogans admit of no *definite* interpretation, so ultimately every examination falls short.

President Trump is an incorrigible spitballer. It is thus no surprise that his favored communications outlet is Twitter, a platform that permits only slogans. And his performance in longer-form interviews confirms our diagnosis. He is infrequently well-informed or temperate, but what he lacks in quality, he makes up for in sheer quantity. He is never at a loss for words, and he is a wellspring of slogans, many of which vaguely suggest underlying commitments that seem outrageous. Since entering the arena of national politics, he has accrued a substantial public record of claims which do not form a coherent set. And for the most part his critics are perpetually overwhelmed; they do not know where to start with substantive evaluation. Whenever a critic voices an objection to one of Trump's pronouncements, Trump indignantly protests that he has been willfully misrepresented and treated unfairly. Indeed, that's the central value of political slogans—they're moving targets. So, to cite only one familiar example, back in 2016, while he was still a presidential candidate, Trump called for a "temporary ban" that would "suspend immigration" from nations "tied to Islamic terror."[1] To this day there remains ambiguity about what, precisely, his view comes to. Unsurprisingly, it has shifted opportunistically. Sometimes the view seems to be that there should be a "total and complete shutdown of Muslims entering the United States" until "our country's representatives can figure out what is going on."[2] On other occasions, the proposal is that the United States should allow persons coming from Muslim countries entry only following "extraordinary screening."[3]

This deliberate imprecision makes Trump's proposal impossible to evaluate according to its feasibility, costs, and probable effectiveness. And those who have tried to assess the proposal along these metrics have been rebuffed by Trump representatives; again, any assessment must fix on some particular interpretation of the Trump slogan, but the entire spitballing strategy depends upon escaping precision so that every criticism can be instantly dismissed as a willful and unfair misrepresentation, thereby creating opportunities for introducing new slogans, which then draw critical responses that are again swiftly dismissed. Consequently, the spitballer controls the discussion by *derailing* any attempt to scrutinize what he has said; thus, in a very real sense, he always speaks unopposed and yet is perpetually the *subject of the discussion*. In this sense, spitballing is a *marketing technique* retooled as a simulation of argument.

Consider next a different, though related, technique that is also rampant in contemporary public political discussion. *Swamping* is a tactic for *controlling* public discourse. Like the spitballer, the swamper introduces into a discussion multiple pointed, self-contained, and overtly provocative statements. Yet the swamper's aim is not that of derailing the discourse by overloading his interlocutors; rather, he aims to *dominate* the political conversations conducted by others. The swamper's intention is to say something so overtly bizarre, outrageous, or inflammatory as to compel others to discuss what he said. In doing so, the swamper seeks not to deflect criticism, but rather to direct political discussion away from the ideas, proposals, policies, and platform of his political competition. As a consequence, the swamper places himself at the center of the conversation, forcing every other topic to the periphery. One important motive for swamping is that, in making oneself the topic of conversation by being overtly either vague or controversial, one crowds out time for critical exchange about other issues. Where news reporting is tightly constrained by the need for regular advertising breaks, the successful swamper effectively controls the news by forcing reporters and journalists to focus attention on deciphering what he said. Competing interests, stories, and events are thereby swamped, crowded out of view.

We said above that President Trump is a perpetual spitballer. He is also an inveterate swamper. The swamping tactic, after all, is largely responsible for his securing the Republican nomination and his eventual electoral success. During the GOP debates, for example, the pattern was recurrent and blatant: Trump would say something disgraceful about one of his competitors (or his critics, or a journalist, or a private citizen), and then the political discussion in the days following was nearly entirely devoted to discussion of Trump's ridiculous pronouncement. For example, in 2015, when Carly Fiorina (former CEO of Hewlett Packard) was leading in the polls for the Republican nomination for the 2016 Presidential, Trump said of Fiorina in an interview with a *Rolling Stone* reporter, "Look at that face ... Would anyone vote for that?"[4] Significant time and bandwith was then devoted to discussion of Trump's disparaging remarks about the appearance of one of his Republican rivals. And Trump's response to criticism of the remark was to backpedal; he claimed to have been talking about Fiorina's "persona" rather than her "look."[5] To be sure, the discussion stimulated by even his silliest remarks contains a good deal of cogent criticism of Trump. But it's important to note that any time that was devoted to criticizing Trump's statements was time *not* spent on discussing the ideas of Trump's competition for the Republican nomination. Arguably, Trump won the GOP nomination by winning a war of attrition; many of the others who had been seeking the Republican nomination simply could not get their message out to the relevant public. Trump's swamping effectively drowned them out.

Since ascending to the presidency, Trump's deployment of the swamping tactic has not abated. The president's favored avenue for public communication remains his Twitter account, and his posts most often feature cryptic and ambiguous pronouncements. This in turn compels journalists around the world to report on Trump's latest tweet, even if only to note its ambiguity. In this connection, consider Trump's early morning tweet on

May 31, 2017: "Despite the constant negative press covfefe." Almost immediately following the tweet, the nonsense word *covfefe* became the focus of television news programming for several days. Journalists asked the president's press secretary everything from what the tweet means, why Trump tweeted a nonsense word, what word he intended to use, and why the tweet was not deleted. Interestingly, the official responses were similarly enigmatic, culminating with a further tweet from President Trump: "Who can figure out the true meaning of 'covfefe'?? Enjoy!" [sic]. This then generated another round of news reportage.

This example raises a further feature of swamping. In order to be effective, the swamper must have a willing accomplice in the media and onlooking audiences. So even if a news outlet or commentator aims to critique the president's comment, the president still drives the news cycles and directs the voices of the journalists and pundits. Recall that it is the *job* of a journalist to report on the president's public pronouncements. Thus, once in a position of sufficient power, the swamper's tactic becomes especially effective. The swamper simply needs to utter something puzzling or inscrutable, and that sets for an entire profession the task of commenting, reporting, and discussing the utterance. Yet while the journalists, reporters, and commentators are busy focusing on the swamper's puzzling remark, they are thereby *not* discussing other news items. And, since the television news cycle is only so long, an effective swamper can cause the media to entirely overlook certain items by providing for them diversionary material to fixate on.

In this brief chapter, we have identified two argumentative tactics that have emerged in the midst of a media environment where substantive news items must be fit in between advertisement breaks, and where a premium is thereby placed on getting the last word in an exchange. The spitballer seeks to *derail* argument by overloading her interlocutors with multiple provocative slogans. The swamper, by contrast, seeks to *dominate* argument by setting himself, and his enigmatic pronouncements, up to be the sole topic of conversation.

What is to be done in the face of a political media environment that incentivizes swamping and spitballing? At least as an audience, we should try to avoid contributing to the phenomenon. Responding to controversial claims is always appropriate, but our attention must be directed also to the detailed and serious policy proposals, ideas about how to stimulate lagging economies, explanations for why domestic and international conflicts persist, and so on. Again, we, the onlooking public, contribute to the success of swamping and spitballing by devoting our attention and time to the swamper and the spitballer. Rewarding those who argue seriously and who try to communicate clearly with our attention is a significant step forward, but it also requires those who direct news stories and political discussions to focus on substantive issues, too.

But perhaps there is a further step that should be taken. Recall that swamping and spitballing thrive due to the constraints inherent in televised news media. As we have stressed throughout this chapter, when news is presented by means of televised argumentation among a panel of commentators, the discussants must jockey for the last word before the station cuts away for a commercial break. Perhaps, then, the real problem is the medium of commercial television itself. Maybe we should stop tuning in to televised new programming—especially of the kind that is found on 24-hour cable news channels—and turn to other sources, including radio and print. It is worth noting that data suggest that the degree to which one is misinformed about political matters is correlated not only with the *source* but also the *kind of medium* from which one mainly gets one's news. Those who get their news mainly from television tend to be *more* misinformed than those who get news mainly from print or radio sources.[6]

There is, of course, an irony to our recommendation. This chapter has *itself* been focused on the very tactics we are claiming ought to be ignored. In pointing out how swamping and spitballing strategies draw disproportionate attention away from other issues, we have been paying close attention to swamping and spitballing. This, of course, is testament to the power these strategies have over us, but this unavoidable inconsistency is endemic to any attempt to identify what one should spend less time thinking about. After all, the sensible advice, "don't dwell on the past" invites its own violation—we can't help but ask: what about the past are we not thinking about, now? In the same way that one can have well-wrought reasons for not liking impressionist painting or sushi only if one has had a good bit of experience with them and has attended to their details, so it is with swamping and spitballing. We must think about these phenomenon in order to identify why they unduly attract and maintain our attention. There are no perfect ways to break these spells, but seeing them as spells is a good start.

For Further Thought

1   It seems that steamrolling is the activity of the argumentative bully, but are there occasions where it is better to try to make sure the other side can't get their view out at all? Is it sometimes better just to talk over someone? Is this a version of Simple Truths?
2   Is spitballing always vicious? Could it be, also, the expression of an active and ambitious mind? How could one distinguish between virtuous and vicious cases of spitballing?
3   Swamping is a strategy for staying at the center of attention, but can it (perhaps like steamrolling) backfire? Are there cases in the public sphere where this has happened?

Key Terms

Steamrolling   Getting the last word in a critical exchange by talking over one's interlocutors.

11 Language, Spin, and Framing

Do you ever get the feeling that every piece of information about contemporary politics that you get is just spin? Do you suspect when watching an interview with a politician that the interview is only an occasion for the politician to get the pre-approved talking points out? Does political reporting on television and in print sometimes seem to you no different in kind from advertising? Do political debates strike you as dances among people with differing opinions that have been carefully choreographed to avoid any actual *contact* among the participants? More generally, do you sometimes wonder if people on opposite sides of the issues are really just speaking different languages—that it's all English only on the surface, but in fact two totally different systems of meaning underneath? We, the authors, have these thoughts all the time. So did George Orwell. In his deeply insightful essay, "Politics and the English Language," Orwell highlights these concerns, and he tries to combat the phenomena we catalogued above. He observed:

> In our time, political speech and writing are largely the defense of the indefensible. ... Thus, political language has to consist largely of euphemism, question-begging and sheer cloudy vagueness.

If it is correct about political speech, Orwell's observation has chilling consequences. In this book, we have been focused on political argument, and arguments are expressed, evaluated, and conducted by means of language. Now ask Orwell's question: What if the language we use to discuss politics makes fair argument impossible? What if, by using certain special words, by never stating what's really at issue, by deploying only compelling phrases, we make political speech impervious to real argument? What if there's no logic or reason in politics, but only vagueness, evasion, flattery, and spin?

To start, *spin* is a biased interpretation of an event or fact, one that is presented in a way that manipulates its audience's opinion of it. So euphemism masks errors, dysphemism highlights them, damning details are glossed over or given prime place, and the focus of critical attention is shifted to one's opponent. A handful of commentators on the contemporary scene have accepted Orwell's view that politics and political discussion is more a battle of spin than rational consideration. They depart from Orwell, however, in thinking that this fact about current political discussion is lamentable. In their view, the fact that contemporary political discussion is really just a fancy kind of advertising is nothing objectionable. You might be tempted to call these folks *cynics*, but, well, that would be to play their game. Giving them a name that already puts them at a disadvantage because of its negative connotations is itself an act of spin, you see. Specifically, this would be to employ a *dysphemism*, which is *euphemism's* evil twin. Dysphemism and euphemism are two of the main tactics, actually, of those who think that argument doesn't matter, but only packaging counts.

Let's not play their game, at least not just yet. Instead, let's call those who hold this view the *realists*, which is a term they themselves like to employ to describe their own views. The realist takes on the perspectives which do not paper over the gritty realities of our political lives. They decisively reject the ideals of reason and rationality in political debate. They will find nearly everything we have written in this book objectionably naïve, idealistic, out of touch, and therefore silly. We all bring our biases to the game of debate, and really the objective isn't to get over our biases, but for our biases to be shown to be right. It's about winning. Okay, so that's realism.

Realists recognize that not everything, if not nothing, happens perfectly. They recognize that the real world of democratic politics is nasty, dirty, and often ruthless. In fact, realists hold that vanishingly little goes even well. Realists admit that sometimes (and perhaps very often), the irrational side of our nature wins. Realists acknowledge the ugly truths about politics, again, that spin and rhetoric are what wins. And they hold that when one plays the game of politics, one must be out to win. So be it, they say.

Our plan for this chapter is to engage with two arch-realists about political discussion: the conservative realist Frank Luntz, and the liberal-progressive realist George Lakoff. Here's what we aim to show: *You can't consistently be both a realist about political argument and loyal proponent of your own political point of view.* To put the thesis in slightly different terms: *It is impossible to think that your own political views are correct when you also think that all political views are the result of manipulation, spin, and propaganda.* So every consistent realist must, in the end, be committed to the value of proper argument, at least with respect to his or her own views. And so, the question looms for the realist: Why isn't that value extended to others and their political views, too? Consistent realism, if it's maintained in the face of this challenge, is revealed to be deeply anti-democratic, and further, it is inconsistent with itself if it is taken as a manner of supporting any substantive view. Realism isn't just bad for democratic politics, then. It's also self-refuting.

Frank Luntz was one of the architects of the 1994 Republican revolution, which gave the Republican Party in the United States control of the House of Representatives for the first time in over 40 years. He helped draft Newt Gingrich's *Contract with America,* and he remains an influential public relations strategist for political parties and various corporations. He heads a polling firm fittingly called The Word Doctors, which helps to craft campaigns with exactly the right messages and slogans. He is a self-described "political and commercial wordsmith" (2007: xi), and his advice is posited on the thought that "every human interaction is an opportunity to connect, and then to sell" (2011: 5).

Luntz's books, *Words that Work* (2007), *What Americans Really Want … Really* (2009), and *Win* (2011), all have the same theme: *If you can say the right words in the right way at the right time, you can get what you want.* Not all of Luntz's suggestions are focused on political strategy, but all of his advice is nonetheless strategic. He offers suggestions about how to apologize effectively, how to get out of a speeding ticket, and even how to get onto an airplane after the cabin door has been closed. He has thoroughly researched the words that are most effective to say when you want something from someone or when someone wants something from you. Luntz describes his project as follows:

> I have built a company and a career by finding the *exact* word for my clients to create the *exact* context and therefore provoke the *exact* response they want.
>
> (2007: 46)

Luntz observes that "ad copy is conquering more and more of our brains' territory." More people can recognize a McDonald's jingle than can name the framers of the Constitution. It is easier to recall what "Snap, Crackle, Pop" is about than any reference to Shakespeare or Homer. Luntz proposes to apply this model to political messaging:

> Almost every Presidential debate is won or lost not on substance or even style, but on a single phrase that catches the public's ear and is replayed again and again.
>
> (2007: 125)

This point is then generalized to the political issues of the day. Are you against the *estate tax*? Simply re-name it the *death tax*. Calling the policy the *estate* tax evokes an estate: a house and largesse of wealth. People have no problems taxing an estate—better to tax the wealthy than those in poverty, as that's where the money is, after all. But once the policy is branded as the *death* tax, the association with grand estates no longer obtains, and it seems suddenly that the proposed policy attempts to tax only some people for something that happens to everyone, namely, death.

But it's not right to tax only some for something that happens to everybody. Thus the lesson: The same policy can elicit different reactions from people, depending solely on the name or description attached to it.

Consider a few other examples. Casino owners should endeavor to change *gambling* to *gaming*. Bar owners and the producers of alcoholic beverages should use the term *spirits* rather than *liquor*. Wall Street brokers should speak of *free markets* instead of *capitalism*. Those who seek to dismantle New Deal social programs should talk about *personalizing* Social Security rather than *privatizing* it. And when talking about spending programs they oppose, politicians should call them *pork-barrel programs*, rather than *ear-marked* or *set-aside* spending. Luntz's general lesson, again, is that "those who define the debate will determine the outcome" (2007: 170).

Luntz's books are all about how to convince *others* that you are right, that they should adopt your views or do as you tell them. The question, however, is whether one can take Luntz's advice all the way home. Can one adopt Luntz's view that it's all just clever marketing in the case of one's own views? Perhaps you can convince *others* to adopt your view by employing clever rhetorical techniques, but can you *convince yourself* with what you know is a purely strategic linguistic maneuver? Put most starkly: Can one advertise to oneself?

Surely it would seem strange to turn the tools of wordsmithing on oneself. It is clear that when we support a political policy or view, we take it that we have not been sold on it strictly by its slick marketing; rather, when we adopt a political view, we take it that the view in question best serves justice or the common good. Luntz, by the way, anticipates this point, too:

> Sure, I seek to persuade. My goal is to fashion political rhetoric that achieves *worthy goals*—to level the linguistic playing field and to inform Americans of *what is truly at stake* in our policy debates.
>
> (2007: xviii)

But here we must press the questions of what constitutes a *worthy goal*, and what makes something *truly at stake* in a debate. These are especially salient, since all of Luntz's attention seems explicitly aimed at developing tactics that are designed to make something *appear* better or worse depending on the language that is used to describe it. Luntz is clearly committed to the values and ideals he works on behalf of and provides rhetorical ammunition for, but he never explains what makes those values actually good or even better than those he tries to undermine with his rhetorical strategies. He cannot hold that his views are the right ones simply because the rhetoric favors them. Rather Luntz must hold that his rhetoric should favor the views he thinks are right. But that is to admit that the rightness or wrongness of a view depends upon something other than the way it is described. Yet Luntz's entire ad-man program is premised on the thought that only the descriptions count in deciding what views to adopt.

On this score, Luntz pauses to note that "actual policy counts at least as much as how something is framed" (2007: 3). Shouldn't what makes the policy correct be part of the case for it? Shouldn't the truth about what's at stake in our discussion play a role in clarifying what's at stake? Shouldn't what makes our goals worthy be what we appeal to when we make our cases in defense of them? Of course, the answer to all these questions should be "yes," and Luntz sees that. He knows that the techniques of rhetoric can only be directed outward, toward others you wish to convince; they cannot work when turned inward, toward one's own attempts to figure out what views to adopt. You can't *knowingly* pull the wool over your own eyes.

Consequently, when figuring out what kinds of views you would wish to use rhetoric to defend and promote, you can't use rhetoric. You must use your reason. You must look for the best arguments. The problem for Luntz's position, then, is that of explaining why one should use *rhetoric* when trying to persuade others when one already has *arguments* that favor one's views? If you take it that reason is on the side of your views, why should empty marketing techniques be appealing at all?

The realist's answer is that rhetoric is effective, while argument, for the most part, is not. But this answer betrays an objectionable attitude. Recall in our first chapter our discussion of the aims of argument. When we argue, we aim not merely to gain the agreement of others; we aim also to win their assent *for the right reasons*. Effective argument, when it is successful, brings others to not only *say* what we believe, but to *believe* what we believe, and, crucially, to *see* the rational basis for believing as we do. Luntz's marketing techniques aim at something different. The effectiveness of rhetoric consists simply in its getting people to adopt the views you want them to adopt; it has nothing to do with the rational evaluation of the reasons that can support a belief. When we argue, we have to address objections, consider new data, and respond to people with questions and concerns. Of course, that's messy and time-consuming. With rhetoric, however, none of this matters. When rhetoric is successfully deployed, everybody simply nods their heads, and we're done.

But notice something. The reason why argument is perceived to be ineffective by those who, like Luntz, engage in rhetoric, is that the people addressed by argument are encouraged to express themselves, ask for clarifications, raise objections, and, generally, give and receive reasons. And if they aren't satisfied by our arguments and reasons, we all must go on arguing. That makes argument inefficient in a certain sense; it often takes a long time to get arguers to come to agreement. But argument aims at something beyond efficiency. When people do come to agree by means of argument, they hold their beliefs on their own terms and for reasons they recognize as good ones. Contrast this with the merely rhetorical strategies endorsed by Luntz. By means of rhetorical marketing techniques, we may be able to secure agreement quickly, but the agreement comes at the cost of having no real dialogue about the reasons that support our views. On Luntz's model, the naming does all the work. But that's not the kind of reason that people can reflectively see as good reason for belief. Again, imagine someone claiming that they vehemently support President Obama's re-election because they like the way his name rolls off the tongue. Or that they are against *pork-barrel spending*, because that just sounds like a bad thing. You'd be right to say that this is the wrong kind of reason for supporting a political candidate or policy.

But now consider a further feature of the result-side look at rhetoric and argument. If a person's views are in place only because of a catchy phrase, then all it takes is another catchy phrase to undo the commitment. Arguments aren't like that, since if the belief is the result of arguments, with considerations, counter-considerations, and all the reflection argument entails, then the beliefs will be considerably more stable in the face of a good deal of feedback. This, by the way, is exactly what we rely on when we can acknowledge that the other side has good rhetoric but a bad argument. That is, presumably, you've likely had the experience of having someone massively wrong on an issue nevertheless turn a good phrase or put things in a way that you say to yourself, "that person just put her view quite nicely there, but she's still wrong." Without the difference between rhetoric and reasons, that thought couldn't be possible.

Now, one can of course concede to Luntz that many people do in fact hold beliefs on the basis of considerations that are irrelevant to their truth or falsity. Perhaps citizens frequently choose how to vote on the basis of considerations owing strictly to the ways in which candidates are marketed with inspirational slogans, glossy images, and slick catch phrases. One needn't deny this in order to criticize the realist's manipulative turn on the matter. In fact, books like *Why We Argue* (the one you're reading now) or most any other book about critical thinking wouldn't make much sense if Luntz's observation weren't right on this issue. The point we have been pressing is that when one adopts Luntz's realist view about argument generally, one must come to see one's fellow citizens as merely objects of manipulation, forces to be swayed one way or another, things to be moved around like pawns on a chessboard. One can no longer see one's fellow citizens as equal participants in a collective project of self-government. Luntz's form of realism is deeply anti-democratic.

A similar form of realism has surfaced recently on the liberal-progressive side of contemporary politics. In fact, a version of the view that all political thought is strictly spin has been elevated to the level of a philosophical theory in the work of cognitive scientist turned political strategist George Lakoff (2002; 2004; 2006; 2008). Lakoff begins from the observation that

Contemporary American politics is about worldview. Conservatives simply see the world differently than do liberals, and both often have a difficult time understanding accurately what the other's worldview is.

(2002: 3)

According to Lakoff, this difficulty derives from the fact that our world-views, and thus the language we use to formulate our political opinions, are couched in conceptually thick systems of meaning and metaphor. Accordingly, although liberals and conservatives may employ the same *terms* to articulate their views, the *meanings* of those terms differ so greatly that liberals and conservatives are in essence speaking different political languages. Consequently, they do not even disagree about anything; they simply and inevitably talk past each other. Argument in the sense we have been discussing in this book is not possible among political opponents.

One might presume that the difficulty each side has in understanding the other's worldview is the problem to be overcome by a cognitive-scientific analysis of political discourse. But this is not the case according to Lak-off's analysis. The trouble, as Lakoff sees it, is that the conservative worldview dominates contemporary American politics. This means that the conservative system of meanings and metaphors "frames" the policy debates in American society. To use one of Lakoff's more nifty examples, consider that policies that cut taxes are popularly characterized as "tax *relief*" (2004: 23). He notes that the very notion of *relief* already presumes the conservatives' *moral* conclusion that taxes are a *burden* that should be lifted. The trouble is that once the public policy debate concerning taxes is framed in such terms, the liberal position is at a loss, for liberals are stuck with the ungainly task of arguing that *relief* is something to oppose. In this way, "progressives have ceded the political mind to radical conservatives" (2008: 2).

Lakoff's advice to liberals is to invent and promulgate their own frames, ones that embed decidedly liberal values and policies (2006: 245ff.). That is, according to Lakoff, the lesson to be learned is that the liberal and con-servative positions are "impossible to compare because they presuppose opposite moral systems" (2002: 385). He continues,

There are no neutral concepts and no neutral language for expressing political positions within a moral context. Conservatives have devel-oped their own partisan moral-political concepts and moral-political language. Liberals have not.

(2002: 385)

Lakoff suggests that "the best thing that can be done for the sake of a balanced discourse is to develop a new language—a language about the concepts and language used in morality and politics" (2002: 385). Else-where, he emphasizes the need to reach a "higher rationality" that is able "to step outside of our own political beliefs and to see how moral and political reasoning works for both ourselves and others" (2006: 15). He calls this set of views "The New Enlightenment" (2008: 245).

The problem with these suggestions should by now be familiar. It is not clear why Lakoff should presume that such a new language would be itself "neutral"; surely, if his view about language in general is correct, a second-order language *about* the language of moral and politics should be subject to the same ideological influences as any first-order worldview. Similarly, a "higher" rationality or "new" Enlightenment would be subject to all the same framing effects and metaphorical influences of the *lower* rationality and *old* Enlightenment view we typically employ and hence could not "step outside" of it. That is, any attempted new language (or "higher rationality" or "New Enlightenment") will be subject to the same analysis that Lakoff has developed of our first-order moral and political language. If Lakoff's right, we're stuck with framing. Indeed, it's frames all the way down.

Hence one can easily develop a Lakoffian critique of Lakoff's proposed new language. Lakoff characterizes the conservative–liberal divide in terms of two moral systems. According to Lakoff, conservatives subscribe to a "strict father morality," and liberals hold a "nurturant parent morality" (2002: 33f.; 2006: chs. 5 and 6). Surely a critic would be right to point out that these characterizations are themselves not value-neutral and are therefore objectionable on the same grounds that Lakoff criticized the conservative framing of tax burdens earlier. A conservative critic will object to the association of conservative politics with a moral vision that is based in a decidedly male role. According to the conservative, this image is objectionable because it embeds into a purported description the normative judgment—a popular one among liberals—that conservatism is chauvinistic, misogynistic, or the politics of the "old boys club."

To be clear, our point is not to dispute Lakoff's characterization of the moral tendencies driving conservatism. We honestly take no view on the matter. Rather we are suggesting that if one accepts Lakoff's claim that "There are no neutral concepts and no neutral language for expressing political positions within a moral context" (2002: 385), there is positive reason to extend that same analysis to the concepts employed in the new language he proposes. To employ Lakoff's own language, *he has simply proposed a new frame within which to describe two influential ways of thinking about politics.* However, since, according to Lakoff, there is no "neutral language for expressing political positions within a moral context" (2002: 385), there are no descriptions that are not also prescriptions. That is, on Lakoff's view, all purported descriptions embed normative judgments about the things described. Hence the entire framework of the "strict father" and the "nurturant parent" embeds the moral judgment that the conservative moral system is antiquated, paternalistic, male-oriented, anti-egalitarian, oppressive, and authoritarian, while the liberal morality is supportive, liberating, egalitarian, loving, encouraging, and caring. This is a description that no conservative would embrace.

Amazingly, this is precisely the point of Lakoff's analysis! Recall, as we mentioned above, that the salient implication of Lakoff's view is that honest and sincere debate between liberals and conservatives is impossible (Lakoff 2002: 385). On Lakoff's view, since moral and political terms are themselves deeply embedded in the more general liberal and conservative worldviews, there can be no rational give-and-take among the contending parties; indeed, he claims that liberals and conservatives employ "two very different forms of reason" (2006: 15). Hence, his advice to liberals is to create a "moral discourse to counter conservatives"; in order to do this, liberals must "get over their view" that "straightforward rational literal debate on an issue is always possible" (2002: 387; cf. 2006: 255). The implication is, again, that liberals and conservatives *need not* engage each other, because they frankly *cannot*.

Apply this line of Lakoff's analysis to the 2016 election. President Trump ran as a candidate who was the paradigm of the strict father model for government. And this involved him perpetually asserting that the world is increasingly dangerous, but he alone could adequately protect the country. Trump also regularly affirmed that the U.S. government is overrun with lazy and dishonest people who deserve overt scorn, and that we as a country need discipline and internal strength. Thus Trump was able to insult his way to the top of the Republican ticket. He played up his love of the military, how much he loves confrontation, how weak his opponents are, and what an excellent and decisive businessman he is. As Lakoff notes,

> In the strict father family, father knows best. He knows right from wrong and has the ultimate authority to make sure his children and spouse do what he says, which is taken to be right.
>
> (2016)

It's the displays of strength and the actions of claiming power and authority that make it so that those who hold this model of politics think that Trump is right. The details of a policy argument don't matter when it's all messy give-and-take of namby-pamby eggheads getting in the weeds on an issue. Someone needs to take charge and make a decision. Lakoff laments this in the midst of the 2016 election, and in particular, how it bears on Hillary Clinton's reception by those committed to the conservative frame for politics.

> This is the basic Clinton argument. Hillary has all the experience, policy know-how, she can get things done. It's on her website. And it's irrelevant. Because Trump supporters [...] could not care less, and for good reason. Their job is to impose their strict father morality in all areas of life.
>
> (2016)

Of course, if there's no room for real argument, only a clash of frames, then the contrary is exactly what the Trump supporters say of Clinton—that she and her campaign did not reply to their ideas, but only wished to impose their progressive, globalist, identity-based politics on them.

Accordingly, Lakoff's discussion about "how to take back public discourse" (2004: ch. 1) contains no examination of the respective merits of liberal and conservative arguments or positions; it instead presents a strategy for replacing the conservative frame for a liberal one. More importantly, the moral question of the worth of characteristically liberal policy initiatives, as compared with conservative alternatives, lies beyond the scope of possible debate. Similarly, the question of why one should be a liberal rather than a conservative is rendered nonsensical. In the end, then, Lakoff is offering a strategy by which progressive ideals can come to dominate American politics, but the strategy requires relinquishing the belief that those very ideals are worth striving for. For Lakoff, as for Luntz, it's not about being right, it's just about winning.

Democratic politics is, on Lakoff's realist view, simply a matter of two worldviews competing for dominance. The "higher rationality" and "New Enlightenment" he calls for are purely tools designed to identify effective strategies for persuading people to adopt your views. Yet Lakoff's view proceeds from a theory of moral commitment which precludes the task of giving an account of why one's worldview is morally better than any other. Indeed, Lakoff's view altogether denies the possibility of moral reasoning in the face of moral disagreement. That is, on Lakoff's view, democracy can be nothing more than an ongoing propaganda contest among incommensurate and hostile moral standpoints. In this way, Lakoff's view suffers from the same defects that we identified with Luntz's.

Let us press the two points here very clearly. First, Lakoff's view is deeply incoherent. Surely he thinks that the liberal-progressive commitments are morally superior to the competing conservative commitments. Yet he also thinks that the two represent incommensurable and self-enclosed worldviews that allow for no external standpoint from which one can evaluate their respective merits. In other words, on Lakoff's view there is no reason, only frames. One of the consequences is Lakoff's procedural suggestion that "framing precedes policy" (2008: 115). Thus the central question that we put to Luntz now must be pressed against Lakoff. Can one adopt Lakoff's stance in the case of one's own political beliefs? Can one recognize that one's own beliefs are merely the products of effective framing strategies, and yet still remain committed to them? Recall, once again, that on Lakoff's view, it's framing all the way down. So why, then, does Lakoff think that the liberal and progressive agenda is on the right track? Why does he even think that it matters whether liberal-progressive policies are enacted? What reason does he have to be a progressive rather than a conservative? In the end, all he can say is that his brain is simply wired to jibe with the progressive agenda rather than the conservative one.

That, again, seems like the wrong kind of reason for holding political beliefs. It may explain why he has his beliefs, but it neither justifies him holding them nor does it show that they are right.

The second point we need to make is about the political consequences of Lakoff's program. Specifically, we want to highlight its antidemocratic implications. Just as we saw with Luntz's view, the Lakoff view requires one to take a very dim view of one's fellow democratic citizens. In order to adopt the practice of framing rather than arguing for your views, one must see one's fellows as something less than partners in self-government by means of reasons. Instead, one must come to see one's fellow citizens as consumers of advertising, nearly mindless objects toward which marketing campaigns are directed, things to be pushed around with well-crafted frames. Lakoff pictures voters as follows:

> They vote against their obvious self-interest; they allow bias, prejudice, and emotion to guide their decisions; they argue madly about values, priorities and goals. Or they quietly reach conclusions independent of their interests without consciously knowing why.
>
> (2008: 8)

Lakoff then turns this realistic view of the voter into advice about how to get the mindless citizen to vote your way. He advises political operatives to endeavor to channel citizens' emotions and unconscious cognitive machinery toward action that produces the operatives' desired political results. Given that most of it will be unconscious, they won't even know what hit them.

Or maybe they would. Lakoff does consider the consequences of making the fact of framing public and explicit. That is, he considers the possibility that if everything is indeed framing designed to fit with the way your brain works, then it likely doesn't matter if it is generally known that what politicians are doing when they appear to be arguing is merely spinning. In fact, Lakoff suggests that the overt adoption of his views may have the effect of making democratic politics more refreshing and open. Lakoff says:

> The framing of issues in public debate would be a matter of public discussion. ... Policymakers would become aware of the moral basis of their policies and would be expected to specify that moral basis explicitly.
>
> (2008: 269)

But this view seems odd in light of Lakoff's overall position. If, as Lakoff contends, all there is to cognitive life is frames, then what could it mean to specify the moral basis for a particular frame? Such a proposed basis would simply be yet another frame. And that means that there's really no basis, only more and more framing. What, then, would public discussion of the kind Lakoff envisions look like? It would simply be an ongoing competition between different frames. And if, as Lakoff's view holds, proponents of different frames are really speaking different languages, with no frame-neutral standpoint from which to assess the relative merits of different frames, then there's really no political argument to be had. Again, it's all just marketing and spin.

Let us conclude this chapter by pressing our main point once more. The problem with the realism represented by Luntz and Lakoff is not simply that it requires us to take an unhappy view of our fellow democratic citizens. To be clear, we think it does require this of us, and we think it is objectionable. If only because, when they take that view of their fellow citizens, they take that view *of us*. And they must take that view *of you, too*. But that's not our primary objection to realism. Our central criticism is that realism encourages us to take a view of others' beliefs that one cannot plausibly apply to one's own beliefs. When one believes that the death penalty is unjust, one must take oneself to be properly responsive to the reasons relevant to determining the justice of the death penalty. As we said in our first chapter, when we believe, we take ourselves to be properly responding to our reasons, and it is by responding to our reasons that we pursue the cognitive goal of believing the true and rejecting the false. The realist views we have surveyed here reject this view of cognitive life. Luntz takes the view that it is naïve to think that people seek to manage their beliefs rationally. But Lakoff takes things further; he claims that it is a matter of fact about cognition that it's frames all the way down. This strikes us as incoherent. If indeed it is frames all the way down, then there's no way for Lakoff to coherently appeal to such things as *facts about cognition*. If Lakoff is correct, then there are no such facts, and his entire enterprise is simply another advertising campaign, destined to attract the favor of a certain demographic while leaving others utterly unaffected. But it is clear from the content of Lakoff's books that he takes himself to be reporting the truth about cognition, language, and politics, too. He claims for himself (and perhaps himself alone) a standpoint from which he can assess what's really going on in the political world. But the view he professes is officially committed to denying that there could be anything even remotely like "what's really going on"; and so, in the end there could be no position from which Lakoff could deliver what he promises, namely a well-reasoned, thoroughly researched, and objective sound assessment of how the political mind functions. In short, unless he takes himself to stand outside the system of frames and worldviews, all he can offer is just another set of political commercials, not cognitive-scientific theories.

So the realist view must at some point declare for itself the kind of rational and evidence-based status that it denies to every other view, and the realists themselves must claim of themselves that they're not simply selling a political product, but engaging in research and uncovering reasons and arguments concerning how best to sell a product. In doing so, realists unwittingly commit to the claim that argument in the sense we have been discussing in this book is possible and important. They simply deny that *you* are smart enough to engage in it. That strikes us as unacceptable. The issue of who is able to engage in argument is to be settled not by the pronouncements of self-appointed elites and professional political pitch-men, but by the processes of actually trying to engage in properly run, logical, old-fashioned argument.

For Further Thought

1   Could Luntz and Lakoff simply accept everything presented in this book, but then describe it merely as the preferred frame of two academic philosophers? More generally, couldn't *every* objection to Luntz and Lakoff be re-described by them as only one more frame? Does this count in favor of their views?

2   Imagine a confrontation between Luntz and Lakoff. How would that go? Could either describe the other as a *critic* of his own view?

3   Realism begins from the idea that, when it comes to politics, abstract intellectualizing is at best a waste of time and at worst a dangerous distraction. Suppose that the conception of argument that we have been developing in this book proves to be unrealistic in some way. Assume, for example, that it simply demands too much of people. What would this prove? Does the fact that in general people cannot argue properly (assuming for the moment that this is a fact) show that people ought not try to argue properly?

4   It seems right that a good explanation for ongoing and seemingly interminable debate is that the two (or more) sides have framed things differently. But in what way is this explanation a way forward for rationally resolving the disagreement?

5   Is the framing debate another instance of deep disagreement?

6   Does the argument of this chapter entail that self-deception is impossible? Is that a problem?

Key Terms

Spin	The presentation of an interpretation of events that is meant to persuade or manipulate its audience to particular evaluative judgments. Biased retelling of a story meant to bolster the bias.
Framing	Situating a detail of an event or feature of a fact in a larger narrative or context, wherein one knows what further inferences to make or practical consequences to follow.
Argumentative realism	Argument is either ineffective in debate or is a frame by

which one manipulates one's audience. One should frame first, argue later.

References

Lakoff, George (2002) *Moral Politics*. Chicago: University of Chicago Press.
Lakoff, George (2004) *Don't Think of a Pink Elephant!*White River Junction, VT: Chelsea Green Publishing.
Lakoff, George (2006) *Whose Freedom?*New York: Farr, Straus, and Giroux.
Lakoff, George (2008) *The Political Mind*. New York: Penguin Books.
Lakoff, George (2016) *Understanding Trump*. Chicago: University of Chicago Press.
Luntz, Frank (2007) *Words that Work*. New York: Hyperion Books.
Luntz, Frank (2009) *What Americans Really Want … Really*. New York: Hyperion Books.
Luntz, Frank (2011) *Win*. New York: Hyperion Books.

12 Argument Online

Thus far we have been focused mainly on argument between persons in face-to-face settings. Even though many of our examples have drawn from formal material like opinion pages, televised panel discussions, political speeches, and newspaper articles, the emphasis has always been on argumentative exchanges between individuals in real time or in well-regulated contexts. But there is another world of argument that occurs online, specifically on web-pages, in blog entries, Twitter exchanges, and on comment threads. In fact, there are a number of argumentative phenomena that are peculiar to the kind of communication made possible by the Internet. Given that online political communication is now pervasive, it is no surprise that there has emerged a rough-and-ready conceptual vocabulary for identifying and discussing various kinds of pathologies that are specific to online argumentation. Our treatment of argument would be incomplete without an analysis of some of these phenomena. Here, we address three of the most prevalent of these pathologies: over-the-top parody (Poe's Law), comparison to Nazism (Godwin's Law), and comment-thread trolling. That two of them have come to be known as *laws* is, of course, suggestive. We will then turn to a particular phenomenon of objection-swamping, called the Gish gallop, and the regular reply of *TL;DR* as standing in the way of productive argument.

Invoking Poe's Law is a mainstay of discussion of religion on the Web. Poe's Law states roughly that online parodies of religious views are indistinguishable from sincere expressions of religious views. Nathan Poe is widely credited for formulating the law in an entry on a Christianforms. com chat page regarding creationism:

> Without a winking smiley or other blatant display of humor, it is utterly impossible to parody a Creationist in such a way that *someone* won't mistake [it] for the genuine article.[1]

This is to say that unless there are unmistakable cues that one is being ironic or sarcastic, many parodies are not only likely to be interpreted as earnest contributions, they will, in fact, be identical in content to sincere expressions of the view.

The website LandoverBaptist.com has had headlines that run from the goofy ("What Can Christians Do to Help Increase Global Warming?" and "New Evidence Suggests Noah's Sons Rode Flying Dinosaurs") to the chilling ("Satan Calls Another Pope to Hell") and offensive ("Trade Us Your Voter's Registration Card for Free Fried Chicken from Popeye's"). The site is designed to parody the racism, scientific illiteracy, and religious bigotry widely attributed to American fundamentalist and evangelical Christians.

But the site's posted mail hardly reflects public awareness that the site is parodic. Most email responses begin by chastising the site's authors for not knowing the true meaning of Christianity, for having misinterpreted some quoted Bible passage, or for being hypocrites about some point of contention. Very little of the posted mail actually confronts the owners and writers at Landover with what they are actually doing: presenting a grotesque, overblown, and bombastic parody of Christian religious life. LandoverBaptist.com's mail bag has entries from its first days, and there has been a consistent failure on behalf of the writing public to determine that the site is a parody.

Parody is an interesting phenomenon in itself. Crucial to the success of a parody is that it must be received by its intended audience as humorous (or at least an attempt at humor), and in a particular fashion. The humor of a parody is usually found in hyperbolizing a distinctive and objectionable feature of that which is parodied. When a parody succeeds, it occasions a critical assessment of that which is parodied. The humor employed in parody is often dark; the parody presents an exaggerated or extreme version of some tendency or feature (allegedly) lying just beneath the surface of its target.

LandoverBaptist.com is exemplary in this regard. Pastor Deacon Fred insists that he "cannot wait to see people burn in Hell" and that modern Christianity is on an unfortunate track of "sissification," because there are no longer holy wars. Regarding science, Pastor Deacon Fred holds that "being familiar with the Holy Bible gives you more authority than anyone who holds a post-graduate degree!" Thus he reasons that, given the contents of the book of Revelation, we should have no concern for global warming:

> Why should we give a lick if our thermometers are edging up a bit, when the Lord promised he is going to turn the whole planet into a fireball any minute now?[2]

It turns out those at LandoverBaptist.com can be both global warming deniers and downplayers. This is parody, and it is extreme, indeed.

Again, the humor and point of this kind of parody is to present religious bigotry and scientific illiteracy in a fashion that exaggerates it and thereby highlights its vice. The question, though, is how exaggerated the parody actually is. Even the most casual websurfing yields similar, if not more shocking, scientific illiteracy and religious bigotry among actual Christian sects. At freesundayschoollessons.org, global warming is refuted by God's promise in Genesis 8:22 that the climate will never change.[3] Republican U.S. Representative John Shimkus of Illinois explicitly denied global warming on the basis of his literal interpretation of the same Biblical passage, saying: "The Earth will end only when God declares it's time to be over."[4] Ann Coulter famously insisted in her *National Review Online* opinion that once the United States has investigated the 9/11 hijackers, "we should invade their countries, kill their leaders, and convert them to Christianity."[5] Fred Phelps of the Westboro Baptist Church and his followers have been protesting at soldiers' funerals and posting videos of the protests at godhatesfags. com. A header for one reads, for example:

> These soldiers are dying form [sic.] the homosexual and other sins of America. God is now our enemy, and God Himself is fighting against America.[6]

Phelps preaches that because the United States tolerates the sin of homosexuality, God justly punished the country with the 9/11 attacks. Hence his followers display placards that read "Thank God for 9/11."[7] This is *not* parody, and it is extreme, indeed. Hence Poe's Law.

Without the cues that the parodies are parodies and with equally extreme material available on the Web, the casual websurfer is in a unique cognitive position. That is, from the perspective of an informal websearch, it seems that for any parody page with extreme and shocking content, there is at least one non-parodic page with equally (or more) extreme and shocking content. Given that parodies can be distinguished from that which they parody by either overt cues or hyperbolic content, there are no positive reasons to ever take parodic statements as parodic when the targets are all extreme. So if you stumble onto a webpage with shockingly extreme religious or political content, and if there are no overt cues of parody, you have no more reason to infer that the site is a parody than you have to take the site as sincere. Poe's Law entails that the fact that a site's authors express ideas that are heinous, irrational, or even buffoonish is not yet a reason to infer that the site is a joke, because for every parody there are equally extreme but non-parodic expressions on similar issues.

Suppose that Poe's Law is true. What follows? And what occurs when one affirms Poe's Law in the course of argument? It is clear that when one accepts Poe's Law or invokes it in critical discussion, one overtly makes an assessment of the quality of one's intellectual opponents, specifically, a judgment of their poor quality. If you accept Poe's Law, you hold that religious believers are indistinguishable from their parodies. This is a decidedly negative assessment of religious believers or at least a particular subset of them. Invoking the law, then, has consequences for argumentation. To be more specific, Poe's Law functions like other dialectical tactics that are aimed at overtly affirming negative evaluations of one's interlocutors.

Consider the straw man fallacy. In Chapter 6, we discussed the straw man as a variety of what we called *pushover arguments*. One commits the straw man fallacy when one takes an opponent's views and arguments, distorts them in ways that make them indefensible, refutes the distortion, and, finally, presents oneself as having refuted the opponent. One *constructs* a new, less defensible opponent and engages with that construction (the straw man) instead of one's real interlocutor. As we mentioned earlier, straw man arguments not only do our dialectical opponents a disservice, they do audiences for these exchanges a disservice, too. Audiences, unless they themselves are as knowledgeable as the parties to the argument, rely on the speakers to accurately represent the dialectical situation that pertains between those who are arguing. Straw-manning misinforms listeners with respect to the difficulties of the issue under discussion and the state of deliberation on it.

Cases in which Poe's Law is invoked are similar. On the one hand, the existence of parody sites seems vicious for the same reason why straw-manning is vicious—they not only fail to engage the other side in their refutations, but they populate the dialectical space with imaginary buffoons. Lampooning one's opponents with grotesque portrayals of their unrepentant intellectual and moral vice has real chances of distorting one's view of the dialectical situation. One comes to see oneself locked in battle with an opponent beyond reason and unredeemable. This is destructive of further positive contributions to resolving any disagreement between the sides, and, in fact, leads to fewer and fewer attempts at any cooperative communication.

Pause to consider how memes work on this front. The regular representation of a political opponent in a meme is of their least defensible, least sophisticated versions of their views. And so, social justice warriors are represented as college bohemians or destructive radicals with no care for culture or awareness of any consequence of their do-gooderism, and religious conservatives are represented as bumbling and credulous rubes. Usually, it's some hypocrisy or ignorance that's easily targeted. So a regular meme about social justice warriors is a white person's face with the text: "People of color are strong and have a voice. That's why I speak for them." Or a meme about conservatives has a son asking his father, "Dad, What's Science?" The father replies, "Son, we don't believe in Science. We're Republicans." The point, again, is that the way those with whom one disagrees are represented has an effect on how one will appreciate and thoughtfully reply to the things they say. Poe's Law and the phenomenon of meme-versions of pushovers are ways of representing the situation with political disagreement over matters that are complicated and conflicted. If one's view of the opposition is that they are no better than the parodies and mean-spirited memes that represent them, then that's a worse reflection on one's understanding of the intellectual situation. (One wonders whether this point could be a meme.)

On the other hand, if the thought driving Poe's Law is correct, then the parodies do not *distort* the current state of affairs, but instead are *reflective* of the current state of play with extremists. In other words, since the parodies are indistinguishable in content from the real things, the parodies are not *misrepresentations* of how dire the intellectual situation has become. In fact, memes and Poe-style situations with parodies can be a good indicator of how badly developed the views are on all sides. To put it expressively: *No matter how crazy or irrational a straw man of a religious fundamentalist or political extremist one constructs, there will always be an equally crazy and irrational defender of a religion or ideology one could have simply googled up.* In essence, if Poe's Law is correct, one does not really straw-man the extremists with one's parodies, one just doesn't directly refer to them; rather one engages with them indirectly, as if under pseudonym. It seems then that if Poe's Law is correct, straw-manning is impossible. We are all, as it were, dialectical pushovers. The dialectical consequences of this commitment are severe.

Perhaps this is overstated, but it is close to the point. Straw-manning is the rhetorical strategy of depicting one's opponents as dumber than they actually are. The trouble is that Poe's Law states that no matter how badly one portrays one's opponent there is someone (and perhaps there are many) in the same camp as one's actual interlocutor who really is that dumb. One, thereby, cannot successfully portray the competition as dumber than they actually are, since (by hypothesis) there are members of the opposition that are as bad as (or even worse than) the portrayal. Consequently, accepting Poe's Law effectively places any discussant in a uniquely difficult position: If one believes the other side of a dispute cannot be straw-manned, then how is one to take the other side's case seriously at all?

One danger that looms for those who embrace Poe's Law is group polarization. Recall our discussion of this phenomenon from Chapters 2 and 3. When groups hold each other in cognitive contempt and, as a consequence, regularly refuse to cooperatively communicate, they have a tendency to become more extreme in the views they hold as a group. And as groups begin to ignore opposing viewpoints, their argument pools shrink, and the variety of data contracts. As a consequence, this limited perspective on issues yields more extreme views, because once most objections no longer are recognized as legitimate by a group, members are no longer inhibited and begin to speak not only more freely but progressively more extremely. Since there are no corrective objections arising, previously contentious views become normalized. In turn, groups that have no room for dissent tend to polarize so that they almost univocally hold extreme views.

The invocation of Poe's Law contributes to the polarization of online discussion, particularly of religion and politics. First, non-believers are often already inclined to think that religious believers are irrational, and Poe's Law feeds that inclination. If one takes it that religious believers are of the same stripe as one's caricatures, one cannot seriously engage with them. The same goes, really, for any ideology. Second, religious believers have become aware of the role that Poe's Law plays in online discussion, and so the more reasonable among them are regularly frustrated to the point of giving up in many discussions because they feel that they are not taken seriously. They then are further disaffected, because they feel that there are no serious attempts to understand their position. As a consequence, they simply prefer discussions with other religious believers. This leads directly to further insularity and Balkanization of discourse, and as a consequence, a deepening of the divides that group polarization has wrought. Consequently, the dialectical environments of mutual regard are undercut and made so toxic that neither side would even consider a cooperative exchange with the other. Just try refuting a meme that represents your side of a debate in a way that implies that those who agree with you are morons. So Poe's Law and the escalation of memes is a consequence and contributing cause of polarization.

It seems a paradox. We have uncannily efficient means of communication and dissemination of information. Yet we seem to consistently fail to engage with and understand each other. Poe's Law is, on the one hand, reflective of how extreme enclaved discourse has become on all the sides of polarized ideologies. On the other hand, the dialectical situation has become this way because of the regular invocation of that law and the prevailing attitude that religious believers and non-believers have become parodies of themselves. Neither side, given this attitude, is capable of argument with the other. And polarization not only breeds contempt, but further polarization.

This is complicated further by the structural features of the Internet. The interconnections between webpages not only allow, but positively foster insularity, as the links featured on any site tend overwhelmingly to carry one to like-minded sites, rather than sites where one could find intelligent opposition. This is magnified on social media, given the ways the sites serve up news and links fitting our tastes. And when those who have conflicting views interact, on the comment pages of YouTube or in a social media exchange, very few of the discussions are helpful. We'll have more to say about that feature of Internet argument later, when we consider trolls.

Thus far, we have focused on the application of Poe's Law to the context in which it originated, namely, debates over religion. But Poe's Law has been invoked beyond parodies of religious extremism. Political parody sites abound, and there are regular discussions concerning which are parodies and which are not. And there are many cases of confusion. For example, in 2007 a commentator on *Fox and Friends* famously cited as legitimate an article from the spoof news site, AssociatedContent.com.

The commentator, in reviewing the story of how a school district in Maine is instituting a "ham task force" to ensure that Muslim students would not be offended by their schoolmates' sandwiches in the lunchroom, insisted that he is "not making this up!"[8]

Further, during the 2008 presidential campaign, a Sarah Palin parody site went up, thepalindrome.com. It purported to be the blog of the Republican vice presidential candidate, enabling her to communicate with her supporters beyond her political rallies. In it were stories about how she met awkwardly with world leaders and how many were from countries that were "not very important anyway," and how she was lectured by Henry Kissinger but "knocked off early for some McDonalds soft serve ice cream."[9] Numerous emails and blog entries with reference to the site circulated as if it provided further evidence of Palin's incompetence.[10] Further, during the campaign, it was widely reported that Sarah Palin thought Africa was a country, and an overwhelming majority of the people who believed the rumor were self-identified Democrats (Sunstein 2009: 6 and 86). Once we antecedently believe that our political opponents are wrong and thereby stupid, we'll believe anything about them that supports that view.

In the wake of the financial crisis of 2008, Cindy Jacobs wrote at the Christian Broadcasting Network site for the 700 Club that:

> We are going to intercede at the site of the statue of the bull on Wall Street to ask God to begin a shift from the bull and bear markets to what we feel will be the "Lion's Market," or God's control over the economic systems.[11]

This is to say that she is calling on Christians to come pray around a large bronze statue of a bull for market recovery. The liberal webpage DailyKos. com picked up the story, and blogger dhonig (already having posted entries with titles such as "Their reality has lapped our satire") posted a photo from the gathering, and ironically intones:

> "Christians," praying at a golden calf, for economic wealth. Seriously, people, how the f*#k do you satirize that?[12]

The point, of course, is that such a ritual seems positively backward for those who are readers of and believers in the Bible. This is exactly what those who self-identify as liberal and humanist come to expect of those who self-identify as conservative and religious. Poe's Law, all over again.

The conservative version of the problem can be seen in the tone and examples of Jason Mattera's book *Obama Zombies*. Mattera's book is filled with vivid examples of twenty-somethings who, in 2008, were enthusiastic Obama supporters, but who also could not state any of Obama's substantive positions. Mattera describes one woman at a gathering at Bowdoin College celebrating Obama's victory:

As one patchouli-smelling hippie on campus exhorted, "It's definitely the most spiritual experience I've had in a while." Meeting Ozzy Osbourne in the flesh was her previous one.

(2010: i)

Mattera interviews another Obama supporter, and he is careful to quote him perfectly:

Mark Buhrmeister, young Obama supporter, had an honest observation: "Having a hip candidate like him makes it difficult to support someone else. Barack Obama is in style, so if you don't support Barack Obama it's like you're not in style."

(2010: xxi)

According to Mattera's presentation, the Obama Zombie is not interested in policy, reason, or any particular political issue. Obama's supporters are instead motivated by fashion. Once we are properly cued, Mattera provides examples of reporters and political pundits in the same vein, and then he turns to politicians themselves. He claims that all of Obama's supporters are zombies, all "lobotomized." The objective, again, is to portray the opposition in a way that makes their sincere expressions appear equivalent to parodies. Let your opposition talk, the thought goes, and *they satirize themselves.*

The polarized discourse of the 2016 presidential election was even more remarkable. In the "Pizzagate" conspiracy at the end of the election (and into the months after it), numerous Twitter and 4chan users falsely reported that emails leaked from Hillary Clinton's campaign revealed that the Clinton camp was deeply involved with a child-pornography and sex-trafficking operation, all secretly run out of Washington pizza parlors. According to their reports, "cheese pizza" was code for the production and distribution of child pornography. From there, the whispers got louder, with Alex Jones at *InfoWars* claiming that Pizzagate is real, and international news organizations reporting on the story. After multiple debunkings of the conspiracy theory, Edgar Maddison Welch decided to "self-investigate" one of the pizza parlors rumored to have a sex dungeon filled with children. He shot three rounds of his AR-15 assault rifle into the restaurant, and he was later arrested. For the record, the pizza parlor Welch attacked did not have a basement.

It all sounds like a joke, right? That there was a right-wing conspiracy theory that the Democratic Party's leaders ran a child pornography ring, and they ran it out of the basements of DC pizza parlors. And they referred in their emails and texts to it all as "cheese pizza." And on top of that, people actually believed it all, and one went and shot one of the pizza restaurants up with a semiautomatic assault rifle. Is this parody? Or is it real life? Was this story a Poe?

Well, it was real.[13] But that's the thing, isn't it? Unless you already knew about Pizzagate, you probably had a few moments while reading the description above where you were asking: *Is this a parody? Is this for real? These guys are putting me on!* And that's the worry about Poe's Law. If it's true, it's hard to tell when we're making things up about the other side and when we're telling the truth. And even if it's not true, our suspicions that it is true make it hard for us to make sense of reports of how wrong those we disagree with can be.

This sampling of the netscape of religious and political commentary and satire paints an unhappy picture—due to polarization, citizens often cannot tell (a) when they are being lampooned or sincerely engaged, or (b) when their opponent's positions are being parodied or presented honestly. That is, Poe's Law encourages a kind of insularity and polarization that yields the reactionary view that all (or at least most) of those with whom one disagrees are beyond reason and thus not worth talking to.

Ad Hitlerum arguments are arguments by analogy—you criticize your opponent's views on the basis of alleged similarities either to those of the Nazis or Hitler himself. And so: *Vegetarianism? No way! Hitler was a vegetarian.* Or: *The Nazis favored euthanasia, therefore it must be wrong.* The crucial premise for these arguments is the claim that Nazis or Hitler favoring X entails that X is morally unacceptable. But, as morally and politically pernicious as Nazism is, this is a pretty unreliable method of detecting immorality, as the Nazis also were avid promoters of physical fitness, environmentalism, and classical music. *Ad Hitlerum* arguments regularly suffer from problems of relevance. Yet that failing hardly ever prevents folks from employing that form of argument.

Godwin's Law, one of the oldest of the eponymous Laws of the Internet, runs as follows: "*As an online discussion grows longer, the probability of a comparison involving Nazis or Hitler approaches 1.*"[14] And so the law has it that the *ad Hitlerum* fallacy will eventually be deployed in any critical discussion online. Given that the argumentative strategy has relevance problems, there's a widely recognized corollary to the law: *Whoever makes use of the argumentative strategy has thereby lost the argument.* The claim here is that a comparison to the Nazis is always a last-ditch grasp at straws, and thus an inadvertent admission of defeat.

So far, none of this is news. It is familiar enough to people who are attentive to discussions. We've likely all seen the placards with President Obama's face with a Hitler moustache drawn under his nose. Earlier, there were the regular accusations that President Bush and the Republicans were like the Nazis. It is familiar noise to anyone who knows politics, and the response that such comparisons are irrelevant is familiar enough, too.

But, again, the widespread familiarity with the fact of Godwin's Law and the trouble with *ad Hitlerum* do not seem to yield better arguments. Consider that Hal Colebatch, writing for the conservative magazine *The American Spectator*, urged conservatives not to be deterred by the charge of Godwin's Law when criticizing the policies of then-president, Barack Obama.[15] He claimed that this alleged law of the Internet, instead of improving discourse, has in fact hampered good argument:

> Try mentioning to a euthanasia advocate that the Nazi extermination program started off as an exercise in medical euthanasia. And as for suggesting that Jews and Israel are in danger of a second holocaust if Muslim extremists have their way, just wait for: "Godwin's Law!" "Godwin's law!" repeated with a kind of witless assumption of superiority reminiscent of school playground chants.

Colebatch's argument raises several questions. The first is this: With whom has Colebatch been arguing? Nobody, at least nobody serious, in any adult discussion of abortion or euthanasia chants like that. Recall that in Chapter 6, we identified the *hollow man* as a form of *pushover argument*. One erects a hollow man when one places in the mouth of one's opposition an argument that no one actually gives. Colebatch is deploying a hollow man here, or he hasn't been arguing with any serious critics of his views. The second question is why would anyone serious about the issues, as Colebatch holds he is, even be bothered by "playground chants"? His article urges people not to be "afraid" of being charged with confirming Godwin's law. But who would be afraid of that charge when you believe that the Nazi analogy is apt?

Colebatch seems to think that the opposition's counter-argument is entirely in the chanting. Or maybe in the claim that those invoking the Nazi comparison have thereby lost the argument. But the real point of citing Godwin's law in the course of a discussion with someone who has just deployed an *ad Hitlerum* argument is to challenge the aptness of the proposed analogy. Take Colebatch's own example. The point of bringing up Godwin's Law in this case of discussing euthanasia would be to say something like: *Euthanasia programs aren't out to do anything more than allow some people to die with dignity. They're not a cover for something else, and there are oversight programs to ensure that it doesn't turn into something pernicious. To analogize voluntary euthanasia to the forced killings in Nazi Germany not only gets the policy on the books wrong, but it fails to fully acknowledge the gravity of the crimes of the concentration camps.* Unless it's shown that there are other plans for euthanasia, or that a policy of euthanasia is inextricably tied to a program of genocide, there's simply no relevance to the analogy.

So Colebatch is not being silenced or intimidated when someone raises the charge of Godwin's Law in response to his arguments. He is simply on the receiving end of a counter-argument according to which the analogy driving his position is no good. For some reason, Colebatch doesn't recognize it. He writes:

Personally, I don't intend to be intimidated by chants of "Godwin's Law" or any other infantile slogan, used to smother debate in a way reminiscent of something from George Orwell or, if you'll excuse me saying so, a Nuremberg Rally. I have come up against echoes of Nazi thought-patterns and arguments many times and not only am I not going to be bullied into keeping silent about this, I believe every civilized person has a positive duty to speak up about it whenever appropriate.

But invocations of Godwin's Law aren't aimed at smothering debate at all. The law is invoked as a means to identify a fallacy of relevance, or at least charge a speaker with committing such a fallacy. Since when is criticism of an analogy a form of intimidation or something infantile? If the analogy is indeed apt, one can defend it. If it is not apt, one needs to reconstruct one's argument. And that's what proper argument is about.

Recent discussion, especially after the 2016 presidential election, has had a markedly different valence with Godwin's Law. This is because with Donald Trump's campaign and in the year following his election, much of the support for Trump was revealed to have significant Nazi (and more broadly white nationalist) sympathies. The alt-right leader Richard Spencer, in celebrating Trump's victory in the election, ended a speech with a "Heil Trump" and Nazi salute,[16] and in the wake of a Confederate monument being removed from a park in Charlottesville, Virginia, Nazi sympathizers arrived in violent protest. Trump held that there were "very fine people" associated with that protest group.[17]

These events brought Godwin's Law's creator, Mike Godwin, to suspend the rule that one's lost the argument when one must rely on the analogy with Hitler. Godwin tweeted: "By all means. Compare these shitheads to the Nazis. Again and again. I'm with you."[18] In Chapter 9 we made the observation that arguments by analogy have a particular problem of *backfire*—that one of the things analogized must have stable characteristics recognized by your audience, and if they don't see things that way, your analogy backfires. The trouble with *ad Hitlerum* analogies is that they are based on the assumption that your audience has thoroughly negative views about the Nazis. The trouble with the analogy, then, with Trump supporters is that not all of the audience has negative views of the Nazis. And so when a critic of Trump says, "This is just like Hitler's program," a white nationalist might say back, "Not by any means, because it's not as effective as what the Fuhrer had in mind." This, of course, is not the effect the analogy is supposed to have. In fact, if the programs are similar, it could be used as a reason why the white nationalists support or wish the program changed in ways they see as better (but which would be, in reality, worse).

So far the lesson has been that there are some invocations of laws of the Internet that can impede good argument, and there are others that can facilitate good argument. The crucial difference between the two is their function. Invocations of Poe's Law function like *ad hominem* abuse, which explains why such invocations are detrimental to argument. Invocations of Godwin's Law work as challenges of relevance, which is why they can be conducive to good argumentation. And so it goes. The Internet provides unique occasions for argument, and, accordingly, provides distinctive kinds of argumentative success and failure. Like all things in life, the Internet is a mixed bag. But argument on the Internet can go very badly, and there is a name for those who embrace a deleterious argumentative practice that is made possible by the Internet. We are speaking of the *trolls*.

Thinking one's way into Internet trolling isn't very difficult. There are news stories, blog postings, and opinion pages. Additionally, social media allows you to respond directly to the postings of people in the news. With these, there are comment threads for critical discussion. Sometimes on these threads, there are hundreds or even thousands of comments. Now, when there are many people talking in a room, sometimes the best way to be heard is to raise one's voice. But, alas, there's no volume on the Internet. To be sure, there is the practice of writing in ALL CAPS, which is the written equivalent of shouting. But anyone can do that, and on the Internet, all such shouting is rendered equally "loud." So the only way to be heard on the Internet is to have content that captures the eye of readers, and in a comment thread, few things attract attention better than comments which are rude and abusive. Thus a troll is born.

We should note that Internet trolls come in many shapes and forms. There are some who post unflattering pictures of their exes online, there are others who bully classmates on Facebook, and there are those who intentionally post false information in the midst of natural disasters. We are not talking about these trolls here, but much of what we say will likely be relevant to them. The trolls we are concerned with are those that dominate discussions with overblown objections and personal attacks, who seem immune to criticism, and who thereby derail Internet argument. A further feature of trolls of this kind is that they seem to thrive on the negative reactions they elicit. Responding to them and defending your view causes them to become even more unhinged. It seems that the best thing you can do is simply ignore them.

But there's the trouble. We have been arguing throughout this book that engaging with critics is a good thing. In fact, we have claimed that it is not merely a good thing; it is what one *ought to do*. We have claimed that those who have critical things to say should be of great interest to us, and we should feel deeply obligated to take up with them. We have gone so far as to claim that engaging with our most vigorous critics is necessary for *cognitive health*. So what about the trolls? In a sense, they take advantage of this obligation we have to clarify and defend our views. They present their challenges, often in insulting form, and then expect a properly tempered reply. And when they aren't given the kind of reply they demand, they claim victory and announce that their opponents are weak-minded cowards.

That is to say that trolls are free-riders on proper argument. They flout the norms of argument when presenting their objections while holding everyone else to the highest standards of dialectical conduct. And that's unfair. In fact, we might say that trolls represent the *incarnation* of the dialectical fallacy. The troll's game is to mimic argument; he claims to uphold the standards of proper discussion, but in fact exempts his own contributions from those standards. So trolls are merely playing at argument. It's best not to feed them.

The most obvious reason why it's best to let the trolls go has to do with personal sanity. The world is full of people with keyboards and chips on their shoulders. Taking all of them on is a Herculean task, and it is personally fatiguing. Engaging with the trolls isn't bad only for argument, it's bad for us as arguers, and it's even bad for the trolls. It's bad for the argument, because when we engage with trolls, we get bogged down with nasty invectives that incline us less to rational deliberation and more to personal hatred. It's bad for us as arguers because we can be injured by insults. They hurt our feelings, make us self-conscious in ways we needn't be, and cause us to worry about things that likely don't matter at all. And engaging with trolls is bad for the trolls, too. In replying, we acknowledge and perhaps even validate their behavior. We hence encourage their trolling.

Another reason not to engage with trolls is simply that you will develop bad habits when you take up with them. Think of things here on analogy with sports. Imagine a soccer team full of cheating hackers. Football trolls. They trip players on the other team, they step on their heels, they pull shirts while running, and they are generally unsporting in all their behavior. They try to play up any foul against them as something worthy of ejection, but when they commit a foul, they act as if nothing ever happened. They try to distract referees from calling offsides, and they will use their hands if they ever can get away with it. They are just boors. Now, even if you cared deeply for the rules and spirit of fair play in the game of soccer, it would not take long for their bad behavior to have an effect on you. A trip or a push here, and a rough tackle from behind there. It starts usually with retribution for a bad foul or rough treatment, but it eventually escalates. And then it becomes a habit, it becomes your default. It's not long before you play just like they do. That's why it's important to care for a sport's culture, and that's why it's important to care for argument's culture, too. Sometimes, the best care we can take of a culture is just to refuse to play with the goons.

A further consequence of trolling has recently come to light. Trolling not only ruins the prospects for argument following a post, but it actually skews readers' perceptions of the content of the original posting. Recent research suggests that personal attacks and rude remarks in the comments section following a post on the Internet affects readers' understanding of its content. The phenomenon is called "the nasty effect."[19] So trolls not only tend to mess up argument, they also tend to mess up comprehension. Surely your personal experience bears this out, as what often becomes most memorable about an exchange is the critical reaction that it generated. Consider Mitt Romney's "binders full of women" gaffe from the second presidential debate in 2012. The critical response to the claim overshadowed Romney's original point, which was that he had hundreds of resumes from women under consideration for jobs in his office. Or think about Donald Trump's hovering over Hillary Clinton in their second presidential debate in 2016. Few remember what was said as he loomed over her while she was talking, but all remember his imposing presence. Or consider any dinner table discussion with one side responding rudely to the other. What is more clearly remembered is the rude critical response, not the words that occasioned them. Trolls not only drown out the other discussants, they drown out the original message.

So it's clear that one should not engage with trolls. However, this advice is nearly vacuous. That one shouldn't engage with trolls seems obvious, but how do we sort the trolls from everyone else with an objection? Trolls almost always deny that they are trolls, and it's not easy to tell the difference between a troll and someone who has legitimate concerns but inadequate social skills. Those who fall into the latter category deserve our dialectical attention; those in the former deserve to be ignored. In fact, it's a common refrain from the troll that they are just taking part in a critical discussion but might be a little awkward. How can one tell them apart?

Often it takes a few rounds of sincere engagement in order to determine whether an interlocutor is a troll. And, yes, this means that in cases where an interlocutor is revealed as a troll, one will have wasted one's time in reaching that determination. But trolls have a way of unintentionally revealing themselves. As they are not sincerely interested in argument, but instead are merely posing as arguers, there are a few telltale signs that one's interlocutor is a troll. The most obvious sign, of course, is the abusive tone; or, more specifically, the increasing intensity of the abuse. A troll continually intensifies the offensiveness of his or her contributions to the discussion. A second, and related, sign is repetition. A troll isn't really concerned with the argument, and so typically is not particularly adept at recognizing when his or her critical points have been responded to. So trolls frequently simply repeat the content of their initial contribution in increasingly abusive language. Third, since trolls are interested in maintaining attention, they will in the course of an exchange attempt to change the topic of the debate. Typically, this is attempted by suggesting that one's view on the topic of the original discussion commits one to a particular view on some other topic. Fourth, given their aims, trolls will quickly attempt to get the support of others. They will be quick to read others' comments as supporting their own contentions, and will very politely thank third parties for such contributions. Moreover, trolls are content to merely provide *the appearance* of widespread support for their views. Accordingly, the phenomenon of "sock puppeting"—the practice of a single person commenting on a single thread under several different usernames—is common among trolls. And trolls engage in the related practice of naming supposed authorities, often without citation, that share their view. Finally, when called out on their abusive tone or non-responsiveness, trolls are quick to cry "who me?" or charge the critic with being over-sensitive.

Still, it's hard to tell if someone's trolling, and engaging with trolls is bad for everyone. So when you're confronted with comments on a thread that look like trolling, you should ask yourself whether this person might have a point, and whether this is the best format for a full discussion about the objection on the table. If the answer to both is No, then you should just ignore the comments. If the answer to both is Yes, then you should take up the conversation. The hard cases emerge when the answers are mixed. Recall our discussion at the close of Chapter 7: there we noted that there's no sure-fire way of responding to an interlocutor who takes an objectionable tone. The same lesson applies with Internet trolls. As with *modus tonens*, one can challenge the commenter on the insults and name-calling. Sometimes just noting that the temperature of the discussion is a little too high can bring the heat down. But sometimes it just further inflames things. One can fire back with some invective oneself, thereby giving an interlocutor a taste of the flame. Though that may be satisfying, it is unlikely to help much. And, as we noted earlier, you stand a chance of developing very bad argumentative habits. One can try to be exemplary in response by carefully replying to the criticisms and patiently sorting the insults from the arguments. But that takes a lot of time and effort, and trolls deserve neither.

One outcome of our discussion of trolls is that argument is easy, perhaps all too easy, to mess up. We argue over issues that matter, and so we are deeply invested in the outcome of argument. But we're also often in a hurry to get things out and decided. This means that argument is frequently messy, heated, rushed, and often incomplete. That's why there is a real temptation to replace good argument with personal attacks. Unlike sincere attempts to reason with one's opponents, personal attacks are highly efficient and often effective. You call someone a name; it hurts their feelings; they blink; and you win. All done. It's easy, even, to imagine getting some measure of satisfaction from this technique. But civility and rationality require that we resist this temptation. Well-run argument is devoted to the objective of figuring things out, getting the right answers. And so making it harder for someone to present her case by producing distracting noise that creates attrition for those in the argument undermines those ends.

The Internet is a unique domain for argumentative interaction. In many cases, we find ourselves virtually face to face with views and lines of thought to which we feel compelled to give the most complete critical response possible. Social media often affords us opportunities to exchange with an uncle on gun control, a friend from middle school on taxes, or a friend of a friend about whether white people wearing cornrows is an objectionable form of cultural appropriation. If you're like us, you have views. You think your reasons are pretty good, and you try them out. Others, sometimes, are game to go a few rounds on the issue. And so, congratulations, you've got an argument on your hands.

Now, again, if you're like us, and especially if you've been paying attention to the fallacies and rules of argument in this book, you'll likely have plenty to say back to most people's arguments. In fact, something that keyboards and computer screens encourage, mostly because we can type as fast as we can talk, is a pile-on of objections, a long, lengthy, list of problems with the other person's view. Such a list is called, again in eponymous Internet jargon, a *Gish gallop*, after the creationist Duane Gish (who was, reportedly, a regular abuser of the technique).

The Gish gallop is simply a long list of all the things you can think went wrong in an opponent's argument. It can be from a small error (a misspelling or typo), to a terminological confusion (like mixing up *clips* and *magazines* when talking about guns that can shoot a lot of bullets in a short time), to significant errors in the argument. The gallop is supposed to be a form of taking the other side seriously, or at least it is a way of *appearing* to do so. But it regularly is more a tactic of simply spitballing the other side, overwhelming them with objections and counter-assertions. In Chapter 10 we noted how spitballing works as an objectionable argumentative technique, in just saturating an opponent and audience with more than they can critically digest. The Gish gallop is a particular form of spitballing—in this case, it's covering an opponent with objections. Most are simple to reply to, some more significant. But the overall task is to overwhelm.

The fact that the Gish gallop is so tempting and easy to fall into is easy enough to see. You've got a keyboard, some time to compose a reply, and a desire to do well in replying to an opponent. You just can't let anything go—it's a *critical discussion,* for Pete's sake. But that's the error. In order for criticism to be heard as criticism, it can't be to *everything.* When someone finds *everything* we say as objectionable, it's more likely that the person just is not trying to interpret the things you say in a way that makes any sense. So when you're finding yourself with more objections to a line of reasoning you can keep track of, what's happening is that you've made a vice of a virtue. You've taken the virtue of being in for composing a critical reply and turned it into a list of complaints. Your audience can process only so much in the way of reply, so you've got to keep it short and simple. In the worst cases, the gallop is just a way of holding the floor, making a big show of critically responding to the other side. Either way, it stands in the way of fruitful critical exchange. So what are we supposed to do with Gish gallops?

There's one widespread technique of reply to the gallop that has a tendency to make things worse. It's the reply of *TL;DR*. That's Internet slang for "Too Long; Didn't Read." For sure, it is in the right spirit of reply to the Gish gallop, since the problem with a gallop is that it is just too long. But the reply also has an implication that it is *just because it was too long, you didn't read*. That's not a good reason not to read a reply to your claims, if only because the point of critical discussion is that we can get into long-form series of objections and replies with each other. TL;DR in this regard is an expression of unseriousness. Essentially one says of oneself: *I'd rather talk than listen, I'd rather type than read.* Nobody wants to engage with such a blinkered egotist. And so, though the Gish gallop in some ways *deserves* the reply of TL;DR, to reply in such a fashion makes us worse. That's why we said earlier that it's a danger to participate in polluted argumentative cultures—even if you show up with the intention of exercising the virtues, the trolls will turn you into one of their own.

Instead of simply announcing that you didn't read, it's just best to start with the observation that there's a lot to reply to, but just limit yourself to responding to one or two of the most salient things you see. If you reply to *all* of the objections, you're setting yourself up for a *TL;DR* reply, anyways. But since we are best in thinking things through one or two things at a time, it's good policy to pick up on the things in the gallop worth replying to. The rest you can leave for your interlocutor to bring back up later (and hopefully, in more appropriate fashion).

For Further Thought

1   The case was made that holding that Poe's Law is true of one's interlocutors is dialectically vicious, as it encourages polarization and insularity. But Poe's Law professes to state an empirical fact, namely, that with respect to views of certain kinds, for every parody there is a sincere counterpart with equivalent content. What if Poe's Law is true?

2   Invocation of Godwin's Law was presented as a legitimate argumentative move. Is it always? Can it be abused?

3   Earlier in this book, it was argued that each of us must try to maximize dialectical uptake. The view presented in the current chapter is *don't feed the trolls*. Trolls are insincere arguers, but so what? Does that mean that they cannot have good reasons?

4   How is one supposed to argue with those who are not convinced that Nazism is an unjust and evil movement? Does one argue with such people? Are there limit cases for argumentative optimism? What's the alternative?

5   Try to make a Gish gallop of objections to one of the arguments in this chapter. Once you get past two or three objections, do you start to see a pattern?

Key Terms

Poe's Law   Eponymous law of the Internet that parodies of religiously and politically radial websites will be indistinguishable from genuine websites with extreme content.

Godwin's Law   Eponymous law of the Internet that the longer a critical discussion goes, the greater the likelihood of a Hitler analogy.

Argument trolls   People who pretend to pursue argumentative goals and follow rules of good argument, but in fact use the rules of argument as tools of abuse.

Sock puppets   Internet profiles used by trolls (and some others) to create the illusion that many people agree with them.

Gish gallop   Eponymous term for the Internet argumentative technique of providing an exceedingly lengthy list of objections to an opponent's argument.

Notes

1 http://christianforums.com/showthread.php?p=17606580#post17606580
2 www.landoverbaptist.org/2008/april/conservationsin.html
3 www.freesundayschoollessons.org/practical-theology/environment/global-warming/
4 Reported in the Toronto Star: www.thestar.com/news/world/2010/11/10/god_will_save_us_from_climate_change_us_representative.html
5 www.nationalreview.com/coulter/coulter.shtml
6 www.godhatesfags.com/written/fliers/20081101_nicholas-casey-memorial.pdf
7 www.thesignsofthetimes.net/tgf911.html.
8 http://thinkprogress.org/2007/04/27/fox-parody/. This is not the only case of news organizations reporting and responding to content on parody sites. More recently, Rachel Maddow reported that a number of Christians at ChristWire.org were advocating an invasion of Egypt in the wake of the 2011 political turmoil. The site, however, was a parody. See the discussion on *Talking Points Memo*: http://tpmdc.talkingpointsmemo.com/2011/02/rachel-maddow-falls-for-satirical-web-site-video.php?ref=fpb
9 http://sarahpalin.typepad.com/
10 www.veryshortlist.com/vsl/daily.cfm/review/593/Website/welcome-tothe-palindrome- sarah-palins-blog/;www.ablemuse.com/erato/ubbhtml/Forum9/HTML/003088.html;http://wotnews.com.au/like/fake_sarah_palin/2437045/
11 www.cbn.com/700club/guests/bios/cindy_jacobs102008.aspx
12 www.dailykos.com/story/2008/10/30/145245/63/817/647006
13 For an account of the Pizzagate story, see the *Washington Post's* full account: https://www.washingtonpost.com/local/pizzagate-from-rumor-to-hashtag-to-gunfire-in-dc/2016/12/06/4c7def50-bbd4-11e6-94ac-3d324840106c_story.html?utm_term=.46acf0c3b6ba
14 See the Wikipedia page on Godwin's Law: http://en.wikipedia.org/wiki/Godwin%27s_law
15 http://spectator.org/archives/2010/08/05/dont-be-scared-of-godwinsso-c
16 https://www.theatlantic.com/politics/archive/2016/11/richard-spencer-speech-npi/508379/

17 https://www.theatlantic.com/politics/archive/2017/08/trump-defends-white-na
   tionalist-protesters-some-very-fine-people-on-both-sides/537012/
18 https://www.washingtonpost.com/news/the-intersect/wp/2017/08/14/the-creator-
   of-godwins-law-explains-why-some-nazi-comparisons-dont-break-his-famous-in
   ternet-rule/?utm_term=.a28c469a2637
19 See "This story stinks" in the *New York Times*: www.nytimes.com/2013/03/03/
   opinion/sunday/this-story-stinks.html?_r=0, which reports on the article at
   http://onlinelibrary.wiley.com/doi/10.1111/jcc4.12009/pdf

References

Mattera, J. (2010) *Obama Zombies: How the Liberal Machine Brainwashed My Generation.* New York: Simon and Schuster.

Sunstein, C. (2009) *On Rumors: How Falsehoods Spread, Why We Believe Them, and What Can Be Done.* New York: Farrar, Straus, and Giroux.

Part III
Repairing Public Argument

13 The Owl of Minerva Problem

The Owl of Minerva flies only at dusk. This is a poetic way of saying that wisdom emerges only in hindsight, that understanding is always back-ward-looking. Our explanatory vocabularies are developed to account for and evaluate what has already transpired, what has surprised or offended us. And once we have alleviated one source of surprise or offense, new sources arise, ones that could be foreseen and understood only by means of conceptual tools yet to be developed. Recall that in the opening chapters of this book, we advanced a conception of democracy as the collective aspiration to rational collective self-control. For those who hold this kind of view of democracy, that wisdom takes a fundamentally retrospective orientation presents a problem of particular urgency.

The conception of democracy developed in this book belongs to a more general family of views which may be called *deliberative democracy*. Delib-erative democrats hold that most of democracy's value (its authority, legiti-macy, and justification) depends on how well citizens enact their public role as *political reasoners*. In a deliberative democracy, that is, citizens shape political policy by means of processes by which they exchange ideas, rea-sons, arguments, and criticisms. More specifically, deliberative democrats think that properly enacted processes of public reason-exchange among citizens tend to engender morally and epistemically better political out-comes; and this tendency is held to be the key to understanding democratic authority. That is, deliberative democrats explain the bindingness of demo-cratic outcomes by appeal to the moral and epistemic dimensions of open public argumentation.

The claim that democracy's authority should be based in moral and epistemic considerations would have struck Plato, and many political thinkers since him, as absurd. As we noted in our opening chapters, on many traditional views, democracy is *not* a means for realizing morally and epistemically good results. Rather, democracy is seen as a way of muddling through, a mechanism for achieving political stability among a largely ignorant and internally factionalized population. Though it is the most fully represented view in the tradition of political philosophy, this understanding of democracy is no longer prevalent; indeed, it is rejected not only in theory, but in practice as well. It is not an over-statement to say that contemporary democracy is deliberative democracy, at least in aspiration.

To see this, consider a point we raised in Chapter 2. Many features of democratic political life depend for their intelligibility on the aspirations of good argumentative culture. News is no longer simply read, but is presented in a format of pro-and-con panel debate; journalists ask questions about the reasons politicians have for the policies they favor, and they test politicians' views for internal consistency; public debates are organized prior to elections. These are all in the service of realizing a mode of democratic politics where public argument is a central civic activity. Note further that this deliberativist aspiration drives our criticism of what are generally taken to be democratically degenerative forms of political communication. The phenomena we have been discussing—pushovers, "simple truth" appeals, spitballing, swamping, spin, framing, and so on—could hardly be regarded as deserving of political criticism except against the backdrop of the aspirations of deliberative democracy. These terms would not be *accusatory* were it not presumed that democratic citizens are committed to a politics of epistemically sound public argumentation.

In light of this, take a moment to appreciate the reaction to one of Kellyanne Conway's most memorable pronouncements. On January 21, 2017, in the first White House press briefing following President Trump's inauguration, Sean Spicer, then Trump's Press Secretary, claimed that Trump's inauguration ceremony drew "the largest audience to witness an inauguration, period." This claim was met by a thorough debunking—photographs and other markers of crowd size were offered from various commentators that showed a relatively sparse audience for the event. Appearing on *Meet the Press* on January 22, 2018, Conway, serving as counselor to the president at the time, was pressed on the White House's claim that the crowd was the largest in history; she denied that Spicer had lied about the crowd size, claiming that the White House wished to present their "alternative facts." In response, the program's host, Chuck Todd, pushed back, saying, "Look, alternative facts aren't facts. They're false-hoods."[1] Conway then went on to say that Todd's reaction was "over-dramatic," and that if he continued to respond so negatively, the White House was going to "rethink" its relationship with the Press. The resulting chill that was felt by many suggests that one of democracy's central aspirations is to be a mode of political governance based in the open and honest exchange of ideas and reasons. Without that aspiration of honesty and good argument, democratic norms are not feasible. And when people who hold political power brazenly flout those norms, they thereby threaten democracy.

Though the deliberativist aspiration is widespread, and arguably constitutive of contemporary democracy, it remains an aspiration only. As we have been arguing through this book, public argumentation among democratic citizens is at best a mixed bag. Hence attempts to deliberativize democracy are fraught with hazards. For one thing, democratic citizens tend to discuss politics mainly with like-minded others. This occasions the difficulties associated with the phenomenon we discussed in Chapter 2, those of *group polarization*: as like-minded people speak to each other about their shared views, their positions shift toward more extreme versions. Put otherwise, under conditions of intellectual homogeneity, deliberation produces extremism. And as one's views progress toward extremity, one grows increasingly unable to countenance the possibility of reasoned, informed, and sincere disagreement. That is, group polarization feeds what the conservative columnist Julian Sanchez has described as *epistemic closure*, the incapacity to see views that run counter to one's own as even intelligible.[2] And as one's views become epistemically closed, one will increasingly find one's critics to be incompetent, insincere, dishonest, and ignorant. Their points will appear as mere noise or petulant emoting. Eventually, one will see fit to simply stop listening to those who espouse opposing views. As a result, there will be progressive all-around marginalization of unorthodox, unpopular, and unfamiliar political views. Those already least likely to get a hearing will be increasingly regarded as incapable of intelligible speech. Accordingly, under existing conditions, the deliberativists' central democratic mechanism seems to undermine democracy.

It's worth taking a moment to underscore the thought behind the last paragraph. We have claimed that deliberative norms can contribute to cultural trends that undercut democracy. That's a strange thought, so here's one more way into it. Democracies recognize and protect certain basic individual freedoms, and among the most fundamental individual freedoms are those of expression and association. These freedoms are especially important for democracy because they are necessary in order to preserve a social order in which citizens can engage in the activities that enable them to govern themselves according to their best reasons. The trouble is that the freedoms of speech and association enable citizens to deliberately silo themselves into like-minded groups, exposing themselves only to material that reaffirms and reinforces their previously held beliefs. In a democracy, no one *has to* talk to anyone with whom they disagree, and no one is required to listen to dissenting arguments. Consequently, given what we know about epistemically homogenous groups, democratic citizens tend to polarize, and this in turn yields attitudes that undercut deliberative norms. Citizens grow to see those with whom they disagree as beyond the pale, and hence they fail to develop the skills of arguing with those who disagree. The great irony, then, is that the institutional rules that make all this mess possible are ones that are instituted in the service of promoting deliberation.

Of course, these difficulties become only more pronounced once it is recalled that public political deliberation is of necessity largely *mediated* by various modern communicative technologies. No deliberative democrat explicitly calls strictly for face-to-face discussions among citizens; public deliberation must be facilitated by intermediary institutions, such as social media, television news channels, websites, and online forums of many other kinds. Despite the fact that these communication platforms all offer the potential robust argumentative exchange among citizens who may be geographically and politically distant from one another, in practice, they tend to exacerbate the vices outlined above. A casual survey of the comments thread of nearly any news site will show that polarization, closure, and marginalization are the norm. As we discussed in Chapter 12, well-run argument is scarce on the Internet.

Again, the Owl of Minerva flies only at dusk. Only after we have identified these pathologies and suffered their consequences can we think about how to mitigate them. Hence there are many fixes on offer among theorists of democracy. Some argue in favor of new and demanding civic duties that require citizens to read widely across the political spectrum. Others propose institutional interventions, ranging from the enactment of "equal time" laws for news outlets and websites. And there are those who hold that we must create a new national holiday devoted to professionally orchestrated public deliberation events. Deliberation Day, they call it (Ackerman and Fishkin, 2002). Empirically minded theorists of deliberative democracy are working vigilantly on these matters. Still, it is safe to say that there is no easy way to inoculate deliberative democracy against these pathologies, especially given that they arise from the democratic norms that we value. But even if there were ways to inoculate them, we worry that another, even more foreboding difficulty lurks. There is reason to think that public argument itself, even when institutional distortions do not pervert it, yields its own pathologies.

To begin, let's review some of the fundamentals with which this book began. Some arguments fail because they proceed from false premises. Other arguments fail because they draw an unwarranted conclusion from their premises, much in the manner in which a magician pulls a rabbit out of his hat. The difference between the magician and the arguer is that there's no magic allowed in argument. In such cases, it often isn't difficult to see that something has gone awry. But sometimes the error isn't so obvious. These are cases of *fallacious* argument. Fallacies are arguments that we tend to regard as good, but in fact are not. We have to *work* to see them as failures, and developing the ability to see them as failures requires us to craft concepts with which to *diagnose* the ways in which they go wrong.

The need to systematically identify and diagnose bad but apparently good arguments calls us to *theorize* argument. The task is notoriously difficult, as the proliferation of textbooks and college courses on Critical Thinking suggests. One difficulty is that the variety of seemingly good (but in fact bad) arguments is considerably wider than the variety of diagnostic names we have for them. Some textbooks have 12 fallacy forms, others 18. Some more, some less. Exactly how many fallacies are there? Is there an upper limit to them? One lesson is that this variety is itself continually moving and growing. Our apparently endlessly creative linguistic capacities occasion a similarly capacious field for the creation of new forms of fallacious argumentation. As a consequence, it is often only in retrospect—after the inferences are embraced, the debates are over, the votes are cast, and the decisions are made—that the illusions can be revealed to be the fallacies that they are. And with the proliferation of communication outlets and argumentative forums, argumentation theory can hardly keep up with the proliferation of counterfeits of good argument.

One reason why our theories have a hard time keeping up is that our best models of argument take them centrally to be *dialogues*, between two people or parties, who exchange reasons, each with the purpose of changing the other's mind. But this dyadic (two-sided) model is no longer fitting. It leaves out of its purview the fact that argumentative dialogues, especially when occurring by means of modern technological mediation, are performed largely for the sake of *onlooking audiences*. The two discussants may reply to each other, but their objective is actually to move *the audience*. Once we see this *triadic* (three-sided) structure to political argumentation, many otherwise strange phenomena start to make sense. Thus we introduced in our opening chapters the idea of a *dialectical fallacy*.

Consider, once again, the textbook straw man fallacy. In the case of the straw man, one takes one's opponent's view and restates it in a form that is more easily criticizable. One then successfully criticizes the new (and worse) version of the view. And then one closes the discussion. For sure, this would not convince *the opponent*, as they would only say that this criticized version of the view is not their own. But a straw man argument can nonetheless move an *onlooking audience*, those who may not be familiar with the issue under debate, who may not be particularly sympathetic with one side, or who may just be looking for a moment of easy clarity with the issue. The straw man strategy gives them what they are looking for.

Consider, further, that much of the textbook vocabulary concerning fallacies has made it into the vernacular. One of particular note is that of the *ad hominem*, the fallacy of inferring that someone is wrong from the fact that they exhibit some irrelevant personal vice. It is common to find in popular political discourse charges of the *ad hominem*. To be sure, the prohibitions on name-calling and insulting an interlocutor's person in the midst of a debate are very old; but now that we have a name for the prohibited strategy, we have a critical tool to invoke in the midst of argument. It is not uncommon to hear in an argumentative political exchange one of the interlocutors charging the other with having deployed an "ad hominem attack." And all of this is largely to the good. That the vocabulary of "*ad hominem*" and "straw man" has entered the political vernacular means that public arguers have additional means with which to sort the good reasons from the bad.

But notice that the argumentative strategy of invoking a fallacy name can be deployed as yet one more move in the developing argumentative exchange. After all, one charges one's interlocutor with having invoked a straw man or deployed an *ad hominem* as a way of *criticizing* him or her. In this way, charging one's interlocutor with having employed a fallacy can become just *one more move* available to an arguer who wishes to sway an onlooking audience.

Donald Trump was often criticized in the Republican Primary debates for his use of the *ad hominem*. When criticized in this way, Trump interpreted the criticism simply as more pushback from his opponents. That is, he did *not* take the criticism to be targeting his *arguments*, but he took the criticism to be *of him*. And the irony is that most of those making the criticism took the critique that way, too. Three specific examples are of note. First, in a debate among those seeking the GOP presidential nomination on September 16, 2015, when Senator Rand Paul chastised Trump for insulting people for their looks, Trump responded, "I have never attacked him (Paul) on his looks, and believe me, there's plenty of subject matter right there." Second, Donald Trump was absent from the January 28 debate in Iowa among the GOP hopefuls, and Senator Ted Cruz opened the evening with an impersonation of Trump. Here's Cruz: "Let me say that I'm a maniac, and everyone on this stage is stupid, fat, and ugly. And Ben [Carson], you're a terrible surgeon"; Cruz then said, "And now that we've got the Donald Trump portion out of the way." Third, at the very late March 10, 2016 debate in Texas, Trump acknowledged the effects his attacks on others, and noted, "So far, I cannot believe how civil it's been up here."

What is troubling in these cases is that the vocabulary for criticizing the *mode* of argumentation is being deployed merely as a tactic *in* the argument, one more way to discredit another's views. The whole point of developing the diagnostic language of fallacies is to create a vocabulary with which we can examine and evaluate each other's behavior in arguing, rather than continue disagreeing about the claims at issue within the argument. Here the Cruz example is important, because, in accusing Trump of relying on the *ad hominem*, Cruz is himself attacking Trump, the person. That is, the impersonation of Trump's *ad hominem* is itself a form of *ad hominem*! And so, instead of being a tool for evaluating the mode of debating employed by Trump, the fallacy-charge falls back into the debate itself; it becomes yet one more tactic internal to the dispute. Trump obviously saw this point very clearly in the midst of the debates, as he plays with insulting (by saying he won't insult) Rand Paul, and goes out of his way to acknowledge and congratulate himself that he (and the others) haven't been name-calling in the Texas debate.

Now for the philosophical upshot. We argue in our natural languages, and so when we argue, we argue over economies, animals, environments, poverty, and so on. But arguments are structured collections of statements that are alleged to manifest certain kinds of logical relations; consequently, those alleged relations, too, can be the subject of scrutiny and disagreement. And often in order to evaluate a claim about, say, poverty, we need to attend specifically to the *argument* alleged to support it. In order to discuss arguments *as arguments*, we must develop a language about the argumentative use of language. That is, we must develop a *metalanguage*.

The objective in developing a metalanguage about argument is to enable us to talk about a given argument's quality without taking a side in the debate over the truth of its conclusion. Accordingly, with the metalanguage in place, we can assess the quality of a given argument without reference to our own view of the matter under dispute. Among other things, the metalanguage of logic enables us to criticize the arguments offered by people with whom we agree, and it similarly allows us to recognize that sometimes a powerful argument can be produced for a conclusion that we know is false. But perhaps most importantly, the metalanguage enables certain crucial critical self-assessments; it is by means of the metalanguage that we can assess our arguments as lacking *without* thereby adopting a skeptical stance with regard to our own conclusions. Put more simply, it is by means of the metalanguage about argument that we can stand above the fray of our first-order disputes, as it were, and ascend to a relatively impartial plane from which to assess not the matter under dispute, but the manner in which the dispute is being conducted. One might say that rationality itself depends upon our ability to competently wield a metalanguage about reasoning, debate, and argument.

The problem is that when the concepts of the metalanguage are used as first-order tools in an ongoing argument, the impartiality of the metalanguage is dissolved. And so with Trump, the entire language of fallacies has become, for all involved in the GOP debates, yet one more competing view about which to wrangle. The metalanguage for assessing the ways in which their disputers were being conducted was dragged into the dispute itself, and, predictably, the rationality of the exchanges dissolved precipitously.

Now we see the full force of the adage with which we began. The Owl of Minerva flies only at dusk. Only after the day is done, after the argument is over, are the tools of wisdom available. The tools of argument assessment, when applied in the midst of the argumentative rough-and-tumble, are mistaken for, or are appropriated as, yet more first-order claims. They are entered into the breach, and thus can no longer assess it. Subsequent debate flies free of evaluative and rational constraints. And what passes for argument then is mere power.

Call it the Owl of Minerva *problem*. Our vocabulary for assessing public argument must run behind the practices of public argument. By the time our evaluative tools are fashioned, the tactics they were designed to diagnose have already had their effect. What's worse, the metalanguage for assessing argumentation needs to be somewhat technical, precise, and unwieldy. This renders the concepts in the metalanguage especially vulnerable for first-order cooptation and deployment.

And all of this poses an acute difficulty for democracy. Citizens in a democracy must be able to argue well. And in order to argue well, citizens not only need to be able to share, exchange, and evaluate first-order reasons; they need also to be able to scrutinize each other's argumentative performances. That is, in a democracy, citizens need to develop a command of an adequate metalanguage about argumentation. However, in the heat of instant online political debate and constant inducements to "sound off," "call in," and "be heard," there is little occasion for stepping back and reflecting on the prevailing modes of political argument. The metalanguage enters the political vernacular almost always as a first-order deployment, and so is most often already distorted. The deeper and dimmer worry is that proper public argumentation is too demanding for creatures like us, since it requires that we be double-minded about ourselves in the midst of argument about things that matter most—we have to see ourselves as standing up for the truth in argument, but also open to having our minds changed by argument. That double-mindedness may not be something we can consistently maintain. Perhaps there's a slight consolation in the thought that the bleakest implications of the considerations offered above would challenge not only deliberative democracy, but political association as such.

Another way to appreciate the Owl of Minerva problem is to think a little further about metalanguages. Let's start with what a metalanguage is. Consider the language of grammar. There are *nouns, verbs, adverbs*, and *adjectives*. And then there's the notion of their *agreement, conjugation, declension,* and so on. Now, the vocabulary of grammar is a vocabulary that's designed to capture the norms of a language as a language, so the language of grammar is a language *about language.* So were someone to say *the cat are on the mat*, instead of *the cat is on the mat*, we'd say that the error isn't that the person is wrong about the cat, but that the sentence is wrongly put together—the *noun* and the *verb* form don't *agree*. In criticizing a speaker in this way, we aren't talking about cats or mats, but *the words* the speaker used to talk about cats and mats. In criticizing a speaker along these lines, we perform a kind of ascent from our language and see it from above, we look at it as a tool that we can think about and work on. And so, literary criticism is a similar metalanguage. Poems are about love, spiders, sunbeams, ancient plazas, and other such things, but when one talks about a *stanza* or a *rhyme scheme* or a *metaphor*, one is talking about how the poem does what it does with language. Again, we're deploying a metalanguage.

Now, notice something important about the two metalanguages (grammar and literary theory) we've discussed. They are, for the most part, *descriptive* of the norms of the languages they are about. Grammar captures the rules of a natural language, and literary criticism describes how poems and literature do what they do. They, as theories about how the practices work, in a way, trail behind and record the languages they are about. You can't have the languages of grammar or literary criticism if you don't have people speaking natural languages and writing poetry. What value these metalanguages provide, then, is that they make the workings of these first-order languages clear to us, and they provide us with a set of tools to correct and improve particular performances. So grammar helps us identify and correct failed subject-verb agreement, training in literary theory can help a poet produce a profound metaphor or an interesting rhyme scheme. Without these concepts, we wouldn't be able to make reflective improvements in these practices or identify them as such.

Logic is a metalanguage. It is one that is out to describe the norms of reasoning that we try to embody when we argue and think things through. Again, when we argue and reason, we normally argue and reason about things. And so we do so in our first-order language about objects, properties, and their relations. So we ask whether the cat is on the mat, when's dinner, whether the president should be impeached, who's in charge of an important work project, and how we can fix the economy. We give and take reasons, and we weigh them. Logic is a language about that practice. As we said above, with grammar, the issue of noun-verb agreement has nothing in particular to do with the cat and the mat but with how the *words as words fit together*; and so it goes with logic—we are looking at how *the reasons as reasons fit together*. And that's how we get the idea of a *premise, conclusion, inference, fallacy*, and so on.

Now notice something important about how metalanguages are developed. They depend on the first-order languages for their development. And so in order for us to have a useful notion of a fallacy, we need to see some instances of it around before we can identify it as a fallacy in the first place. So, we would not have had the resources to develop the notion of *ad hominem* fallacy if people hadn't developed the bad habit of insulting each other as a means of arguing. Luckily for informal logicians and fallacy theorists, people *just love to insult each other* when they argue. That not only makes it so that logicians have something to theorize, but they have relevant things to say about our reasoning.

And the Owl of Minerva problem arises. Once the informal logician has arrived to correct all those arguers who insult each other with the new fancy term, *ad hominem*, the arguers have a new tool to use in their exchanges with each other. Thus they are able to use the accusation of using *ad hominem* arguments as a way of attacking their opponents. Our tales of the Republican primaries bears this out. Instead of being a concept that corrects the reasoning on the first order, the fallacy concept offers yet another way for people to reason badly.

The fallacy fallacy is a good way to appreciate this wrinkle of the Owl of Minerva problem. The fallacy *fallacy* occurs when one starts seeing fallacies everywhere. In the same way that the college sophomore taking

Abnormal Psychology becomes convinced that everyone in her dorm suffers from some disassociative disorder, the student of informal logic becomes convinced that fallacies are everywhere. That's fine, in a way. There *are* lots of fallacies and bad reasoning. That's because reasoning well is hard, and humans may not be good at it. But once you start seeing fallacies everywhere, you are tempted to think that those who commit the fallacies are *thereby wrong about the things they say.* But, you see, *that inference,* too, is a fallacy. Here's the basic scheme:

> S is committed to p
> S gives argument A for p
> A is a fallacy
> *Therefore,* S's claim that p is false

The conclusion does not follow. Just because people have terrible reasons for some conclusion, it doesn't mean that the conclusion is false. Your uncle may believe something on the basis of wishful thinking, but that doesn't make it a false belief. So if he believes that the sun will rise tomorrow because he just can't go on in the dark, he's got a dumb reason, but his conclusion's still right. That's why we evaluate reasons *as reasons* independently of evaluating the conclusion. That's the whole point of critical thinking—keeping those questions separate. (In our early chapters, we were careful to distinguish *material* and *logical* success—and it turns out that material and logical failure, too, are distinct.)

This point about the fallacy fallacy is important because it is a case where training in informal logic and fallacy detection actually creates a new kind of error. Nobody could commit the fallacy fallacy if there were no vocabulary of fallacies to begin with. The metalanguage of logic, which was supposed to help make us *better reasoners*, ended up making possible a new particular kind of argumentative pathology. From the project of fallacy correction arises a new fallacy. Now, if that ain't ironic, we don't know what is.

The whole point of developing our critical vocabularies and skills of reflection was to have them then return to our first-order reasoning to improve it, to be a tool for correction. But when we return to our reasoning, these tools are still in the hands of fallible, hasty, easily distracted creatures such as ourselves. And so, logic helps and corrects, and it may even direct us to new ideas. But it brings with it its own set of problems, and it turns out that we can understand and correct them only in hindsight. This is what makes the problem a deep and abiding problem with argument repair, because it is a problem that arises from the tools we use to repair argument.

The Owl of Minerva problem, however, has some good news mixed in with its bad news. The bad news, of course, is that the tools we have for argument correction will contribute to new problems that need new corrections. In a sense, we create problems with our solutions. The good news, however, is that the problems to correct are often before us, open to our reflective awareness, because they are products of our reflection and attempts at correction. We can detect them, and we have ready to hand tools for thinking about them and moving to correct them too. The process is, by this analysis, endless. But, really, that's the job. In the same way that bodily hygiene is about the regular quotidian efforts of cleanliness and healthiness, so it goes for intellectual hygiene. Nobody would believe you if you said you had a product that made it so that you'd never have to shower or brush your teeth ever again. Well, so it goes, too, for intellectual health.

For Further Thought

1   If metalanguages are merely descriptive, then can they *really* correct any instance of first-order language use?
2   Is the Owl of Minerva problem a problem for grammar and literary theory, too? Is that good news or bad news for those domains?
3   Does politics have a unique version of the Owl of Minerva Problem, because with it, we are not just talking about things like taxes, resources, and so on, but we are also talking about how we live with each other?
4   Could one solution to the Owl of Minerva problem be to keep the metalanguage of argument entirely separate from the arguments altogether?

Key Terms

The Owl of Minerva Problem	Wisdom can only be in hindsight, because our knowledge of norms itself creates new problems.
The Fallacy Fallacy	The fallacy of inferring that the conclusion of a fallacious argument is false merely on the grounds that the argument is fallacious.
Metalanguage	A language about a language; a language that represents and records the components and norms of another language.

Notes

1   https://www.nbcnews.com/meet-the-press/video/conway-press-secretary-gave-alternative-facts-860142147643
2   http://www.juliansanchez.com/2010/04/07/epistemic-closure-technology-and-the-end-of-distance/

Reference

Ackerman, Bruce and James Fishkin (2002) "Deliberation Day." *The Journal of Political Philosophy* 10: 2. 129–152.

14 Argumentative Responsibility and Argument Repair

Throughout this book, we have endeavored to make explicit the nature, norms, and aims of argument. We think there are several reasons why this is an important exercise. The most significant reason is that as we make our argumentative practices clear to ourselves, we come to understand them better and thus can reflectively improve them. The project of improving our practices of argument obviously involves developing strategies for *avoiding* bad styles of argumentative engagement. But this is only part of the task. Improving argument also involves developing strategies for *repairing* the flawed arguments we give and receive. And given the cognitive interdependence we emphasized in the opening chapters, the project of repairing argument requires us to tend to the *culture* of argumentation and deliberation that we share. Accordingly, thus far we have been developing a critical vocabulary for the improvement of our shared culture of argumentation. We've talked a lot about *pathologies* of public discourse, *fallacies*, and *pseudoreasoning*. It's certainly a good first step in improving argument to develop an account of how argument *goes wrong*. But that enterprise is strictly *negative*. We also need a positive path forward. How can we do better at argument?

Telling the positive story about improving argument requires some stage-setting. So let's begin by introducing the idea of *argumentative responsibility*. Here, the claim is that there are ways of failing to argue well that are also instances of *irresponsibility*. That is, we sometimes fail at proper argument in ways that render us also *blameworthy* as arguers. As we explained in the previous chapter, the purpose of the vocabulary of fallacies is partly that of *assessing* each other's argumentative performances. When we claim that an interlocutor's argument is fallacious, we do not merely indicate that his argument is bad; most frequently, we also *charge* him with having committed a fallacy. And in charging an interlocutor with having committed a fallacy, we *blame* him for argumentative foul play; we indict him for having committed a distinctive kind of *wrong*. The vocabulary of fallacies, then, provides a way to *hold each other responsible* for our behavior in argument.

We see, then, that argumentation has an agential element in that some instances of bad argument are also instances of *irresponsible, reckless,* or *wrongful* behavior. To be more specific, instances of irresponsible argumentation are cases in which one *could have* performed responsibly, but did not. Accordingly, it makes sense to think of argumentative responsibility in terms of the exercise of one's *argumentative skills.*

To get a handle on the idea of argumentative skills, consider first practical skills. There are situations where things go badly because one fails to exercise one's skill properly. Take the professional soccer player who shanks a shot over an easy goal, or the bartender who over-pours a drink, or the teacher who mishandles a simple question in class. In these cases, it is appropriate for these people to *blame themselves.* By their own reckoning, they failed to live up to a standard appropriate to the skills they have; they fell short. The failure was not due to some overwhelming obstacle within the situation, but rather to their failure to effectively engage the skills at their disposal. And so modestly negative assessments of their performances are appropriate. A person with the relevant skills may kick themselves for squandering a shot on goal, wasting delicious Irish whiskey, or missing a pedagogical opportunity. And others may react similarly. Sports writers may speak of the soccer player's "whiff," the barfly may mock the bartender's "party foul," and a student may resent that a question was inadequately answered. Notice also that the degree of negative reaction and fault-finding is proportionate to the skills we assess these agents to have—the more skilled the soccer player, for example, the more blameworthy the shank. Mundane practical failures of skill are not uncommon. And so it goes for argumentative skills, too.

Consider the skill of extrapolating a range of deductive entailments from a few pieces of information. The following task, **Republican Friends**, provides a nifty example:[1]

A is a Republican
A and B are friends
B and C are friends
C is not a Republican

Now a question: *does it follow from this that there is at least one Republican with a non-Republican friend?* Give yourself a minute to think about it. Here's the answer: It does, since (hint!) B is either a Republican or not. If B's a Republican, B is the Republican with a non-Republican friend; and if B's not a Republican, A is the Republican with a non-Republican friend, namely, B. Challenging, yes, but not impossible to figure out, right? Now, insofar as we're competent language-users, we have all the skills we need in order to make the necessary deductive inferences to see this follow. Notice also that if you consider yourself good at logic, but struggled with the case or were flummoxed (or worse: got the wrong answer), you might kick yourself a little bit afterwards. [Full disclosure, we were stumped by the puzzle until we were given the hint, and it seems reasonable for us to be a little ashamed about it. Don't tell our students!]

So there are cases of what can be called *skill blame*; this is blame that is grounded in an agent's failure to engage appropriately the skills she or he possesses in addressing a problem or a task whose resolution calls precisely for the deployment of those skills.[2] Thus there are cases of *argumentative skill blame*; these are cases where one fails to appropriately engage one's argumentative skills. When one forms unjustified beliefs, fails to form justified beliefs, or fails to effectively deploy one's reasons because of some failure of intellectual or argumentative capacity, one renders oneself liable to argumentative skill blame. Similarly, one renders oneself deserving of *argumentative skill praise* when one proves especially adept at employing one's argumentative skill. For example, one might gain an especially deep command of the evidence related to some pressing problem, or one might display a high level of conscientiousness in responding to the counter-argument of one's interlocutor. Those are cases where you would deserve some praise for the exercise of your intellectual skills.

We can now draw from the examples above a few rough criteria for assessing how responsibly someone has handled a situation relative to their skills. Consider:

> The more skilled the person is, the more wide-ranging the person's responsibilities are.
>
> The more difficult the task relative to the skill level, the less blame we should give for failure, and the more praise for success.
>
> In tasks where the stakes are high and errors are costly, we might go so far as to blame some for *not having developed the necessary skills for addressing the task*, and praise those who have.

Thus we would blame the professional soccer player more for the shank than the amateur, we would praise the teacher for skillfully answering a particularly difficult question more than for an easy one, and we might blame the unskilled bartender for even trying to make a complicated and expensive drink without having prepared or looking up the recipe. And so it goes for argument, too. Responsible arguers develop their skills so that they can exchange reasons with others on the issues that matter, and those skills should be on display whenever argument is engaged.

As we laid out in our opening chapters, argument is a *practice* in the sense that it is a coherent and complex form of socially established human activity, which (a) involves standards for excellence in its performance, (b) promotes goods internal to the practice achievable only through the pursuit of the practice's excellence, and (c) results in extending our conceptions and powers of excellence in its development.[3] This idea of a *practice* calls for some elaboration. Regular examples of practices are chess, farming, portraiture, and baseball. Take the practice of baseball. There are certain kinds of actions that are *possible* only within the game. Consider that there is no such thing as a strike out *as such*; a swing of a bat can result in a strike out *only* when one is playing baseball. The same goes for a "no-hitter," a "homerun," a "bunt," and so on. But notice also that, given this, there are certain actions that can be *admirable* or *desirable* only within the game. The beauty of a double-play, a clutch strikeout, or a grand slam are things that can be appreciated only *internally* to the practice of the game of baseball. And so what it is to *know* baseball is to know what those acts are, and why they're to be appreciated. Similarly, what it is to excel at baseball is to have developed the skills that make it possible for you to perform acts of those kinds. And the ability to perform excellently in baseball is precisely what is cultivated within the domain of that practice.

Further, practices develop over time, and they extend our conceptions of excellence as they develop. The crucial thing is that they have goods internal to them that are definitive of them and which become more refined and developed as one acquires the skills of the practice and appreciates the practice's evolution. As we have said, argument is a practice that has developed over time, which involves skills and excellences that uniquely achieve its internal and definitive goods. And so, the deliciousness of a successful counter-argument, the successful detection and displaying of relevant evidence, the satisfaction of building a solid case for a conclusion—these are all goods internal to, definitive of, pursued by the skills belonging to, and consequences of developing the practice of argument. All practices have standards for skill, and entering into any practice means taking on the authority of those standards—taking on the criteria of evaluation and submitting to be judged by them. Practices cannot flourish unless the goals internal to them are valued and those who value them can judge themselves and others in their capacities to pursue them. And so, every practice—including argument—requires that we master a critical vocabulary, one reflecting not only how we achieve those goods in the exercise of our skills and excellences, but also how our failures of skill in the practice prevents achieving those goods. As we emphasized in the previous chapter, the metalanguage of logic and the vocabulary of fallacies are designed to serve this very purpose. They arise naturally from the care we have for the goods internal to the practice of argument.

As we have said, the vocabulary of fallacy theory provides a collection of concepts for identifying failures of skill in presenting and developing arguments. So we have *asserting the consequent, ad hominem* abusive, and *false dilemma* as diagnoses for particular lapses of argumentative skill. And when we use those terms to evaluate an arguer's performance, we hold them accountable for the bad arguments they gave. Just as one may kick oneself upon discovering one has constructed a straw figure of one's interlocutor, so others may think one blameworthy for engaging in that argumentative practice.

The fallacy of *petitio principi* (begging the question/circular argument) is of particular importance for our purposes. Recall two important points about circular arguments. When an argument is circular, it has a conclusion that also serves as one of its premises. Note next that an argument is valid when it is impossible for its premises to be true but its conclusion false. Therefore, circular arguments are always valid: for any circular argument, if the premises are true, so is the conclusion, because it's one of the premises! But more importantly, some circular arguments are also *sound*. Nevertheless, as we observed in our opening chapter, circular arguments are rubbish, at least in the *practice* of argumentation. This is because when we argue, we strive to resolve disagreements, address questions, inquire into or deliberate about an issue. Argumentation requires *progress*, and circular arguments defeat that progress, because they fail to meet their audiences where they are. Circular arguments just go around and around. They are, as we've said, *insufficiently dialectical*.

In order to be successful, arguments must be appropriately dialectical, and in order to be appropriately dialectical, an argument must live up to three requirements: (i) its premises must be propositions the audience accepts, can accept, or are introduced on the basis of acceptable authorities to the audience; (ii) its premises are relevant to the conclusion in a way that is accessible and acceptable to the audience; and (iii) it addresses the voiced concerns about and objections to the conclusion (and previous versions of arguments for the conclusion). Arguments must be up to date with the state of dialectical play on an issue; arguments that are not are dialectically defective. We have been calling this complex norm *the dialecticality requirement*.

Generally, arguments that beg the question fail requirement (i) or (iii) of the dialecticality requirement. That is, question-begging arguments are either posited on premises that are just as controversial in the domain as their conclusions, or else they fail to address standing criticisms of their conclusion. Accordingly, there are two explanations for why arguers give question-begging arguments. They may either not have sufficient awareness of the audience's commitments on the issue, or they may have awareness of those commitments but not engage the requisite skills in addressing them. That is, the question-begging arguer may either *be ignorant of* or *ignore* the commitments to be addressed. Ignorance has been well-canvassed in this domain, and the range of culpable ignorance is often best conceived as defined by intellectual and argumentative negligence, and we've surveyed the problems with this in Chapter 2 in our discussion of group polarization.

We must ask, though, what assessment is appropriate in a case where a speaker is sufficiently aware that her audience rejects her conclusion, and nonetheless presents a question-begging argument. Some who argue this way intend to overtly express their lack of interest in addressing opponents. And there are others who pose question-begging arguments to particular audiences because they believe that anything other than a question-begging argument concedes too much to the opposition.

Recall our discussion of deep disagreement from Chapter 4. Deep disagreements are the limit cases for the dialecticality requirement. A disagreement between two parties is deep when the parties do not share enough commitments in common for them to produce arguments that can rationally resolve the issue. But notice, further, that we should expect deep disagreements to occasion high degrees of contempt among the disagreeing parties. That is, when parties deeply disagree on an issue, their attention strays from that issue to other issues, and then eventually to each other as arguers. And when two sides share little in common and have significant and frequent conflict, it stands to reason that they will develop negative attitudes about one another. The creation of such attitudes contributes to the escalation of hostility in argumentative contexts. In fact, once the depth of disagreement is manifest, it seems clear that there may even be reasons internal to one's commitments not to live up the dialecticality requirement for arguments. That is, if one sees one's opposition as so beyond the pale that *even trying* to address their reasons would concede too much to them, an attempt to meet the dialecticality requirement would feel like a betrayal of one's own rationality and the truths one holds dear. Moreover, given that argumentation frequently occurs within view of an onlooking audience, willfully attempting to meet the dialecticality requirement can be taken as *legitimating* the opposition's viewpoint. In cases of disagreement that is both deep and with an opponent that one takes to be championing a truly *odious* view, the risk of seeming to be legitimating the opposition is significant.

Deep disagreements are intractable because of the dialecticality requirement, and because of their depth. As the argumentative exchange progresses, the disagreeing parties have continually diminishing motivation to attempt to live up to the dialecticality requirement. In fact, they, given the presence of an onlooking audience, may have an escalating motive *not to live up to the dialecticality requirement*. And so, because the disagreement appears deep and the sides bear antipathy, they argue in ways that will beg the question. Finally, because offering question-begging arguments is a blameworthy argumentative behavior, the interlocutors contribute to their mutual resentment.

Consider a few examples of this phenomenon:

- The consistent refusal of "New Atheists" in the late 2000s to take any theistic argument seriously.
- The complaint that the #metoo movement has stigmatized flirting and has turned victimhood into a virtue.
- The objection that the statement "Black Lives Matter" means that black lives matter more, and so must be rebutted with the statement "All Lives Matter."

In these cases, we can see the internal calculation of those using the argumentative tactics. Their strategy is not to concede any ground whatsoever, since even the slightest concession will seem to raise the respectability of one's opponent. To concede or to take seriously the other side—even if only for the sake of argument—seems to taint the argumentative agent. And so, one is incentivized to stick strictly to one's talking points.

The Greeks had a notion of moral pollution, *miasma*. Our colleague Larry May developed this notion with what he called "metaphysical guilt" (1992). The core idea is that there are deeds (and even thoughts) that when performed pollute and ruin an agent, and even associating with those who are polluted can pollute us as well. From this perspective, our deep disagreements are deepened by the attitudes we take toward each other, and in some cases, *those attitudes are of a kind of moral pollution*. When we have these attitudes toward each other, this yields a view that the other side *must not* be given serious consideration, because doing so would taint or pollute us in engaging with them. And so one overtly refuses to even countenance the opposition as reasonable.

This point about intellectual pollution occasions a story. Imagine an earnest supporter of the Democratic Party in the United States named Gerry. It was his birthday recently, and one of his neighbors, who doesn't know Gerry too well, gave Gerry a "Make America Great Again" Hat (a *MAGA hat*, for short). It was a gift, and one given in genuine belief that Gerry would appreciate it. Because it was a gift given with a generous heart, Gerry tried the hat on, and it fit quite well. Still, Gerry felt disinclined to wear the hat. This occasioned some soul-searching for Gerry. He reasoned: *I own hats even for sports teams I don't care for, but I will wear them on occasion. I do have a bald spot, and I need to cover my scalp on sunny days. So why not wear this hat?* Why should Gerry spurn a hat that fits so well (and prevents painful scalp sunburn) simply out of party loyalty?

Gerry's story has a second act. Gerry wore the hat home from the neighbor's house, and he showed his wife and kids his new hat. And he shared his practical reasons for wearing it. His wife refused to allow him in the house, and the kids wouldn't look at him. "It's just a hat!" Gerry complained from the porch. His wife locked the door.

We (your authors) have conducted an experiment with similar valences of reaction. One of us owns a MAGA hat, given to him as a gift, under circumstances not altogether different from Gerry's. At recent lectures we've given together, we asked our academic audience (who generally skew pretty well Left of center): *Who wants to hold this hat? Who would wear it for a minute?* We've found that some people—and only after seeming to summon their energies as if to prepare for a great act of bravery—are willing hold the hat or put it on. But others react as though the hat was made of poison or rat feces. They can't touch it, and they have a hard time looking at it without reactions of disgust on their faces. Often, those who hold it or put it on will, when we take the hat back, breathe a sigh of relief, slump in their chairs as though some Herculean task has been completed. But wait a minute. It's *just a hat!* What's the big deal?

The *miasma* phenomenon of intellectual pollution is alive and well. It assigns to red hats something like a magical power. And it's not just limited to MAGA hats. It has similar (but perhaps less profound) effects with conservatives and *pussy hats* (the pink knitted hats worn by women to protest President Trump's sexism), and it occurred with Republicans and Obama stickers in 2008, and in 2004, Democrats had bad reactions to the letter W (associated with President George W. Bush). It's a striking thing, that even *touching* or *looking at* a representation of an opposing political program has an effect on people. Now, if this is the way we respond to hats, then how do you think we are going to do with ideas and the people that articulate them?

This occasions another story. Once, on a family vacation to visit some distant relatives, one of us (Aikin) let the other family members know about his policy of reading widely across the political spectrum. He affirmed to his family that he regularly read work from the Right and visited websites like Alex Jones's *Infowars*, and *Breitbart*. He claimed also to read things on the Left, like *DailyKos* and *Alternet*. Some in his family expressed concern that he would be "converted" by reading so much material from the Right. They asked if he needed to shower after reading the Right-wing sites. The idea, again, is the odd one that one *is made dirty* by allowing one side of a political discussion to speak or to take them seriously enough to try to think of reasons why they are wrong.

Recently *Huffington Post* ran a story titled "I'm a Liberal Feminist, and Next Month I'm Marrying a Trump Voter," telling the story of how a woman came to see past the political divide once she saw the man she was dating was a decent human being.[4] She, herself, is conflicted about the issue, but her story is one that shows something about the hope one might have of creating a civil space for disagreement. It does not take much imagination to predict what the comments for the piece were like. They ranged from analogizing the relationship with a Trump supporter to one with a drug addict who needs to be reprogrammed to simply denying that the woman *really* holds the views she says she does. "You're not a liberal feminist—you just play one on the internet," runs one comment.

Alex Jones's *InfoWars* has a post about how many Trump supporters have been "disowned" by their families.[5] Some of the stories reported in the post are quite sad: A son is no longer welcome at his parents' house because of his political views; two brothers refuse to share Thanksgiving dinner because one voted for Trump; and a grandmother is disallowed from seeing her grandchildren. It's pretty terrible. Of course, after reading the sad stories, all one has to do is go to the comments section for the posting to see why many Trump supporters and readers at *InfoWars* find themselves unwelcome at family occasions. They shout that the "libtards" have ruined civic culture, and that they would never put up with a house of "cucks," and that too many of their own families are brainwashed slaves to the mainstream media and need to be *confronted* about it. The irony of it all is that in complaining about how uncivil their political opponents are about their disagreements, these *InfoWars* folks manifest the incivility they claim to abhor.

Our goal here is not to score a point about hypocrisy on one side or the other of the political spectrum, but rather to show that the reason why political discourse is dysfunctional is that we do not share a culture of proper argument; in the absence of such a culture, our disagreements inevitably escalate and spin out of control. As the intellectual pollution phenomenon we mentioned above suggests, once polarization has set in, argumentation among those who deeply disagree yields only further polarization, and escalation. The lesson is that if we don't know how to argue well—if we don't have the skills, or are disinclined to exercise them properly—engaging in argumentation exacerbates our divisions.

As we noted earlier, deep disagreement presents a limit case for the dialecticality requirement for argument. When disagreement is sufficiently deep, any attempt on the part of one interlocutor to *engage* the other side constitutes a kind of *concession* to the opposition. The problem magnifies once our other argumentative responsibilities are brought into view. We must sustain our fidelity to the truth as we see it, while also maintaining appropriate community norms of interpersonal exchange. However, as one becomes more familiar with the views with which one deeply disagrees, one grows more inclined to see the opposition as pathological; and exchange with such dysfunctional interlocutors will seem to involve a kind of *miasma,* or pollution. And so responsible exchange becomes almost impossible. Importantly, this inability to engage responsibly arises from our aspirations *to be responsible*, to know more about the other side, to engage with them and to hold them to the norms of exchange that we (purportedly) share! When disagreements are sufficiently deep, argumentation is like quicksand—the harder one tries to engage well, the more one finds oneself unable to do so.

Thus a striking puzzle emerges: How can we responsibly address a problem with argumentation that itself arises from our attempts to argue responsibly? Simply engaging in further argument is obviously not sufficient. Is argument doomed?

We have already said that, in order to address properly disagreements that are especially deep, argument must be conducted against the background of a healthy culture of argumentation. The thought is that proper argumentative practice might be sustainable, even in cases of deep disagreement, if the disputants can see their quarrel as arising from their mutual fidelity to common cognitive aspirations and norms. That is, when those embroiled in disagreement can nonetheless see one another as striving to find the truth, respond to evidence, and track the best reasons, they might be able to overcome the tendency to pathologize each other. With that tendency held at bay, there could be opportunity for productive engagement. So the question now is how such a culture could be cultivated and sustained.

Argumentative practice can remain healthy only within an environment of broader social coordination and cooperative activity. In order to argue well together, we must be able to trust one another to be honest, to value good reasons, to listen carefully, and to remain respectful. We might encapsulate the ways in which our present cognitive environment is troubled by saying that we are no longer willing to *trust* those with whom we disagree to live up to the demands of authentic argumentation. The question is whether there are argumentative means for reestablishing the requisite kind of trust. We believe there are, but it requires two converging alterations in our current political argumentative practice.

First, we must devise ways of tempering the blame we place on each other in argumentative circumstances. When trust is scarce, we tend to see our opposition's errors as either *tricks* or *ineptitudes* rather than simply mistakes; thus we *over-ascribe* blame for our opponents' errors. Meanwhile, our opponents see our over-ascription of blame as opportunistic moralizing, and this in turn breeds their resentment and hostility. Argumentation then devolves rapidly, and trust is further dissolved. It is far better to *under-ascribe* blame in cases of severe disagreement, to incline to regard the opposition's errors as *merely mistakes* owing to the many hazards that one confronts when trying to think through difficult and complex issues. To put the suggestion in a nutshell, in order to reestablish the kind of trust necessary for a healthy culture of argument, we should adopt a policy of explaining our opposition's errors by appeal to *honest mistakes* whenever possible. Attributing incompetence or dishonesty to our argumentative opponents should be a last resort.

Second, in order to reestablish trust, we must also temper the negative reactions we tend to have regarding those one our own side who attempt to engage seriously with the other side. The tendency is to think that, in order to be an *authentic* advocate for one's political views, one must see the opposition as more than simply mistaken; one must also attribute the opposition's mistakes to some kind of irremediable depravity. Thus there is now a robust nomenclature for "calling out" those who are otherwise allies for "accommodating" and "platforming" those who espouse opposing views. Again, the *miasma* phenomenon is at work. Consider the term *RINO* ("Republican in name only"), which is most often applied to GOP office holders who seem too cooperative with their Democrat colleagues. The idea is that one who is *truly* committed to "Making American Great Again" wouldn't bother trying to cooperate with liberals. On the other side of the political spectrum, there is the view that one who is *not merely posing* as a feminist wouldn't attempt to understand Natural Law arguments against abortion. To be sure, where there is a lack of trust among disputants, a premium will be placed on in-group loyalty, and intellectual purity (the opposite of pollution!) is a metric of loyalty. But the effect is not only the undermining of our capacities to productively argue with our opposition, and thus the further dissolution of trust; the demand for intellectual purity is itself a recipe for inauthenticity and posturing. As we lose the capacity for proper engagement with our opponents, we also lose the ability to be reflective and intellectually responsible spokespersons *for our own views*. Consequently, it is no mystery why political factions based in demands for ideological purity frequently dissolve amidst internecine clashes over minute doctrinal details. If we are to reestablish the kind of trust necessary for a healthy argumentative culture, we must give up the bunker mentality that condemns those on our own side as inauthentic posers when they express anything short of contempt for the opposing view.

One reason why arguments go so badly is because the disagreement and interplay between us, our interlocutors, and our onlooking audiences starts off as fraught. And so, further exchange often makes things worse, instead of better. We call this phenomenon *argument escalation*. Again, we've all seen it happen—a difference of opinion about some small matter grows into an argument, an argument becomes a verbal fight, and the verbal fight becomes a fight involving more than merely words. Half of the time, we want to stop it all and say, "We are all grownups here … can't we calm down?" But were one to say this, the interlocutor is liable to respond, "Are you calling me a child, then? And don't tell me to calm down!" How can we repair arguments without further escalating them?

The first thing to notice about argumentative escalation is that it is a manifestation of the broader phenomenon of escalating antipathy, and this pattern proceeds in the presence of a few background conditions. They are:

Iterability: Some, if not all, of the exchanges between the parties repeat or can be repeated.
Irritability: Repetition of a component of the exchange becomes more frustrating the more it is repeated.
Harm: Escalated forms of the exchange cause some harm (or perceived harm) to the practice or the participants.
Heat: As iterations escalate, replying proportionately to harmful exchange appears to be appropriate.
Fog: As iterations escalate, it is difficult, at the time, to determine a proportionate response, so one tends to respond to harmful iterations excessively.

Argumentative escalation happens pretty easily and rapidly. Note that because argument is a turn-taking practice, iteration is built into it. And since argument is inherently critical, there is ample opportunity for irritation, and expressions of irritation are often taken as harming one's reputation. And so arguers commonly express sub- and non-linguistic aggressions toward their interlocutors—sighing, rolling one's eyes, responding curtly, taking a tone. Once the harm or perceived harm is done, turn-taking then allows the other side to push back, perhaps with more tone, or enhanced sarcasm. Things then get heated, and that's when they get ugly, since it's hard to tell, in the midst of a hot argument, whether the other's implication that you're stupid is proportionately rebutted by your insinuation that they are closed-minded. In that case, one might think it better to also imply that the opponent is dogmatic and ugly, too. And so an exchange can escalate from a sigh of impatience to a full-on insult exchange in just a few rounds.

One way to repair an argument exchange and the background argument culture is just to help folks practice not being dismissive in the midst of exchanges. Gestures of frustration get in the way of good argument, and though it's appropriate to be frustrated with someone who's not arguing correctly or is being dogmatic, it only escalates the situation to start rolling your eyes right off the bat. Or even after a few rounds. Moreover, it's important to recognize that people will respond to being challenged in various ways. Indeed, there are some cases of eye-rolling that should be received not as an attempt to belittle an interlocutor, but as a signal that one's interlocutor regards what you've said as less than relevant. In this way, an eye-roll is an expression of one's interlocutor's investment in the quality of the argumentative exchange.

As teachers, we've developed a pretty thick skin for student rudeness in class conversation. It took some time before student *harrumphing* in the midst of a lecture didn't bother us much. What it took was a kind of change of view. Expressions of frustration are implicit signs of investment in the conversation, and they are also incompletely formulated objections. Pausing to let folks emote in the midst of an argument can actually be pretty useful. Here's a reality: sometimes, argumentative exchanges aren't just for the sake of getting to the bottom of an issue. Sometimes they are for the sake of just clearing the air between two sides—they are, as our friend and colleague John Casey puts it, occasions for *the airing of grievances*. Only once we've got them out, and they are properly interpreted, can we really proceed with the critical discussion.

This point about grievance and adversariality reflects the fact that escalation is a natural outgrowth of our investment in our views and our commitment to proper argument. The irony, again, is that those very commitments are what seem to undercut well-run argument. The key is that they needn't always do so. Remember that *arguments are instances of both confrontation and collaboration*—we argue with people with whom we have a disagreement urgent enough to call for settling, but we have to work together in a cooperative exercise of figuring out the best way forward. Submerging the confrontational element, denying it or prohibiting it isn't feasible. Argument needs to have its adversarial edge. So we must endeavor to focus and work on the skills of cooperation and collaboration in the midst of the disagreement. Consider that athletes walk this line all the time. Athletes must be competitive, but they also must uphold the virtues of sportsmanship. They must play to win while also respecting the game. For sure, it is possible, as a fan of or player for one team, to acknowledge how excellent a goal just scored by the other team is. There is no danger of outing oneself as a "poser" fan of Team X when one credits Team Y with a good play. It's that spirit—we might call it the *sporting spirit* that we see in athletes—that needs to be made part of the culture of argumentation. Good argument requires that we develop the capacity to concede a good point, even if it hurts our case. We must be willing to let an objection be fully stated before cutting it off. We must be prepared to admit that not all of our opponents are stupid and ignorant. That's how the arguer-as-good-sport handles controversy.

We have been talking about steps we might take in order to improve our *practices of argument*, and we have fixed on the idea of rehabilitating a broader *culture of argument*. There remains the question of how we can improve our individual arguments—our performances in the particular argumentative exchanges that we have with specific others. Call this program of looking at arguments as performances that can be improved that of *argument repair*. Again, when we argue, we engage in an activity that is both confrontational and collaborative. The confrontational aspect of argument is where a lot of the trouble resides. But in order to fix arguments, we need to emphasize the collaborative dimension of the enterprise. Again, as teachers, this is a task we take on all the time. We have students try out arguments in class, and sometimes these arguments are crashing failures. Sometimes we get term papers that aren't very good. Our job, as teachers, is not only to diagnose what's gone wrong (or right, on occasion); we must also provide guidance on how the student could revise. We often suggest that a conclusion's force be weakened to fit with the support the premises provide, or we suggest that a salient objection needs to be addressed, or we highlight a consideration or piece of evidence that's been overlooked.

Now, the model of the teacher reading student essays is a useful one for argument repair. It has some benefits, but it also presents some limitations. The benefits are that the teacher is all about the *process* of turning a not-so-great paper into a better one, regardless of whether or not the teacher likes the conclusion. This is because the issue isn't in the end just about the conclusion of that argument, but about developing the skills of arguing together and developing the trust to share one's reasons about things that matter. We get the skills we are responsible for enacting only if we practice them, and we can practice them only if we have a culture that values them. That's a pretty noble line to take, and that's where the problems start. When taken as a model for argument repair more generally, the model of the teacher is unfitting. Few people will tolerate the tone that can come along with taking the attitude of being a schoolteacher reading student papers. They often resent it, in fact. Why? Well, because *you're acting like their teacher*. That's going to alienate folks. And so, taking oneself to occupy the role of the *teacher* casts one's interlocutor as one's *pupil*, and that is bound to cause argumentative escalation. Further, the teacher model requires the teacher to give helpful feedback to people with whom he or she has significant disagreements. The problem, of course, is that the best and most useful objections to arguments also provide a path forward to argument improvement. That's a strange thought, but it makes sense if the point of argumentative exchange is to bring our reasoning up to date with the best evidence and lines of thought. And so, the best way to *hear* an objection and the best way to *pose* it is in terms of making the reasoning at issue reflective of the best thoughts we have on the matter. Again, that's the spirit of a teacher's comments on a term paper (ideally), and that's the spirit of argument repair. The trouble is that this ideal commits us to repairing the arguments on the side of issues that we reject. In order to argue well, we must *join forces* with our opposition to try to *fix* their arguments. That's a hard pill to swallow.

Again, the background problem is that the broader background of civic trust that must be in place for argument to make sense has been significantly eroded. As we said earlier, practices expand our capacity to think about excellence only if they themselves are valued in the broader culture. Baseball, music, and journalism make sense and have their internal values only if they are themselves valued in the culture they inhabit. The same goes for argument. If the broader culture doesn't value proper argument and its goals, then the goods internal to the practice lose their vitality for us. Well-run argument can help reinforce those norms, but ultimately proper argument depends on those norms and values already being robustly in place and widely prized. So a teacher's comments on a student's paper don't mean much if the students can only interpret the comments as just pedantic carping. The same goes for the sporting spirit in athletics—one cannot maintain the attitude of a good sport in the midst of games with those who seem only to be out to win and hence will cheat to do so. One's sporting behavior will come off as some kind of bluff or naïve nonsense. The problem is that well-run argument, in contexts where the necessary trust is lacking, seems pointless, if not impossible.

With this point about the necessity of trust (and our worries about its erosion), there is some good news amidst the bad. First, let's recapitulate the bad news. It's not surprising to hear that political polarization has yielded a good deal of civic distrust, and that has had adverse effects on how we argue. The comments on any of the major online news articles of the day bear this out. But there is good news lurking within this bad news: nobody is happy with the situation. The degree to which our politics is plagued with polarization, mutual incomprehension, and distrust is frequently lamented from all corners of the political landscape. Even the most polarized in the polarized groups lament the fact that few are open to genuine arguments. Recall the folks at *InfoWars* lamenting the fact that their families don't invite them to Thanksgiving. Even though they, in expressing their complaints, exhibited the behavior that explains why they were un-invited, they nevertheless saw the same problem. The ideals are still alive, but they are neglected. How can they be rekindled?

One way to make this happen is to try to think of arguments about politics, where to have dinner, and the existence of the divine as all happening amidst a community of people who can't help but think not only about such issues, but also about what others think about these issues. That's just part of being the social animals we are: we cannot help but be other-regarding. And this means that we cannot help but formulate and adopt views about others; and, in turn, we cannot help but formulate and adopt views about others' views. What's more, we inevitably formulate and adopt views about the *merits* of others' views. Consequently, assessing each other's thinking—how they came to adopt the views they hold—is inescapable.

When considering vexed but highly significant matters—what we earlier in the book called Big Questions—we often find ourselves overwhelmed. When it comes to Big Questions, there is too much complexity, too much evidence, and too many reasons to lead us swiftly and unambiguously to any resolution in particular. And so we must exercise our *judgment*; that is, we must take our best shot at *weighing* our evidence and *ordering* our reasons. And any honest view of this process must concede that, with respect to any Big Question, there will be several Big Answers that reflect a responsible handling of the relevant reasons and evidence that are nonetheless incompatible with each other. To use a fancy philosophers' term, reason and evidence *underdetermine* Big Questions. When it comes to the most important issues in our lives, we all ultimately take a risk with our commitments—we must do the best we can with what we have, realizing that there's no guarantee that the impeccable exercise of our faculties will necessarily lead us to the truth. Add to this the fact that we are incurably *dependent* cognitive creatures. Our endeavors to settle Big Questions require us to rely on others. And sometimes others can let us down, not only because they can prove dishonest or careless, but because they, like ourselves, are inherently limited, frail, and fallible. A lot can go wrong.

And yet Big Questions are, well, nonetheless *Big*. They *matter*. We not only *believe* some set of Big Answers, we *live by them*. Accordingly, we form *investments* in our Big Answers. And this means that all of the uncertainty surrounding our efforts to address Big Questions, and all of the attendant risks that the uncertainty engenders, creates within us considerable anxiety. We do not like to dwell on the thought that our most central convictions about how to live, what's valuable, how the political order should be structured, and what we owe to others could all turn out to be hogwash. This is not only because we don't like to be wrong. When it comes to Big Questions, the discovery that one of our Big Answers is flawed brings the requirement to *change our lives*, often in significant respects. Change is always costly. And if the change comes too late, then it's possible we've wasted parts of our lives. That is a heavy thought.

In light of this, we have developed cognitive strategies, many of which we are barely aware of, for *sustaining* our current Big Answers. These are largely strategies for insulating our Big Answers from unsettlement, and the insulation consists largely in *avoiding* occasions where our ideas could be challenged. However, as we emphasized in our opening chapters, explicit challenge-avoidance is *itself* a recipe for the unsettlement of our commitments. To see this, recall that when we believe, we *take ourselves* to have satisfied a series of unshakable cognitive norms. In order to *believe* that p, we must take p to be true. And, what is more, we must take p's truth to be something that is indicated by the best evidence we have; further, we must take our belief that p to have been formed *in response* to that evidence. An interesting result follows. A successful strategy for sustaining Big Answers by avoiding occasions for unsettlement must *mimic* the processes by which we gather, weigh, and evaluate evidence and reasons. In other words, if we seek to ease the anxiety of having to confront Big Questions with uncertain methods by shoring up our confidence in our own Big Answers, we must engage in a certain kind of self-deception. We must trick ourselves into thinking that our Big Answers are *the only cognitively responsible answers there are*. To call upon our discussion from Chapter 5, we must surreptitiously impose on ourselves the Simple Truth Thesis.

As we have emphasized throughout this book, argumentation so often misfires not because we are vulnerable to overt irrationality, but rather because we are insufficiently attuned to the clever ways in which proper reasoning can be imitated. Now we want to add the further observation that our susceptibility to reason's counterfeits—the dialectical fallacies and other strategic maneuvers we catalogued and diagnosed in the preceding chapters—arises out of something within ourselves, namely our drive to manage the uncertainty and insecurity that stem from our cognitive limitations. Because we seek the comfort of surety and unshakable confidence, but must also see ourselves as properly reason-responsive, we are driven to embrace views according to which there is no reasonable opposition to our preferred Big Answers. This is what makes us easy marks for purveyors of Pushovers and the other mimics of argument; they gratify us because they feed a deep-seated psychological need to feel secure. And yet, as they are counterfeits, they cannot really satisfy us. We may be staggeringly adept at self-deception, but there is always a sense in which self-deception cannot be total; there is always the part of us that must *realize* the deception.

And so we find ourselves in an odd arms race against ourselves. Part of us recognizes the need to uphold proper cognitive norms, to be critical and self-critical of our attempts to reason, and to honestly assess the evidence and reasons we can access. But another part of us reacts to the potentially unsettling consequences of endeavoring to reason and argue well and in earnest. That part creates the Owl of Minerva Problem; it perpetually turns the tools of argument against themselves, morphing the concepts we develop for evaluating argumentative performance into new ways of mimicking argument.

And so, in the end, the conflicted result we reached above—that the proper argumentative ideals are still alive, but are at the same time neglected—is perhaps not so surprising after all. We are anxious about argument because proper argument is cognitively risky, and yet we cannot get beyond the need to see ourselves as successful arguers. But being a successful arguer means embracing the risks. We are conflicted about argument and its cognitive norms because *we* are cognitively conflicted creatures. So, again, the norms are still alive, but they're neglected. We now can see why this is the case. But what can be done?

Back in the heat of the 2016 presidential race, once of us (Talisse) conducted an experiment. Everywhere he went, people were talking about Trump, Clinton, and the coming election. Often strangers would ask each other who they planned to vote for, and what they thought about whatever news-making pronouncement or event had just occurred. Talisse decided to just say "I'm not sure" in response to any such question. The overwhelmingly common reply is telling: the "I'm not sure" response was constantly heard as "I don't know what you're talking about," and so after saying "I'm not sure," Talisse's interlocutors would launch into a short recapitulation of, for example, Trump's *Access Hollywood* tape or Hillary Clinton's "basket of deplorables" remark. The overriding assumption was that *to not have an opinion* is *to not be aware of the facts*. Most frequently, this response was simply an expression of the Simple Truth Thesis: to know the facts is to know what to think about them, so anyone who disagrees with one's own opinion must not know the facts. But in a few (all too few) occasions, the "I'm not sure" response opened an occasion for his interlocutor to state their views in a way that involved none of the adversarial features of argumentative exchange. Sure, the interlocutor was trying to *present a case* for adopting his opinion, but did not see the need to base that case in a demonstration of the *flaws* of the other side's perspective.

Of course, Talisse indeed had views about many of the issues that he claimed to be unsure of (though he did not always have a view in which he placed a high degree of confidence), and the exchanges did not result in Talisse changing his mind about very much. However, these rare episodes showed something interesting. There's a value in hearing someone articulate their position when they are speaking to someone who they do not perceive to be a member of the opposition. When reasoning is disarmed in this way, the reasons become more apparent, as do the lapses and the leaps. Moreover, in conversations of this kind there are occasions in which we can remind each other that *being undecided* is not equivalent to *being uninformed*; as Talisse argued in these encounters, sometimes there's *good reason* to be undecided because sometimes one's reasons pull with roughly equal force in opposing directions.

Note how unlike our standard modes of political argument these engagements were. The content of the interlocutors' positions was not announced in advance, the task was not that of vindicating one's own position by means of overcoming an opposing view, and the ideas of suspending judgment and having inadequate basis for judgment were easily put into the mix. The experiment left Talisse with the sense that he had gained a better sense of why fervent Clinton and Trump supporters held their views, and he claims to have formulated a more sympathetic view of those who embrace the positions he rejects. And when these conversations eventually did turn into argumentative exchanges, Talisse found them more productive.

We are inclined to think that big problems always call for large-scale interventions. But perhaps this isn't always the case. Maybe there are big problems that can be addressed effectively by taking small steps. Perhaps the best we can do to rekindle our fidelity to the argumentative norms that we already embrace is simply this: get your view of others' commitments directly from them, within a context where they can, initially, articulate them non-defensively and in a way that does not prompt them to begin by lay out their negative assessment of their opponents' views. Once a view is put on the table in this way, perhaps a proper argument can more readily commence.

For Further Thought

1   Are there reasons to reject the dialecticality requirement? What if your intellectual opposition seems to reject everything that you see as good? Can't it just be the case that you've got a good argument even if they can't see it as a good one?
2   Argument, if it is a practice, requires skill. And in order to acquire a skill, we must allow people to practice it when they do not yet have mastered it. (Like with sports—dribbling a basketball, for example.) Does our culture offer spaces to practice and refine the skills of argument before they have perfected them?
3   The preservation and development of a practice requires a broader culture that honors or at least can acknowledge the values of the goods achieved in the practice. Are there ways that contemporary culture shows its value for argumentative skill? Are there examples where argumentative skill is explicitly disvalued?
4   Why do arguments escalate? Must depth of disagreement be a contributing factor? Can't disagreements escalate independently of the depth of disagreement? Think of escalating disagreements between siblings, couples, and among mostly like-minded people? What are the other contributing factors?
5   Are onlooking audiences a consistent problem with arguments made in public? Making an argument not for the interlocutor but for some third audience listening in seems to distort the exchange, but it also

makes it so that it has a broader scope. Are there non-vicious ways to integrate the onlooking audience?

Key Terms

Skill responsibility	A person has skill responsibility for a task when that person has a skill that should be brought to bear in that task. Skill praise and blame reflect the domains in which we hold people responsible for the use of their skill.
Practices	A coherent form of socially complex human activity with goods internal to its performance that are achieved only by the development of skills definitive of the practice. The result of this interplay is that practices, as they develop, expand the horizons for human excellence.
Dialecticality Requirement	Arguments must have premises and support relations their audience can accept (or find acceptable), and they must address any standing concerns or objections the audience or interested others have.
Intellectual Pollution (Miasma)	The phenomenon of feeling as though one has been made unclean by having only thought about, been aware of, or having contact with views one rejects.
Argumentative Escalation	The phenomenon of arguments becoming less and less focused on the issues and more contestations between antagonistic parties.

Notes

1 Thanks to Catarina Dutilh Novaes for this illuminating example.
2 See Gunnar Björnson's work on skill blame (2017a and 2017b).
3 See Alasdair MacIntyre (1984: 187) and Lorraine Code (1987: 183) for the development of the notion of a practice for which and within which we are responsible.
4 https://www.huffingtonpost.com/entry/liberal-feminist-marrying-a-trump-voter_us_5ac3cc81e4b00fa46f874949
5 https://www.infowars.com/have-you-been-disowned-by-your-family-friends-over-politics/

References

Björnson, Gunnar (2017a) "Explaining Away Epistemic Skepticism About Culpability." In *Oxford Studies in Agency and Respnsibility*. David Shoemaker (ed.) Oxford University Press. 141–164.

Björnson, Gunnar (2017b) Review of Rik Peels, *Responsible Belief.* In *Notre Dame Philosophical Review.* October 17.

Code, Lorraine (1987) *Epistemic Responsibility.* Hanover: University Press of New England/Brown University Press.

MacIntyre, Alasdair (1984) *After Virtue (Second Edition).* Notre Dame: Notre Dame University Press.

15 Civility in Argument

In this book, we have moved briskly across a broad field of philosophical issues, ranging from conceptual matters regarding our most fundamental cognitive goals, to foundational questions about the nature of democracy and political authority, to empirical concerns about the ways in which reasoning is deployed in real-world social contexts. This has been a short book, yet we have covered a lot of ground. But it is important to emphasize that we have aimed throughout not to settle once-and-for-all the questions regarding the nature and role of argumentation in our individual and collective lives. To be sure, in this book we have presented a systematic conception of argumentation in both its individual and social dimensions that we take to be highly attractive philosophically. But we have done so with the intention of beginning—not ending—an investigation. In short, we have tried to start an argument about argument. Of course, we are not the first philosophers to have undertaken the study of argument. That honor probably belongs to Aristotle. We do not pretend to have started an investigation into argument in that sense. But we have tried to present the philosophical issues in ways that would enable those without years of training in philosophy to begin thinking deeply about argument. In this brief concluding chapter, then, we take up the issue of civility as a means for presenting a distilled version of the central themes that have run through the book. In the previous chapter, we addressed the problem of a deteriorating culture of argument and the question of how to repair it. But what, exactly is the goal of that repair? What is the value of civility in the first place?

One distinctive feature of our approach bears special emphasis straightaway. A common view of argument has it that we argue *after* we have individually settled on our own viewpoints. Argument is engaged strictly as a matter of defending our views from criticism. Success in argument is thought to consist in shutting down such criticism, thereby sustaining our original beliefs. According to this common view, success at argument means never having to change your mind. This is argument construed on the model of the high school debate team, a model that in turn is based on the example of team sports. The aim is to win, and winning consists in defeating or dominating one's opponent.

Whatever one may think of team sports, it seems clear such a model for argument brings with it a good measure of danger. The game is adversarial, and even if sportsmanship requires a level of mutual regard between players, sports regularly have an "us versus them" mentality that all too often dominates. Argument, for sure, arises very often from disagreement, and so there is something right about the sporting metaphors. As we said in Chapter 14, because it is rooted in disagreement, argument must have a confrontational edge. Disagreement begins with the basic thought that at least one person in a disagreement is mistaken, and argument is out to determine which one it is. But properly run argument is also collaborative. To be sure, we can see argument on the model of sports competition, but the fact that argument needn't be about winning suggests that argument aims at other ends that are worth striving for. As we have been emphasizing throughout this book, we humans argue because we aspire to believe what is true and reject what is false. We pursue this aspiration by striving to believe in accordance with our best reasons and evidence. The attempt to keep our beliefs on track with what is supported by the best reasons and evidence reveals our inescapable mutual cognitive dependence. That is, pursuit of our fundamental cognitive aim requires cooperation with others, especially those who disagree with us about important matters: for those who disagree may have reasons and evidence that we have not yet considered or understood the force of. In this sense, then, argument is the process of maintaining cognitive health among mutually dependent rational creatures. Argument is how creatures like us enact and maintain our rationality.

Accordingly, argument is not what people often say it is. Argument is not merely fighting with words. Nor is it simply a competition for verbal dominance over others. Nor is it merely the art of persuasion. Argument is ultimately the attempt to examine beliefs with others by means of our reasons and evidence. None of those other conceptions of argument would even be a little appealing were this not the case. Were argument not primarily about the assessment of reasons, it wouldn't be persuasive or be effective as a means of doing anything else. This means that when argument is done well, one often comes to change one's mind, either about the question under discussion, or the strength of one's position, or the force of the opposing views. In proper argument, then, we come to better understand those with whom we disagree. That is, we come to see more clearly how our fellow rational creatures could hold views that oppose our own; and even when we come in the course of argument to see those with whom we disagree as mistaken or wrong, we still inoculate ourselves from the thought that their failure to see the truth entails that they are stupid, benighted, dim, irrational, or worse. All of this is to say that argument, properly understood, is not a means for shutting down one's critics or ending a discussion. Argument is how to conduct an ongoing discussion.

As we have also emphasized throughout this book, democratic politics is all about argument. We have said that democracy is the social and political manifestation of our individual aspiration to manage our cognitive lives according to reasons. We have noted several times this view of democracy is bound to strike many of our fellow academics—and our fellow citizens, too—as absurd. Even the casual observer of contemporary politics will find many occasions to doubt the rationality of democracy. Back in Chapter 3, we called the *Plato Principle* the tendency among those who lose out in democratic elections or decisions to express the thought that democracy is merely the rule of an irrational mob. What we have tried to argue in the foregoing chapters is that the most obvious *failings* of contemporary democracy can be understood as examples of *failure* precisely because they fall short of an ideal to which we are all committed. A core aspect of that ideal, we have contended, is *epistemological*. To repeat, the democratic ideal is in one fundamental respect the ideal of collective self-government by means of shared reasons. In other words, democracy is the rule of argument.

Our suspicion is that those who claim to find this idea absurd are actually pressing a different kind of point, one about the character of contemporary public discourse in our democracy rather than one about the nature of democracy as such. Indeed, we are writing this concluding chapter in the wake of the 2016 presidential election in the United States. During the campaigns and continuing now into the legislative battles that are the focus of the first year of Donald Trump's presidency, commentators from across the political spectrum are offering the familiar lamentations regarding the sorry state of our popular political discourse. Often these critiques express a yearning for a mostly fictitious past in which opposing candidates and parties addressed their differences of opinion by means of calm and reasoned discussion rather than with attack-ads, smear campaigns, and dirty tricks. One popular way of posing the complaint is to say that in contemporary U.S. politics we have lost our collective sense of *civility*.

Everyone agrees that civility in political argument is both good and increasingly scarce. But it's not clear precisely what civility is. On some accounts, civility is equivalent to conflict aversion. One is civil insofar as one is conciliatory and irenic in dealing with one's political opponents. Civility in this sense seeks to deal with disagreement by squelching its public expression. Civility of this kind is little more than a call for compromise or silence at the expense of one's own commitments. Hence this kind of civility might be inconsistent with actually believing anything. It's certainly inconsistent with *believing in* anything. Now, to be sure, compromise among clashing viewpoints is frequently a fitting avenue to pursue, *once argument has reached an impasse.* Compromise then isn't about reasons, it's about hashing out a workable resolution in the face of an unsettled disagreement. So when taken as a fundamental virtue of *argument itself,* compromise is vicious.

Another prevalent account of civility is focused on the *tone* one takes in arguing with one's opponents. The thought is that when arguing, one must avoid overly hostile or antagonistic language. On this view, a paradigmatic case of incivility is name-calling and other forms of expression overtly aimed at belittling or insulting one's opponents. Now, there is no doubt that maintaining a civil tone when arguing is generally good policy; indeed, we addressed cases of inappropriate tone in Chapter 7. But a civil tone is not always required, and there are occasions where aggressive language is indeed called for. As we have argued, argument is sometimes a form of confrontation, one with words instead of weapons, and any norm that prevents argument from displaying the critical edges of our disagreements thereby undercuts what inspires the argument to begin with. Furthermore, it is possible to fail at proper argumentation and yet maintain a calm and respectful tone of voice. In fact, as we again noted in Chapters 7 and 14, under certain circumstances, one *patronizes* one's interlocutor precisely by sustaining one's composure. If civility of tone has a purpose, it is to maintain conditions under which proper argument can commence. Thus it is not itself a component of proper argument.

In order to get a clearer view of what argumentative civility is and why it is important, we need to reflect again on why we argue. Argumentation is the process of articulating our reasons for holding our beliefs. The point of articulating our reasons is to put them on display so that they may be examined and evaluated. When we argue specifically in response to disagreement, we supply our reasons for the purpose of demonstrating to our interlocutor their strength, and the comparative weakness of the reasons that support opposing views. Argumentation hence has within it the idea that one should believe only what the strongest available reasons support; it is, again, the activity of supplying reasons for the purposes of testing and evaluating them. This means that arguers are committed to the possibility of finding that their reasons are weaker than they had initially thought or that their opponent's case is in fact stronger than expected; and when one's reasons come up short, one may have to revise one's belief. Unless conducted against the background commitment to the possibility of revising one's views, argumentation is pointless.

We now are able to identify argumentative civility with those tendencies that enable the exchange of reasons among disputants. Chief among these concerns is the need for those who disagree to *actually engage with each other's reasons*. This requires arguers to earnestly attempt to correctly understand and accurately represent each other's views. It also demands that arguers get their conception of their opponents' views *from the opponents themselves*. Civil arguers must go to the source. For similar reasons, arguers must also *give a proper hearing to their opponents' reasons*, especially when the opponent is responding to criticism. In addition, when making the case for their own view, arguers must *seek to present reasons that their opponents could at least in principle see the relevance of*. We can summarize these ideas by saying that civility in argument has three dimensions: *Representation, Reception,* and *Reciprocity.*

To see how this framework works, consider that erecting a pushover argument, harping on a gaffe, or seizing on a clumsily formulated claim made by one's interlocutor without allowing for restatement are all uncivil tactics because they depend upon an inaccurate *representation* of one's interlocutor's view. It is also uncivil to speak over one's opponent, or engage in behavior designed to signal overtly that you are no longer listening. Similarly, it is uncivil to simply repeat your same talking points when your interlocutor has attempted to introduce something new into the debate. And it is contrary to the point of argument to ignore good points made by your opponent. These are all failures to be *receptive* to your opponent's reasons.

Finally, it is uncivil for, say, Christian opponents of same-sex marriage to offer in an argument with secular proponents of marriage equality the reason that the Bible forbids homosexual activity. This is because the secularists' position is premised on the claim that Biblical pronouncements do not determine what the state should do. In our example, the Christian's proposed reason could not count as a reason for the secularist. What the Bible says could of course be the Christian's reason, and thus could help to explain why the Christian has the view she does; but in arguing we are trying not merely to explain our views to others, but to *give reasons to each other.* This requires us to trade in considerations that all parties to the dispute could recognize as relevant, on topic, and worth discussing.

Thus we see that civility in argument is not a matter of being nice, calm, or even polite. It instead has to do with being a *sincere arguer.* Civility is consistent with sharp tones, raised voices, and other forms of adversariality that would in other contexts be inappropriate. But our model of civility also holds that name-calling, impoliteness, and hostility are to be avoided when they would obstruct or undermine a properly run exchange of reasons.

We have contended throughout this book that democracy is all about argument. This is all the more obviously true once we notice that in our day-to-day politics so many of argument's imposters prevail and thrive. Proselytizers, propagandists, bullies, pitch-men, dupers, and manipulators must pose as sincere arguers in order to get their jobs done. Unsurprisingly, it is often these same characters who proffer visions of civility that consist in undue politeness and other forms of conflict aversion. Civility so understood serves to insulate sham arguers from the kind of criticism they most deserve. But democracy's health depends upon the ability of citizens to reliably make the distinction between argument and its counterfeits. If the account we have been developing in this book is correct, our individual cognitive health is bound up with the cognitive health of our social and political environment. A cognitively healthy democracy is necessary for our individual cognitive health. Consequently, it falls to us, individually and collectively, to engage with each other over the Big Questions that divide us in ways that nonetheless acknowledge, exercise, and respect our common rationality.

Index